and price deflation have tended to generate deficits. The question that remains, and to which the last part of the book is given, is whether we can be enlightened in our present-day concern over an unfavorable payments balance through a study of pre-1913 experiences.

Jeffrey G. Williamson was born in New Haven, Connecticut, in 1935. He holds a Bachelor of Arts degree from Wesleyan University and Master of Arts and Doctor of Philosophy degrees from Stanford. Until the fall of 1963 he was assistant professor of economics and assistant director of the graduate program in economic development at Vanderbilt. Dr. Williamson, who currently is assistant professor of economics at the University of Wisconsin, has published articles on American economic history in such scholarly periodicals as the *Journal of Economic History*, the *Southern Economic Journal*, and the *American Economic Review*.

# AMERICAN GROWTH AND THE BALANCE OF
PAYMENTS, 1820-1913

# AMERICAN GROWTH

## A STUDY OF THE
## LONG SWING

CHAPEL HILL

THE UNIVERSITY OF NORTH CAROLINA PRESS

# ND THE BALANCE

## OF PAYMENTS

## 1820-1913

*JEFFREY G.*
*WILLIAMSON*

To K. M. W. and M. A.

# PREFACE

In this era when developing countries find it increasingly difficult to achieve internal policy goals while satisfying external constraints and when even the most advanced of nations, the United States, finds balance-of-payments disequilibrium a most pressing problem, there should be little need to justify the research that follows. This study is concerned with the historical interaction between trade and growth in the American nineteenth-century setting.

Although the result of the pace and direction of internal growth upon a nation's balance of payments is quite inseparable from the effect, in turn, of external trade upon domestic development, the investigation that follows is primarily concerned with the former causative relationship. While pursuing this research, it very soon became clear that another limitation would be necessary. Although the reader is often presented with post–World War I data, nowhere have I attempted to extend the analysis into the interwar years. The time period under examination stops abruptly with World War I simply because the scope of the study would otherwise have been much too ambitious. It should be admitted that the generalizations that are derived from an analysis of American nineteenth-century history do not appear to hold up very well for that unique era between two world wars.

The present volume is a revised and extended version of a Stanford doctoral dissertation, "Kuznets Cycles and Their Effect upon American Balance of Payments: 1820-1913," which was completed in 1961. As the original title suggests, this study in economic history makes full use of a particular temporal separation. The long swing, or Kuznets cycle, is an extremely useful chronological framework for analyzing our balance-of-payments history, and it appears to do the least damage to the historical continuity of change. However, no effort is made here to justify the long-swing hypothesis as an explanation of our internal nineteenth- and twentieth-century development, let alone to debate the question of its self-generating and recurring nature.

Some of the results of my research have already appeared elsewhere. Most of Chapter VI is taken from "The Long Swing: Comparisons and Interactions Between British and American Balance of Payments, 1820-1913," *Journal of Economic History*, XXII (March, 1962), 21-46, while Chapter VII is a revision of "Dollar Scarcity and Surplus in Historical Perspective," *American Economic Review* (Papers and Proceedings), LIII (May, 1963), 519-529.

The topic itself was initially suggested by Moses Abramovitz, and throughout all stages of the research I had the eminent good fortune of working closely with him. My interest in historical investigation is certainly due to his stimulation. Furthermore, any sophistication this book may contain or any contribution it may make to our historical knowledge is due primarily to his efforts to impart to me an understanding of economic research. Whether or not he was successful will be judged by those reading these pages. I am deeply grateful to him whatever the judgment.

During the early stages of this investigation I was also fortunate in having available quantitative research, which was the base upon which my own analysis eventually was constructed. The estimates of United States balance of payments compiled by Douglass C. North and Matthew Simon have been, and will continue to be, very important empirical contributions to American economic history. (A discussion of these estimates appears in Appendix A, and the reader may wish to refer to that section before attacking the rest of the analytical chapters.) These preliminary mimeographed manuscripts were obviously crucial to the pursuit of the research; both Professor North and Professor Simon have also kindly shared their thoughts with me, which have clarified greatly the analysis that follows. Other scholars as well have freely made available to me their unpublished statistical research: among them are Robert Lipsey, Milton Friedman and Anna Schwartz, John Madden, and Simon Kuznets.

Besides those mentioned above, I have also derived considerable stimulation and valuable suggestions from Professors Edward Shaw, Brinley Thomas, Richard Easterlin, and Rendigs Fels. To all of them, and to any others I may have slighted, I express my thanks. I must also express my gratitude for a grant from the Ford Foundation under its program for assisting American university presses in the publication of works in the humanities and the social sciences, for financial and secretarial assistance received during my stay at Stanford, and, of course, for the inestimable services supplied by Nancy, my wife.

# CONTENTS

# LIST OF TABLES

# LIST OF ILLUSTRATIONS

*AMERICAN GROWTH AND THE BALANCE OF*
*PAYMENTS, 1820-1913*

# *I.*

# *INTRODUCTION*

## *The Setting*

The economic growth of the United States, although vigorous throughout the span of the nineteenth century, did not progress without serious interruption. Even if we disregard familiar business cycles, American economic history does not trace out a smooth path of industrialization and development or a consistent response to the challenge of the frontier. Rather, it seems that American development is best described as occurring in waves, each dynamic crest of which was followed by an equally stagnant, but shorter, period of depression, unemployment, and price deflation.

These long swings in the economic growth of the American states usually required two decades to run their course and left their mark upon many facets of our economic and social history. The rate at which population grew to fill our boundaries reflected these alternations in the pace of American development, not only in natural increase but also in the willingness of European immigrants to sever ties with the Old World and to accept the challenge of the New. Nor was the pace of the Western exodus unaffected by the long swing. In every upsurge of rapid growth, internal migration quickened, public land sales on the frontier assumed immense speculative heights, and the romantic expansion of the railroads progressed at feverish levels. Similarly with every stagnant or depressive period that followed, house building and urban development fell to extremely low levels, business incorporations became retarded, and even our inventive genius seemed to languish. In the most severe of these episodes, the promise of this country's future hardly seemed bright.

The investigation of this feature of our history, its Kuznets cycles (as they have sometimes been called after one of their early discoverers), has been limited thus far chiefly to its domestic aspects. Yet throughout American nineteenth-century history our economic relations with other countries were extremely important to this country's growth, not only directly through our absorption of immigrants, but also by our trade in goods and by the willingness of foreign investors to participate in this growth by exporting capital to us. Foreign trade today does not play, and in the *latter* portion of the nineteenth century never played, a leading role in our self-sufficient economy due to our abundant and varied resources. Nevertheless, it did play a great role when the United States was relatively underdeveloped during the formative years prior to the Civil War. What is more, over the nineteenth century as a whole, the financing of American railroad expansion owed a large debt to capital supplied from Europe. During periods of extensive development of the railroads after 1850 and of the canals and state land banks prior to that date, European investors were anxious to purchase those securities which were used mainly to expand our transportation network. Similarly, the liquidity of American business and the state of the money market were related intimately to conditions in our balance of payments. On the upswing of a Kuznets cycle we were able to finance not only an increasing inflow of goods but also of gold, which helped the money supply keep pace with our real growth without severely tightening the credit market.

The evidence of Kuznets cycles in the United States extends at least as far back as the 1820's, but the cycles were not isolated to American experience. Significant evidence of these swings in, for example, British growth begins to appear in the 1860's and the 1870's. At the same time there have been almost no important attempts to extend the long-swing analysis to the international flows of goods, capital, and specie prior to the 1870's, although there has been an extensive investigation into the impressive wavelike rhythm of Atlantic migration by Brinley Thomas.[1] Surely one important reason for the particular lack of attention to American and British balance-of-payments movements over the long swing has been due to our lack of quantitative knowledge about net capital flows over the two nations' borders. This important statistical gap has been filled quite recently by Douglass C. North, Matthew Simon, and Albert H. Imlah.[2]

The purpose of this study, then, is to examine the movements in goods, gold, and capital over American borders, mainly from 1820 to 1913, when this country's domestic development was undergoing significant long waves in its pace of growth.

The evidence and importance of the long swing in American history is not extensively pursued here: we begin with the assumption that the existence of Kuznets cycles in our domestic development, each approximately fifteen to twenty years in duration, is sufficiently clear in the evidence thus far accumulated.[3] A chro-

---

1. *Migration and Economic Growth* (Cambridge: Cambridge University Press, 1954). For a significant exception see Douglass C. North, "International Capital Flows and the Development of the American West," *Journal of Economic History,* XVI (December, 1956), 493-505. North has expanded his early research into an excellent book on early American development which, by necessity, includes the interaction between external and internal development (*The Economic Growth of the United States, 1790-1860* [Englewood Cliffs, N. J.: Prentice-Hall, Inc., 1961]). Unfortunately North's work appeared too late to be of major use in the present study.

2. North, "The United States Balance of Payments, 1790-1860," *Trends in the American Economy in the Nineteenth Century* ("Studies in Income and Wealth," Vol. XXIV [Princeton, N. J.: Princeton University Press, 1960]), pp. 573-627 (this volume is hereafter cited as *Trends*). Simon, "The United States Balance of Payments, 1861-1900," *Trends,* pp. 629-715. Imlah, *Economic Elements in the Pax Britannica* (Cambridge, Mass.: Harvard University Press, 1958). See Appendix A for a discussion of the balance-of-payments data.

3. During the 1950's there has been extremely active interest in the evidence and importance of the twenty-year building cycle in both American nineteenth-century development and British development after 1870. The major sources of research into American history follow: Moses Abramovitz, "Resource and Output Trends in the United States since 1870," *American Economic Review* (Supplement), XLVI (May, 1956), 5-23; U.S. Congress, *Hearings before the Joint Economic Committee of the Congress of the United States,* 86th Cong., 1st Sess., 1959, Part 2, "Historical and Comparative Rates of Production," pp. 411-433; "Long Swings in United States Economic Growth," *38th Annual Report of the National Bureau of Economic Research* (New York: National Bureau of Economic Research, 1958), pp. 47-56; and most recently, "The Nature and Significance of Kuznets Cycles," *Economic Development and Cultural Change,* IX (April, 1961), 225-248. Arthur Burns, *Production Trends in the United States Since 1870* (New York: National Bureau of Economic Research, 1934). Simon Kuznets, "Long Term Changes in National Income of the United States since 1870," *Income and Wealth,* Series II (Cambridge: Bowes and

nology of American nineteenth-century long swings has been constructed from this evidence, and the present study builds on that foundation. Table 1 is intended to give the uninformed reader a very general impression of the timing of those waves in United States development. The Abramovitz series dates economic activity (or gross national product) in rates of change, while the

**Table 1** American Domestic Long-Swing Chronology

|  | Riggleman Building Index[a] (trend removed) | Railway Mileage Added[b] (smoothed data) | Economic Activity or Gross National Product[c] (in rates of change) |
|---|---|---|---|
| Trough |  |  |  |
| Peak | 1836 | 1840 | 1834 |
| Trough | 1843 | 1845 | 1840 |
| Peak | 1853 | 1851 | 1846 |
| Trough | 1864 | 1863 | 1858 |
| Peak | 1871 | 1871 | 1864.25 |
| Trough | 1878 | 1876 | 1874.25 |
| Peak | 1890 | 1881 | 1881 |
| Trough | — | — | 1886.50 |
| Peak | — | — | 1889.75 |
| Trough | 1900 | 1896 | 1892.25 |
| Peak | 1909 | 1905 | 1899 |
| Trough | 1918 | 1922 | 1911 |

[a]Derived from Table B-10.
[b]Derived from Table B-13.
[c]Taken from a statement by Abramovitz in *Hearings before the Joint Economic Committee of the Congress of the United States*, 86th Cong., 1st Sess., 1959, Table 9, p. 411.

Riggleman building index and the railway mileage added series are indices of important components of domestic investment. If one ignores the extra cycle during the 1880's, there appear to be five domestic long swings between the 1820's and World War I. The periods of rapid growth on the upswing of the Kuznets cycle are, very generally, the 1830's, the late 1840's and early 1850's, the

Bowes, 1952); *Secular Movements in Production and Prices* (New York: Houghton Mifflin, 1930); "Quantitative Aspects of the Economic Growth of Nations; I, Levels and Variability of Rates of Growth," *Economic Development and Cultural Change*, Vol. V (October, 1956); "Long Secular Swings in the Growth of Population and in Related Economic Variables," *Proceedings of the American Philosophical Society*, CII (February, 1958) , 25-52. R. C. O. Matthews, *The Business Cycle* (Chicago: University of Chicago Press, 1959), Chapter 12.

late 1860's and early 1870's, the 1880's, and the late 1890's and early 1900's.

### The United States Balance of Payments: 1820-1913

American demands for goods from, and in part supplies of goods to, the international market do indeed reveal long swings systematically related to domestic Kuznets cycles beginning as early as 1820. These long swings in the flow of goods can be clearly distinguished in United States history without resort to the sometimes questionable methods of moving averages, trend removal, and calculated rates of changes; they are easily identifiable in the unadulterated annual estimates.

Chapter III will show that over the nineteenth and early twentieth centuries Kuznets cycles in merchandise imports are positively related to collections of diverse domestic series. After 1860, when better data are available, deflated imports and imports in current values reveal extremely high positive correlations with income, output, and investment using more rigorous sta-

**Table 2** Balance-of-Payments Dating for Long Swings[a] (Smoothed Data)

| | Imports (current value) | Imports (deflated) | Net Capital Inflow (current value) | | Trade Balance (current value) | Exports (current value) | Exports (deflated) |
|---|---|---|---|---|---|---|---|
| Peak | 1817 | — | 1817 | Trough | 1817 | | |
| Trough | 1822 | 1822 | 1825 | Peak | 1825 | 1818 | 1832 |
| Peak | 1837 | 1837 | 1837 | Trough | 1837 | 1822 | 1835 |
| Trough | 1842 | 1842 | 1842 | Peak | 1842 | 1838 | 1847 |
| Peak | 1858 | 1859 | 1852 | Trough | 1855 | 1844 | 1848 |
| Trough | 1863 | 1863 | 1858 | Peak | 1860 | 1858 | 1860 |
| Peak | 1873 | 1874 | 1871 | Trough | 1871 | 1863 | 1863 |
| Trough | 1877 | 1877 | 1879 | Peak | 1879 | 1882 | 1880 |
| Peak | 1891 | 1895 | 1889 | Trough | 1888 | 1886 | 1884 |
| Trough | 1896 | 1896 | 1900 | Peak | 1900 | 1918 | 1900 |
| Peak | — | — | 1911 | Trough | 1908 | (1923) | 1904 |
| Trough | — | — | 1917 | Peak | 1918 | (1927) | 1918 |

[a]The evidence of long swings in these balance-of-payments components was derived from annual data. The dating of their turning points was derived from a smoothing by use of a five-year moving average in all cases. The peaks and troughs are of absolute values and *not* of rates of change. Dating of turning points by annual estimates is in Table 3.

tistical techniques. Furthermore, all the import components appear to move together over the long swing while aggregate imports appear generally to lag behind movements in domestic activity.

Chapter III presents evidence of four long swings in imports prior to World War I and of a period from 1896 to 1915 which reveals a cycle only in rates of growth. Excluding the period 1896-1915, the average duration of these long swings in imports (smoothed data in current prices and from trough to trough) is 18.5 years. The dating of these imports swings, as well as of the

**Table 3** Balance-of-Payments Dating for Long Swings (Annual Data)

| | Imports (current value) | Imports (deflated) | Net Capital Inflow (current value) | | Trade Balance (current value) | | Exports (current value) | Exports (deflated) |
|---|---|---|---|---|---|---|---|---|
| Peak | 1816 | — | 1816 | Trough | 1816 | Peak | 1818 | — |
| Trough | 1821 | 1821 | 1827 | Peak | 1830 | Trough | 1821 | 1821 |
| Peak | 1836 | 1836 | 1836 | Trough | 1836 | Peak | 1836 | 1832 |
| Trough | 1843 | 1843 | 1840 | Peak | 1843 | Trough | 1843 | 1835 |
| Peak | 1860 | 1860 | 1853 | Trough | 1854 | Peak | 1860 | 1845 |
| Trough | 1862 | 1862 | 1858 | Peak | 1862 | Trough | 1864 | 1850 |
| Peak | 1873 | 1873 | 1872 | Trough | 1872 | Peak | 1881 | 1860 |
| Trough | 1878 | 1878 | 1878 | Peak | 1879 | Trough | 1886 | 1864 |
| Peak | 1893 | 1897 | 1888 | Trough | 1888 | Peak | (1892) | 1881 |
| Trough | 1898 | 1898 | 1900 | Peak | 1901 | Trough | (1895) | 1882 |
| Peak | — | — | 1910 | Trough | 1910 | Peak | 1920 | 1901 |
| Trough | (1915) | (1915) | 1917 | Peak | 1919 | Trough | (1922) | 1903 |

other components in the balance of payments, appears in Tables 2 and 3.[4]

Without exception, these long swings in the import of goods, which clearly respond to similar swings in American domestic development, have more violent amplitude than do fluctuations in our exports. Over the period 1820-1913, imports dominate the balance of trade, and exports only randomly affect the timing

---

4. The method of dating time series used throughout this book is much less sophisticated than the National Bureau techniques represented by, say, those of Abramovitz. The dates are picked directly from the series themselves (whether these series are five-year moving averages, rates of change, or annual data is indicated in each case) without recourse to "reference cycle" techniques or other dating methods.

and amplitude of its violent long swings. Thus, during periods of rapid growth on the upswing of a Kuznets cycle in internal development, the trade balance and the current account (see Appendix A) became progressively worse, reflecting increasing excess demands for goods in the American market. These periods of progressive worsening in the trade balance and current account alternated with periods of progressive improvement when American growth was sluggish and seriously involved with protracted depressions and domestic stagnation. The trade balance improved simply because import demands were relatively low following the crest in the wave of domestic expansion.

This description, however, slights the importance of the export market in *conditioning* the pace of American development prior to the Civil War. Although they are less severe in amplitude, the long secular swings exhibited by exports before 1860 are positively related to the pace of United States development. Indeed, some students of American economic history insist that in its undeveloped state American growth was very closely tied to conditions in the export market. From 1820 to 1860 this market was dominated by cotton and, to a much lesser extent, grain. There is support in the present study for the view that long swings in American development (during a period in which the United States had a monopoly on cotton supplies) were at least partially *initiated* by a persistent and endogenous lag of raw material and foodstuff production behind supply price.[5] Nevertheless, after the Civil War export movements do not reveal long swings, and over the nineteenth century as a whole export movements do not interfere with the singular importance of imports in producing the wavelike pattern of the trade balance.

One further comment on export movements is necessary in this introduction. Chapter II discusses what appear to be two definite periods in American growth as reflected in export movements from 1820 to 1913. Somewhere on the development spec-

---

5. North has presented this argument most cogently. See his article in *Journal of Economic History* and also "Location Theory and Regional Economic Growth," *Journal of Political Economy*, LXIII (June, 1953), 243-258. This argument is expanded in North's *The Economic Growth of the United States, 1790-1860*. See also Jeffrey G. Williamson, "International Trade and United States Economic Development: 1827-1843," *Journal of Economic History*, XXI (September, 1961), 372-383.

trum–the 1860's or 1870's seem the most likely dates–the United States underwent a profound change; the export sector and agriculture in general lost their positions of predominance. This is common knowledge. But in the process the American economy gained a measure of stability in its balance of payments which is so obviously lacking in contemporary developing nations. Diversification and a shift in comparative advantages toward manufactures added stability to aggregate exports; the American economy became less influenced by conditions in the external primary products market and less a victim of its own monopolistic control over cotton and, to a lesser extent, grain. Furthermore, not only does the period 1860-1870 reflect a transition in United States export trade and a newly endowed stability, but also a general decline in the importance of foreign trade.

Concomitant with alternations in the pace of real growth over the long swing and alternating excess demands for goods reflected in the trade balance and current account, we should anticipate variations in excess demands for real-money balances. During periods of rapid growth in income and output, there must also have been tendencies toward heavy excess demands for increments in real-money balances and tight credit markets, whereas during periods of sluggish growth and prolonged depression, excess supply of real-money balances may even have been the rule. Under a gold-standard system such as that which existed during most of the nineteenth century, how was it possible to eliminate price deflation or serious deficiencies in aggregate demand which could have cut short our spurts of rapid growth on the upswing of the Kuznets cycle? In the face of the deterioration in the trade balance during periods of rapid growth and concomitant import demand, how was it possible to eliminate gold outflow? What is more, how was it possible during those periods to finance both an excess demand for goods, as reflected by an increasingly unfavorable trade balance, and an excess demand for money and so for gold? Under ordinary conditions our internal production of gold was insufficient to satisfy excess demands for money which tended to cumulate on the upswing.

In Chapter V it becomes clear that long swings in net gold flows do indeed exist (1825-1842, 1849-1862, 1879-1893, 1894-

1914), and in all but one case (1849-1862) they move in sympathy with general business activity, i.e., maximum inflow conforming with peaks in domestic activity. If anything, then, it appears that in the short-run sense, the specie-price mechanism is disequilibrating rather than equilibrating since it normally moves in a direction which would tend to accelerate the long swing rather than dampen it. In a long-run growth model, these gold flows are *equilibrating*. Prior to the Western gold discoveries (that is, in the period 1820-1850) and after the resumption of specie payments (from 1879 to 1913) there was a long swing in the rate of inflow of specie positively related to postulated excess demands for money and also to secular swings in observed changes in the money stock. There is also some evidence that at least during the period 1879-1904 the external flow of gold was of prime importance in determining the rate of growth of the money supply.

Alternations in the rate of import of goods and gold, intimately related to the long swing in internal development, were financed by similar long waves in net capital imports. The evidence in Chapter IV reveals that extensive periods of rapid development during upswings in Kuznets cycles were accompanied by sharply rising, but lagging, net capital imports. Indeed, so sharp were these rises that fluctuations in the trade balance were overshadowed by the flow of American securities abroad. Tables 2 and 3 present a summary of the dating of these long swings in net capital imports. Beginning with the trough in 1827, the first swing rises to a peak in 1836 and falls to a trough in 1840. The subsequent long swings in net capital imports follow closely the chronology of domestic long swings: 1840-1858, 1858-1878, 1878-1900, and 1900-1917. In the last of these swings, the variation is primarily in the rate of net capital export, since the United States becomes a creditor on the margin two decades prior to World War I, but this development does not interfere with the consistent relationship between domestic growth and capital flows.

Long swings in the rate of export of American securities to foreigners are perhaps the most obvious evidence of Kuznets cycles in our balance of payments. The kinds of securities generated in excess supply by rapid American growth and which foreigners, mainly British, were induced to purchase were particularly of one type. From 1820 to 1913 between 60 and 80 per cent of all American securities accepted abroad were either state and municipal bonds (a large part of which was used to finance a developing transportation network) or railroad stocks and bonds. Chapter IV examines in detail how potential increases in balance-of-payments deficits generated by periods of rapid growth were financed by securities resulting from systematic upsurges in transportation development. The construction industry in general and the transportation industry in particular were therefore very intimately related to long swings in American growth. Not only did these long swings in transportation development contribute to the growth of our productive capacity, but they also played two other crucial roles in the long-swing framework. First, the expenditures made in the process of railroad expansion contributed to the growth of aggregate demand during upswings of Kuznets cycles and to retardations in the growth of total investment on the downswings. Second, these upsurges in transportation development generated a flow of securities which were attractive to foreign investors and which financed the accompanying potential increase in our balance-of-payments deficit.

In summary, the major thesis that underlies this book can be phrased in terms of the real-transfer problem. The model is a simple, although unorthodox, one. Given secular variations in the rate of net capital imports, long swings in the merchandise trade balance are hardly primarily explained by the price-specie mechanism of real transfer. Rather, we will argue that it is a long swing in the pace of real domestic development that is the major cause of fluctuations in both net capital flows and the trade balance. The resulting flow of specie acts only as a mechanism to complete the real transfer already initiated. Thus during periods of rapid growth in internal development, especially under conditions where capital movements were relatively uninhibited and exports were diversified and only loosely related to such capital flows, the balance of payments improved.

Phrased in terms of the current discussion of the dollar problem, rapid growth tended to generate dollar scarcity and sluggish growth dollar surplus. Because of this, American balance-of-payments experience during the 1800's can be described as reflecting an alternation between dollar scarcity and surplus, with dollar scarcity or balance-of-payments improvement being typical of the upswing of a Kuznets cycle—quite the opposite of the usual predictions of a simple trade model. Chapter VII pursues this relationship into the twentieth century. The question in that chapter is whether post–World War II conditions are similar enough to the pre–World War I environment to explain in the same fashion the transition from dollar scarcity during the 1940's and 1950's to dollar surplus in the late 1950's and early 1960's. The tentative conclusion is that more rapid growth in the near future may generate another period of dollar scarcity for reasons similar to those that explain the pre–World War I pattern.

Although this study is primarily concerned with American experience, it is necessary to devote some attention to British external and internal fluctuations in order to fully understand the nature of United States movements over the long swing and especially to account for the pattern of American capital imports. Since 1870 at least, the course of British home investment has moved in a path roughly opposite to that in the United States, and this inverse correlation between American and British domestic development explains a great deal about the nature of our net capital imports. British experience with the long swing is, however, somewhat different. Whereas long swings are clearly to be seen in almost all American series of output, income, and investment, British history is more complex. Long swings in British capital exports alternated with long swings in domestic development and so smoothed fluctuations in income and output which would have been attributable, as they were in the United States, to long swings in domestic investment.[6]

6. This relationship has perhaps been most energetically pursued by A. K. Cairncross, *Home and Foreign Investment, 1870-1913* (Cambridge: Cambridge University Press, 1953); Thomas, *Migration and Economic Growth;* and W. A. Lewis and P. J. O'Leary, "Secular Swings in Production and Trade, 1870-1913," *The Manchester School of Economic and Social Studies,* XIII (May, 1955), 113-152. The most recent publications concerning the nature of British long swings are by E. W. Cooney, "Long Waves in Building in the British Economy of the Nineteenth Century," *Economic History Review,* Second Series XIII (December, 1960), 257-269; Jeffrey G. Williamson, "The Long Swing: Comparisons and Interactions Between

In the course of the research, it was found useful, therefore, to examine British balance-of-payments fluctuations over the long swing. It was then possible to compare the external movements of a relatively developed, high income, chronic capital exporter with those of a relatively underdeveloped, capital scarce, net capital importer when both nations were undergoing internal swings in the process of growth. This portion of the study was helpful in clarifying not only the nature of the relationship between domestic development and international trade but also the interesting inverse interaction between these two members of the nineteenth-century Atlantic economy.

Over the last half of the nineteenth century, the development of these two nations was very closely linked by the flow of goods, capital, and people. The general impression of the preliminary analysis in Chapter VI is that there is a systematic inverse relationship between British and American development in the nature of a Kuznets cycle. Furthermore, it seems likely that this mechanism of interaction had its source not in Great Britain but in the United States. The Anglo-American interaction was primarily connected, it seems, both by waves in the migration of people, which eventually had serious effects upon domestic activity in both nations, and by the more direct effect which long swings in American import demands had upon the British export industry.

This, then, is an outline of what this book contains. What follows is a more detailed examination of American balance-of-payments experience during the nineteenth century.

---

British and American Balance of Payments, 1820-1913," *Journal of Economic History,* XXII (March, 1962), 21-46; and H. J. Habakkuk, "Fluctuations in House-Building in Britain and the United States in the Nineteenth Century," *Journal of Economic History,* XXII (June, 1962), 198-230. For two other articles covering nineteenth-century British Kuznets cycles see Cooney, "Capital Exports and Investment in Building in Britain and in the U. S. A., 1856-1914," *Economica,* N. S. XVI (November, 1949), 347-354; and A. K. Cairncross and B. Weber, "Fluctuations in Building in Great Britain, 1785-1849," *Economic History Review,* Second Series IX (December, 1956), 283-297.

# II.

# EXPORTS AND THE
# LONG SWING

## Summary of Findings

An analysis of American nineteenth-century export movements is extremely interesting but, at the same time, very difficult. A history of these secular movements might be divided into three entirely separate and sharply differing periods. From 1822 to 1863 there is indeed striking evidence of two long swings in commodity exports; from trough to trough they cover the years 1822-1844 and 1844-1863. These long swings in aggregate export values are violent in amplitude and similar in timing to Kuznets cycles not only in domestic series but also in imports, the trade balance, and net capital imports. From 1863 to 1886 there is again evidence of a long secular movement in aggregate exports, but it appears to have very little in common with all other indices of American growth and with other components of the balance of payments. Export values do not significantly decline during the depressed 1870's, but they *do* decline during the 1880's, a decade of generally rapid growth. Thus, there is little similarity between the ante-bellum and immediate post-bellum periods. Between 1886 and 1913, aggregate exports not only reveal very little relationship to domestic long swings but also exhibit an astonishingly high degree of stability. Furthermore, we shall see that a large part of the fluctuations in the post-bellum period are due entirely to variations in export prices; deflated exports reveal much milder fluctuations throughout the nineteenth century.

The first problem is to attempt a reconciliation between these stages in American economic history. A good argument can be, and has been, presented which insists that the ante-bellum United States economy was dominated by conditions existing in the export market. Prior to Rostow's "take off" in the 1860's and 1870's, the state of the cotton and grain markets may have been the primary cause of the rhythm in economic growth. As should soon be evident, the present chapter is consistent with the "North thesis"[1] ( as yet unproven) that the domestic long swing may be explained in large part by cotton and, to a lesser extent, grain exports. The ante-bellum period is one stage in our history when the relationship between net capital imports and commodity exports is direct and intimate. In later periods this apparent dependence becomes much weaker.

There is a relatively simple explanation of this secular transition to export stability and to exports' comparative independence of the domestic long swing. As economic development proceeds, two crucial structural changes occur apace. First, the process of industrialization tends to diversify the export bundle. In the American case, this tendency toward diversification was supported by the continual settlement of an expanding frontier and the application of new "slabs" of resources susceptible to the cultivation of diverse primary products. As a result, aggregate exports should become less sensitive to systematic or random shocks from within and without. This secular tendency toward increased export stability should be further strengthened by greater price stability in response to these shocks; that is, industrial products usually exhibit greater short-run supply elasticity. Second, as industrialization proceeds, the interrelationship between the industrial and agricultural sectors becomes weaker as the relative size of the former increases. One would expect, therefore, that both the export of primary products and the products' prices

---

1. Douglass C. North, *The Economic Growth of the United States, 1790-1860* (Englewood Cliffs, N. J.: Prentice-Hall, Inc., 1961), especially pp. 1-14.

would become less sensitive to a domestic Kuznets cycle as development proceeded.

But even if we accept that diversification increases over a period of time, does this still imply that long swings in exports will be nonexistent? If we assume that a domestic long swing of about twenty years' duration does exist, then most certainly there is good reason to believe that exports will be subjected to the same economic pressures which seem to dominate domestic series of all kinds. The problem is not whether a domestic long swing would affect the movements in exports. The difficulty, in theory, is that there are so many diverse factors which may act upon aggregate exports during a domestic long swing that the total effect may be either neutral or inconsistent from one period to another.

More explicitly, does economic theory suggest any prediction about export movements given the existence of a domestic Kuznets cycle? Surely it does. General price movements may be a positive function of real-income movements, discouraging exports in the boom and encouraging them in the slump. Assuming normal elasticities of the Marshallian reciprocal demand curves will result in an inverse relationship between export values and "income." Another situation which could yield this same inverse correlation would be if domestic demand outbid foreign demand for the products of the export industry during the boom period of a long swing and vice versa for periods of sustained low and negative growth rates. Perhaps more important, however, is the possibility that the rate of growth of export values may be a direct function of internal investment rates (primarily in export and related industries, such as transportation) and the direction which aggregate investment takes. Under these conditions export movements may be coincident with domestic activity (rate of capacity expansion) or may lag, since exports are more a function of capital stocks than of investment flows.

The conclusion of the above a priori reasoning is that unless long swings in exports are the dominant *cause* of long swings in domestic activity, it is unlikely that exports would have a consistent response to the Kuznets cycle, especially when each export component will be affected in a different way by these domestic variables.

In fact, when we disaggregate exports into component groupings, we do indeed find inconsistent secular movements among them. The net result, as predicted above, is to produce little evidence of long swings in aggregate exports after the 1880's, since with increased diversification none of the components is important enough to dominate total export revenue over the full length of a cycle. From the 1860's to the 1880's, however, secular movements in aggregate exports are dominated in large measure by the grain market. Why, then, do not aggregate exports reveal long swings during this period as they did with cotton in the ante-bellum years? The answer to this question may lie in America's relative importance in the world trade of these commodities. Part of the North thesis is based upon monopolistic control over supply. This is much less the case for American grains from 1860 to 1880 than for ante-bellum cotton. The nature of the lagged relationship between supply and price was much less direct since American supplies to the world grain market appear to have had less effect upon price than was the case with cotton in the pre–Civil War period.

This chapter also examines the effect of secular movements in export values upon the trade balance. Partly due to the fact that exports exhibit irregular patterns relative to the domestic long swing, the trade balance follows a cyclic path clearly dominated by long swings in merchandise imports. During the nineteenth century—for eighty years of our history—there is a striking inverse correlation between the trade balance and import values with very small discontinuities. The long-swing pattern in aggregate imports is discussed extensively in Chapter III, but we conclude here that exports do not seem to play a primary role in initiating dynamic long swings in the balance of trade. This is especially obvious in the post-bellum period, when exports move almost independently of the domestic long swing. But even in the ante-bellum era import fluctuations over the long swing are far more excessive than those of exports, thus making trade-balance deterioration typical of all Kuznets cycle upswings.

Finally, it should be made clear that our method of analysis of balance-of-payments movements, with respect to long swings in the pace of development, is somewhat artificial. We will examine exports and, in subsequent chapters, imports and net capital flows as if each more or less moves independently of the others while all are functions of income. This is an oversimplification to be sure since, as a problem concerned with variations in growth, the long-swing mechanism must be enclosed in a general equilibrium framework. During periods of accelerated growth on the upswing of a Kuznets cycle, there are excess demands on both the goods *and* money markets while rapid growth generates a concomitant excess supply of securities. After examining import and trade-balance fluctuations (a variation in excess demand for goods) and net capital movements (a variation in excess supply of securities), we cannot treat gold flows simply as residuals. An inflow or outflow of gold cannot be treated as a fortuitous arithmetic residual but must be treated as a partial satisfaction of (exante) excess demands or supplies of money. An integrated general equilibrium approach is presented in our examination of gold flows (Chapter V). The present chapter and the two that follow use partial analysis.

## Export Values: 1820-1913

Prior to the Civil War there are at least two long swings in exports which are easily identified, the first beginning with a trough in 1822. (The dates are derived from the smoothed data: see Table B-1, Tables 2 and 3, and Chart 1.) Aggregate export values fall from the peak of 1818—a major revival of American trade following the serious disruption imposed by the War of 1812 and the Jefferson embargo—to a long period of dull export and import trade which continues into the late 1820's. There is a minor peak in 1825 followed by another relapse troughing in 1829. Exports really begin their first major boom after 1818 with the 1830's. From 1830 to 1838 in the smoothed data (1828 to 1836 in the annual data), a rapid expansion in foreign trade occurs. The first long swing in exports then falls to a trough in 1844, which terminates the cycle.[2]

---

2. In the longer process of secular development, the period of the 1830's is

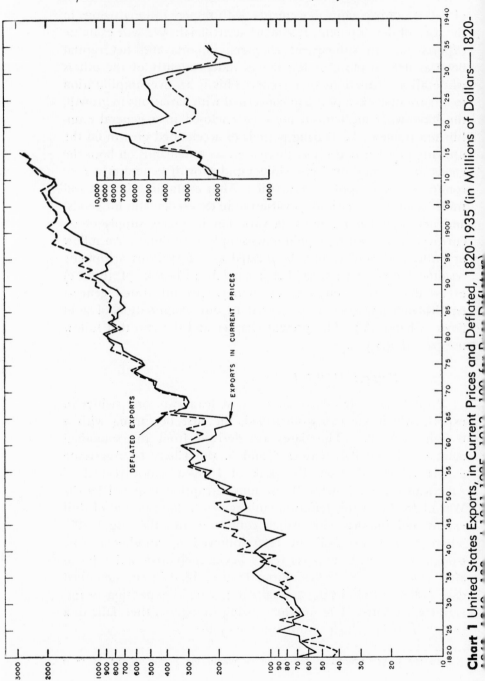

**Chart 1** United States Exports, in Current Prices and Deflated, 1820-1935 (in Millions of Dollars——1820-

The second swing is less clear since exports continue to rise from 1844 to the beginning of war for the Union. When a five-year moving average is applied to aggregate export values, exports peak in 1858 and fall to a trough in 1863. This may be somewhat contrived, however, since in the annual data a terminal peak is less obvious prior to the outbreak of the Civil War. But after 1856 there is strong evidence of an abrupt slackening in the rate of expansion of export revenue. As a matter of fact, except for one good year, export values are relatively constant during the period 1856-1860. It may be argued that the sharp fall from 1860 to 1861 is due primarily to a disruption of Southern cotton exports and to the war, but a reduction in the rate of growth of export values is in evidence as early as 1856. Nonetheless, there is striking evidence of two full swings prior to the Civil War, the average duration of which is about twenty years from peak to peak. The swings themselves have a substantial amplitude and are not reflected just in rates of change but also in absolute values.

These two swings in export values conform strikingly to the movements in other components of the balance of payments. This in itself might suggest causative importance of export movements rather than a response to domestic conditions. In the annual data, exports are synchronous with imports in all cases but one, the Civil War trough, when exports lag by two years; in the smoothed data, exports lag by one year in 1838 and by two years in 1844 while all other turning points are synchronous. Capital imports are positively related to exports with long lags, but the trade balance moves inversely with exports. (The smoothed data for exports in current and constant prices are given in Chart 1.)

After the Civil War the relative time shape of exports changes quite drastically. First, their amplitudes become much more damped; over long periods, export fluctuations are mostly in

---

extremely important as the starting point of United States export expansion. It is interesting to note that it was not until 1835 that export values exceeded those achieved in 1807 prior to the Jefferson embargo and the War of 1812. Clearly, much of the apparent stagnation of American trade during this period was the result of a long secular fall in world prices which was not seriously interrupted until the gold discoveries in the American West during the 1850's.

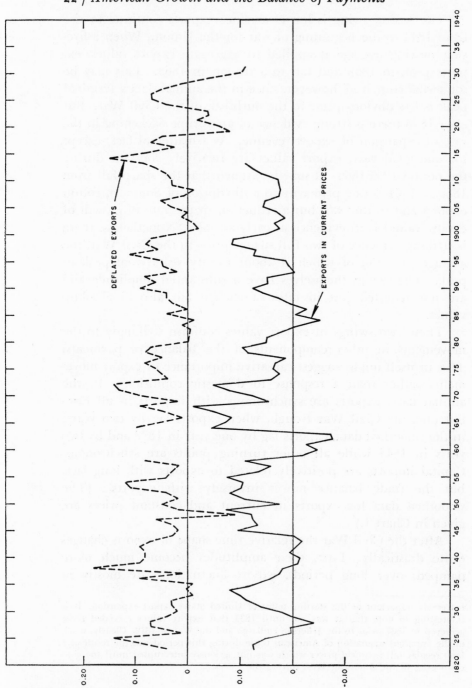

**Chart 2** United States Exports, in Current Prices and Deflated, 1823-1931 (in Percentage Rates of

positive rates of change rather than in absolute values. This is especially evident in the time path of rates of change when smoothed by a five-year moving average (see Chart 2). Second, the evidence of long swings in particular is somewhat lacking. There is one long secular movement from the trough in 1863 to a peak in 1882 and a trough in 1886, twenty-three years from trough to trough. Not only does this secular movement have an unusually long duration, but also it has very little similarity to domestic movements and to the other components of the balance of payments as well. Aggregate exports continue to rise during the depression in the middle and late seventies; they trough in 1886 during a period of secular boom in imports and capital movements. This movement in aggregate exports is not at all like the two long swings prior to 1860.

After 1886 there is little evidence at all of secular fluctuations. From 1886 to the outbreak of World War I, exports expand at a fairly constant rate.

The over-all view would seem to be that exports did have a definite relationship to other balance-of-payments components prior to the 1860's. After the Civil War, exports did not move in any consistent fashion. There is only one secular swing in evidence, and it is not of the same amplitude as those before 1860 nor of the same amplitude or timing as other elements in the balance of payments. This secular movement, 1863-1886, spans one and one-half cycles in imports and capital movements.

### Deflated Exports: 1820-1913

Adequate deflator indices for exports from 1820 to 1913 are difficult to obtain. The index used here is an aggregation of the following (see Table B-4): for the pre–Civil War period, a cotton price index compiled by Hammond in his study of the industry;[3] for the period 1861-1878, an index supplied by Matthew Simon in his balance-of-payments study;[4] for the period

---

3. M. B. Hammond, *The Cotton Industry*, American Economic Association (New York: Macmillan Co., 1897), New Series No. 1, Appendix 1.
4. "The United States Balance of Payments, 1861-1900," *Trends in the American Economy in the Nineteenth Century* ("Studies in Income and Wealth," Vol. XXIV [Princeton, N. J.: Princeton University Press, 1960]), Table 6, Col. 1, p. 650.

1879-1923, Robert E. Lipsey's index.[5] All these series are weighted export price indices except, of course, the cotton price index. The use of the cotton price index to deflate aggregate export values should become clear when we are fortified with the knowledge that cotton revenue makes up about 50 to 60 per cent of aggregate exports even as late as the mid-1850's (see pages 33-35).

When deflated, exports in constant prices have much milder amplitudes, but the export fluctuations are by no means eliminated. We cannot explain the post-bellum movements in export values by appealing to endogenous price movements alone. For the period 1863-1912, and especially from the late 1870's on, exports in constant prices exhibit a great deal of stability when we examine absolute levels (see Chart 1). The swing from 1863 to 1886 in current prices is not washed out by the deflation, but the dating is altered. Not only has the amplitude of this cycle in total exports been reduced by the application of a price deflator, but also the swing now peaks in 1880 and falls to a secular trough in 1884 (the decade of the 1880's is *generally* a period of rapid expansion in all other series).

Another long swing reveals itself in the deflated data, however, rising from the trough in 1884 to a peak in 1900 and falling to a trough in 1904. This movement reveals itself mostly in rates of change and is inversely related to domestic activity. In view of the roughness of the deflators for the latter part of the nineteenth century and due to the rather minor character of this "cycle" in exports in constant prices, we shall tend to disregard the movement from 1884 to 1904 altogether for our purposes.[6]

### Exports and the Trade Balance: 1820-1913

If we examine the dating in Tables 2 and 3, the inverse relation between the trade balance and imports is immediately

---

5. We have used Lipsey's early price estimates since his revised estimates appeared too late for us to take advantage of them: *Price and Quantity Trends in the Foreign Trade of the United States,* National Bureau of Economic Research (Princeton, N. J.: Princeton University Press, 1963).

6. Nevertheless, it is interesting to note the inverse relation between exports and domestic long swings from 1863 until World War I. The seriousness of these exports swings is, however, questionable. This inverse correlation is discussed further on pages 33-35.

clear. In spite of the fact that export values conform positively with imports before 1860, move inversely from 1863 to 1886, and reveal relative stability from 1886 to 1900, exports seem to cause only minor interference with the coincident pattern between imports and the trade balance. This can be explained, of course, by the lack of consistency of export movement in relation to the long-swing schema. From 1820 to 1900 the trough in the trade balance leads the peak in import values by an average of two years: in three out of four cases there is a clear lead, and in one case imports and the trade balance are synchronous. During the same period, the peak in the trade balance consistently lags the trough in imports: three cases lag and one is synchronous (discarding the dating for the Civil War trough).

This variety in the time pattern of export values over the period 1820-1900 seems to have a more important effect upon the *amplitude* of the trade balance. The fluctuations in the trade balance up to the mid-1840's are extremely mild relative to those after that time, although the trade balance *does* reveal vigorous swings during the earlier period. Part of the explanation for this progressive increase in amplitude lies in the fact that exports generally conform to the movements in imports from 1820 to the 1850's. After 1845 exports continue to rise, but the recession of the late 1850's and early 1860's is only reflected in a prominent slackening in growth rates before the start of the Civil War and the Southern blockade (and the resultant sharp fall in cotton export revenues). This is not true of the import series which falls more decisively in the late fifties. And, of course, after 1860 exports either move in an inverse relation to imports, 1863 to 1886 (trough to trough), or do not interfere with the dominance of import movements at all, 1886 to 1900, since exports exhibit relative stability. (Compare trade-balance and import dating in Tables 2 and 3; see Chart 11 for trade-balance movements and Chart 9 for import movements.)

The period 1900-1913 presents quite a different story. Exports begin to play a definite role in dictating movements in the trade balance. It is also true that the evidence of long swings in the trade balance during this period is much less clear—perhaps for the same reason.

Imports fall from a peak in 1891 to a trough in 1896. The trade balance, as in all other swings previous to the nineties, moves inversely, rising from a trough in 1888 to a peak in 1900. But from 1898 to 1908 there is a period of ten years when the trade balance remains at a more or less constant level. When the trade balance falls to a trough in 1908, it is due to the movements in exports. In spite of the fact that the trade-balance cycle 1888-1908 has a relatively mild movement at its termination, it is necessarily the case that the movements in export values cause this termination.

The reason for this apparent importance of exports just prior to World War I is clearly due to the uncharacteristic lack of violent movement in imports. Interestingly enough, this is also a period in which domestic series do reveal a long swing but of rather mild movement. Thus, an autonomous fall in exports during the period 1908-1911 is enough to control the movements in the trade balance and to precipitate an apparent cycle in the trade balance. The swing in the trade balance, incidentally, is of doubtful importance since it has few of the characteristics consistently revealed in other cycles. It has a long period of sustained high trade surplus 1898-1908, and the trough itself is short and extremely abrupt; neither characteristic was exhibited in the relatively smooth swings prior to 1900. (In Chapter VII we shall remark on the similarity between this pre–World War I period and the post–World War II era.)

The conclusion of this brief analysis should be explicit enough. Exports move in either such a relatively stable or such an inconsistent fashion that they have no systematic effect upon long swings in the nineteenth-century trade balance. In normal periods, export amplitudes are mild relative to imports, and their movements lack the consistency in timing and amplitude which is revealed in import movements. Merchandise imports dominate the trade balance during the period 1820-1900 in such a manner as to cause a striking inverse correlation between these two components and an inverse relation between the trade-balance deficit and net capital imports. Exports seem only to act as a random and autonomous element over the trade-balance timing. They influence the amplitude of the trade balance such that over the long swing 1822-1844, for example, when exports conform to the movements in imports, trade-balance fluctuations are milder than in later periods when exports are either inversely related to, or independent of, import movements.

We have said little about the evidence which might lead us to treat exports as exogenous or as functionally related to the building cycle and thus to other components of the balance of payments; this discussion is continued below. What we have concluded here, however, is that exports play a minor role in influencing trade-balance fluctuations during the nineteenth century. During the first portion of the twentieth century, they *do* play an important role: (1) due to the stable growth of imports from 1900 to 1914, which is consistent with domestic movements, and (2) perhaps also due to the fact that the United States was then a net exporter of capital.

### Export Components: 1850-1913

In an earlier section of this chapter, we drew the preliminary conclusion that the movements in aggregate American exports could be treated as exogenous to the long swing schema or, more simply, as not reflecting the domestic long swing. There are two aspects of export movements which merit discussion at this point: (1) the character of the export movement, 1822-1863, 1863-1886, and 1886-1913, for it is mainly on the grounds of the unusual and dissimilar movements of these periods as well as the lack of evidence of endogenous long swings from 1863 to 1913 that we have considered exports as unimportant to the long-swing schema; (2) the components of the export series for the period 1863-1913 (the period during which we have difficulty finding long swings) and in particular the characteristics of the extended movements 1863-1886.

Chart 3 disaggregates exports into five commodity groupings (Table B-7): crude materials, crude foodstuffs, manufactured foodstuffs, semimanufactures, and finished manufactures. Beginning with 1880, it is immediately evident that the export components do not consistently behave in the same fashion as aggregate exports. Rarely do the five series conform during 1880-1913. It is evident that the movement in aggregate exports is

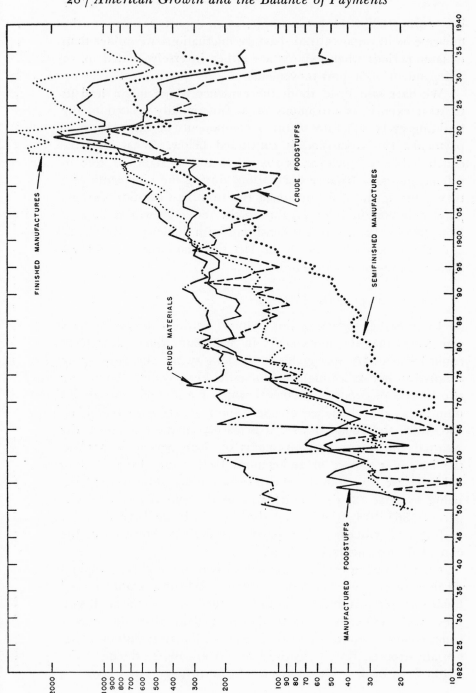

**Chart 3** Five Export Commodity Groups, 1850-1935 (in Millions of Dollars)

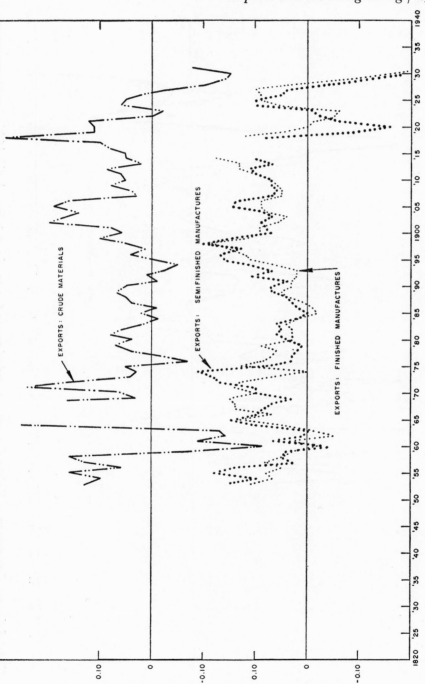

**Chart 4** Export Components: Crude Materials, Finished Manufactures, Semifinished Manufactures, 1853-1931 (in Percentage Rates of Change, Smoothed by Five-Year Moving Average)

*Source:* Table A-7

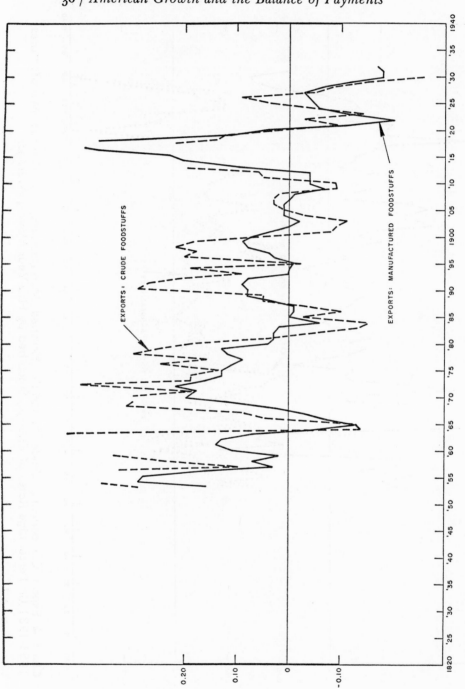

**Chart 5** Export Components: Crude Foodstuffs and Manufactured Foodstuffs, 1853-1931 (in Percentage

hardly common to all export commodities. More accurately, the movements in aggregate exports reflect the dominance of one series or another at any point in time. We shall see that there is some evidence of long secular movements (in rates of change) in each of these components and of much longer duration than the building cycle. But since they rarely coincide, the movements in the aggregate are random and do not exhibit long swings.

In Chart 3 the period 1880-1886 exhibits three series rising and two series, crude and manufactured foodstuffs, falling. Due to the importance of agricultural products in United States trade at this time and since the movement in crude foodstuffs is extraordinary, aggregate exports fall during these six years, indicating the termination of a "long swing." The six years 1886-1892 reveal all the export components growing at a somewhat smooth rate. But 1892-1898 again reflects inconsistency among components: two series are falling, two are rising sharply, and crude foodstuffs falls sharply to 1895 and rises sharply again to 1898. Aggregate export values grow at a fairly stable rate from 1898 to 1906, but this is certainly not the case of all the component series. This stability is the result of offsetting fluctuations in the components: three series are rising sharply, one remains somewhat stable, and one falls sharply. Again, the period 1906-1914 is one in which aggregate exports are rising at some constant rate. However, three series are rising and two series are falling. (These descriptions are approximate. For a more accurate description of the movements in the aggregate and its components, see Charts 3, 4, and 5.)

This exercise certainly underlines the unsystematic aspect of total export movement during the period 1880-1913. The result of this extremely divergent movement in direction and amplitude among the export components is to delete any long swings that might appear in the components themselves. As we have already noted, this is a result we might expect, since United States exports after 1880 become increasingly diversified so that none of the series seems to dominate the aggregate movement over any long period of time. Nor would we expect the direction of domestic investment, supply conditions, price elasticities, and foreign demand to affect each of these varied commodity types, especially manufactured and agricultural products, in the same way.

The movements of these five export components are even more interesting during the two decades or so after the Civil War. By 1870 all of these export components attain their prewar peaks. Crude foodstuffs, manufactured foodstuffs, and crude materials reattain their average 1858-1861 levels. Finished and semifinished manufactures, located in the North and Northeast, seem to have been less affected by the war and rise during the hostilities to 1870. The year 1870 seems to be a fair starting point for an examination of the export components over the apparent aggregate export cycle (1863-1886).

As we concluded earlier, the secular "swing" in aggregate export values over this period has little relation to the balance-of-payments dating as a whole. It also has little likeness to the export swings prior to 1860. But why does this long secular movement persist in both current and constant prices? The answer will be clear after looking at Chart 3. The movement from 1863 to 1886, the upswing of which is often badly termed a "take off" in foreign trade, is mainly a reflection of the unusually rapid opening of the West and the increasing importance of the United States in world grain trade. This is a period in which United States exports are still dominated by primary product export (the movements prior to 1860 are strictly cotton dominated).

From 1870 to 1886, disregarding the mild depression of 1875-1879, crude materials rise at a fairly constant rate. There is no evidence of a long swing in this series by itself nor does its movement conform to that of aggregate exports. This is true of movements both in absolute levels and in rates of change (see Chart 4). The movements in semifinished manufactures and finished manufactured exports do not exhibit long swings in absolute values. They do, however, reveal movements in positive rates of growth, the dating of which conform to aggregate exports at the terminal point 1886. But the relationship is less precise than that. From 1870 to 1876, in absolute values, the export of semifinished manufactures expands at extremely high rates of growth averaging from 10 to 12 per cent per annum. From 1876 to 1888, however, there is a protracted period of relatively low growth rates; when smoothed by a five-year moving average, the rates of growth average about 2.5 per cent per annum. The same kind of pattern is exhibited in finished manufactures which rise sharply to 1877 and remain almost constant over the period 1878-1889. In the light of this evidence, one would hardly say that the three series move sympathetically over the period. But in spite of this somewhat divergent movement, aggregate exports rise rapidly to a peak in 1882 and *fall* to a trough in 1886. The cause of this movement is due to the extraordinary fluctuations in, especially, crude foodstuffs and in manufactured foodstuffs. Thus, in spite of the apparent clarity in the long-run movement of aggregate export values from 1863 to 1886, a movement rejected as part of a pattern of long swings, the export components do not move in sympathy with each other.

**Table 4** Dating for Crude and Manufactured Foodstuff Exports

| In Absolute Values After Smoothing by Five-Year Moving Average | Crude Foodstuffs | Manufactured Foodstuffs |
|---|---|---|
| Trough | 1866 | 1867 |
| Peak | 1880 | 1880 |
| Trough | 1888 | 1887 |
| Peak | 1899 | 1901 |
| Trough | 1911 | 1910 |
| Peak | 1920 | 1919 |

We do not intend to disregard the unique movement during this period; clearly, it may have great implications about the process of growth, its effects upon the balance of payments, and vice versa. The boom in the grain trade surely had its effect upon industrial expansion in the West as well as influencing the movement of net capital imports. What has been attempted throughout this chapter, however, is to make clear that the movement must be considered as unsystematic in relation to our schema in spite of any possible linkage with building and transportation development.

Before we proceed to an examination of the unique movements in export values prior to 1860, each of the export components should be examined briefly over the entire period from the Civil War to World War I. Unfortunately, a disaggregation of this sort does not exist earlier than 1850.

The dating for *absolute values* of crude foodstuffs and manufactured foodstuffs follows below (see Table 4). In rates of
growth there *are* long and protracted movements in these two
series, averaging a bit longer than our usual conception of build-
ing-cycle duration, but the movements are extremely clear (see
Chart 5). From trough to trough, the average duration is about
twenty-three years, and from peak to peak about twenty-two years.
The two series are almost synchronous. But the interesting pattern
of these two agricultural groups is their *inverse* correlation with
domestic activity beginning with the period of Reconstruction.

**Table 5** Dating for Crude Material and Semifinished and Finished
Manufactured Exports, in Rates of Change

| In Rates of Change After Smoothing by Five-Year Moving Average | Crude Material | Semifinished Manufactures | Finished Manufactures |
|---|---|---|---|
| Trough | — | 1860 | 1862 |
| Peak | — | 1874 | 1869 |
| Trough | 1894 | 1885 | 1885 |
| Peak | 1905 | 1898 | 1898 |
| Trough | 1913 | 1900 | 1903 |
| Peak | 1918 | Constant to 1929 (eliminating 1915-1923) | |

Both series achieve rapid growth during deep domestic depression
(the late 1870's and early 1890's) while they languish during
domestic boom (the decade of the 1880's and from 1900 to 1910).
There are, of course, a number of plausible explanations for this
inverse movement. We shall briefly mention four possibilities:
(1) it may simply reflect a long lag of supply increase in agricultural products behind domestic investment,[7] especially in the
railroads; (2) when the export industry no longer plays a major
role in United States development, post-1860, it is possible for
foreign demand, inversely related to American long swings (in
Great Britain at least), to precipitate mild long swings in our
agricultural expansion; (3) Great Britain may reveal evidence of
long swings inversely related to United States development only

---

7. Cotton revenue revealed no such lag during the two long swings 1822-1844
and 1844-1863.

*after* 1870 when this inversion in agricultural exports begins; and (4) this period may reflect support for Cootner's thesis which is considered below.

The dating for rates of growth in the remaining three series are given in Table 5. Although their movements are less violent, both semifinished and finished manufactures also reveal long swings inversely related to domestic activity. Crude material reveals no long movement in rates of growth until 1894, then a movement to a peak rate of growth in 1905 and a trough in 1913. The movements in that component are almost inversely related to semifinished and finished manufactures, both of which have two long movements beginning in the early 1860's. There is no long movement in semifinished and finished manufactures evident after 1900 (see Chart 4).

## Cotton Exports and the Long Swing: 1820-1860

Throughout the discussion, we have pointed to the unique movements in exports during the pre–Civil War period. This section will be devoted to an analysis of that period.

There are two questions that require answering. First, why do aggregate export values exhibit such strong and regular swings from the 1820's to the 1860's and not between 1863 and 1913? The second question is directly related to the first: why do these long swings in export values exhibit systematic relationships with the other elements of the balance of payments? We have found that export and import values (1820-1860) are directly correlated with capital inflows and that exports and imports are also positively correlated. The answer to these questions lies in the fact that the United States was essentially a one-commodity exporter prior to the Civil War, and that this export was extremely susceptible to, *and/or the initiator of,* the same forces that seem to have caused import and capital-flow fluctuations over the long swing. The export is cotton, while grain plays an important secondary role in the middle and late 1850's.

The first task is to quantify our qualitative historical knowledge concerning the extreme importance of cotton in United States export trade. In the five-commodity disaggregate, we have information on the relative importance of crude materials in total

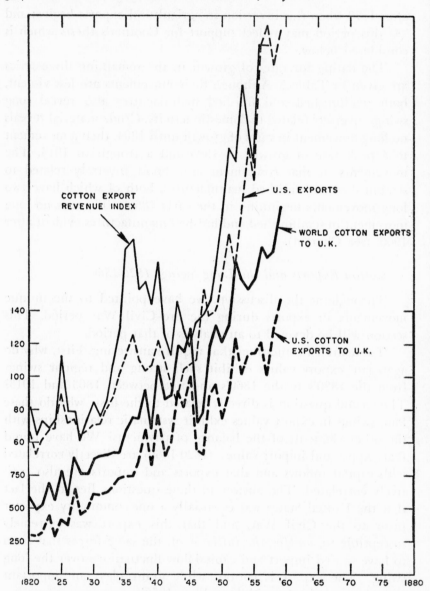

**Chart 6** Total United States Exports and a Cotton Revenue Index (in Millions of Dollars); United States Cotton Exports to United Kingdom and World Exports of Cotton to United Kingdom (in Thousands of Bales), 1820-1860

*Source:* See Text

exports beginning only with 1850. Crude materials (predominately raw cotton) accounted for 63 to 70 per cent of total exports from 1850 to 1853 and 51 to 57 per cent from 1854 to 1858! This fall in the percentage share is, incidentally, a reflection of United States entrance into the world grain trade. But the relative size of raw cotton exports at any point in time is not our main concern. More important to our problem, do movements in cotton export revenues dominate total export movements during the period?

Chart 6 reveals the dominance of cotton in total export movements. Cotton revenue was derived by converting Hammond's report of New York prices of middling-uplands cotton into an index over 1820-1860.[8] This index was then used to derive an estimate of the *movements* of cotton revenue, since quantum data for cotton exports are readily available (see Table B-8). The result is striking. In thirty-two out of thirty-seven years, the movement in the cotton revenue index conforms to official estimates of total exports and has a much larger amplitude than total exports. In 1823, 1838, 1839, 1843, and 1854 there is some disagreement. But the general impression is most certainly either that cotton exports dominate total export movements or that the other commodity groupings in the aggregate follow the movements in cotton with the exception of those five years. Either case has the same implications for our analysis.

The next problem is to determine, if possible, the importance of United States cotton exports in the world market. Chart 6 shows the relationship between total exports of cotton to the United Kingdom by the world and total United States exports of cotton to the United Kingdom.[9] Throughout the period under examination, approximately 85 per cent of United States cotton exports went to the United Kingdom. That we can treat the United Kingdom as the world market for the early part of the nineteenth century appears to be a fairly reasonable assumption.

In thirty-five out of forty years, the movement in United States exports seems to dominate the world market. There are two minor

8. Hammond, *Cotton Industry*, Appendix 1.
9. James A. Mann, *The Cotton Industry of Great Britain* (London: Simpkin Marshall and Company, 1860), Table 27, p. 126.

exceptions in 1829 and 1831, and three more serious ones in 1837, 1847, and 1854. Thus, in spite of the fact that the United States' share in the world market falls slightly over the forty years, the movement of our cotton exports still dominated the market throughout the period 1820-1860. If this evidence is accurate, it simplifies the analysis a great deal, for now we are able to discuss the effect of endogenous United States supply on price and revenue without appealing to autonomous price movements caused by supply changes outside the United States. It seems clear, then, that the United States had a very large monopolistic control over its major export commodity, and thus supply conditions in the American market must have had important repercussions on cotton prices.

Does foreign demand exhibit any movement which could have caused long swings in export revenue? Measurement is difficult, but it is our opinion that consideration of foreign demand is somewhat extraneous. If we find that there are regular and consistent relationships between United States production and world prices (with United States supply revealing much larger fluctuations), then it is very unlikely that demand can play too great a role, *especially* in view of the fact that Great Britian does not exhibit evidence of long swings prior, at least, to the 1850's (see Chapter VI).

In an attempt to measure the change in foreign demand, two indices, both of which are British series, have been utilized. First is the Kondratieff index of annual British textile manufuctures production, and second, British cotton manufactures exported.[10] These are given in rates of change on Chart 7. In reality, both these series are in terms of revenue, and therefore the observations are not independent of the United States supply of cotton (raw material price has an effect upon cotton manufactures and thus on the revenue product of cotton manufactures). The results are still striking and meaningful. In rates of change there is no evidence of long swings in either the Kondratieff or the British cotton

---

10. N. D. Kondratieff, "Die Preisdynamik der industreillen und landwirtschaftlichen Waren (Zum Problem der relativen Dynamik und Konjunkten)," *Archiv für Socialwissenschaft und Sozialpolitik*, LX (1928), 81-82. British cotton manufactures exported comes from Mann, *The Cotton Industry of Great Britain*, Table 3, pp. 97-98.

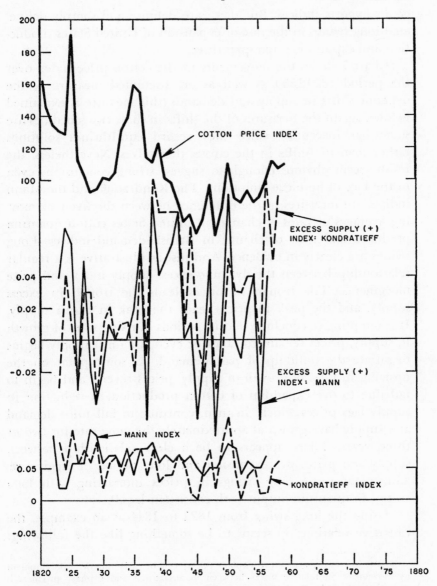

**Chart 7** Cotton Price Index (Imlah): Mann and Kondratieff Indices, 1820-1860 (in Percentage Rates of Change)

*Source:* See Text

goods exports indices. But there are definite and sharply delineated long swings in the rate of expansion of United States production and export of cotton quantities.

Chart 7 shows the movements in the cotton price index over the period 1820-1860 as well as an attempted measure of the dynamic shifts in supply and demand (this measure is explained below). Again the measures of the shifts in these two schedules are somewhat inaccurate since they record equilibrium solutions rather than the shifts in the curves themselves. Nevertheless, the results seem obvious enough to suggest strong conclusions even in the face of heroic assumptions. The Kondratieff and the Mann indices are measures of the difference between the five-year moving averages of rates of change of United States cotton quantum produced and rates of change in British demand indices. Long swings are clearly in evidence. And just as illustrative is a regular relationship between the dynamic excess supply index and price movements. The trough in prices leads the trough in excess supply, and the peak in prices leads the peak in excess supply. It is tempting to conclude that in periods of rising rates of growth in supply, prices remain constant or even rise until supply begins to satiate the build-up of past demand. At some point on the upswing in rates of growth of supply, prices reverse and begin to fall due to overexpansion of cotton production. A reduction in supply lags prices which, in turn, continue to fall until demand and supply have grown at approximately the same rate for two or three years. There appears to be a clear relationship between supply and price: overexpansion and long period of lagging readjustment cause long swings in prices interacting with long swings in quantum output with consistent lags.[11]

Using the long swing from 1822 to 1844 as an example, the causative relationship seems to be something like the following:

---

11. An interesting attempt to explain the process of early American development by movements in relative prices between manufactured and primary products is given in a thesis by Paul H. Cootner, "Transportation, Innovation, and Economic Development: The Case of the United States Railroads" (unpublished Ph.D. dissertation, Massachusetts Institute of Technology, 1953). Cootner's thesis purports to explain secular shifts from cotton and grain production into manufacturing by the systematic movements of raw material prices and supply overexpansion. The initial work on the hypothesis of price and supply lag mechanism in explaining early long swings in American development has been done by North.

quantum cotton exports rise rapidly from 1829 to 1835 and export values rise with them since supply has not yet caught up with past demands. The price of cotton rises to a peak in 1835. After 1835 and up to 1843, the rate of growth of cotton quantum exports approximately sustains itself and prices begin to fall. Export values begin falling (late 1836 and early 1837) since, apparently, the locus of equilibrium points moves along an inelastic long-run demand curve. From 1843 to 1850 export quantum remains at

**Table 6** Indices of Rates of Development in the United States

| Cotton Export Quantities in Percentage Change | (2) Rigbleman's Building Index | (3) Percentage Change in Railroad Mileage in South | (4) Land Sales in South (public) | (5) Steamboat Tonnage Built on Western Rivers | Average lag of (1) |
|---|---|---|---|---|---|
| 1830 T | — | — | 1824 T | — | 6.0 |
| 1838 P | 1836 P | 1839 P | 1836 P | 1839 P | 0.5 |
| 1845 T | 1843 T | 1845 T | 1842 T | 1841 T | 2.3 |
| 1857 P | 1853 P | 1852 P | 1854 P | 1855 P | 3.5 |
| Average lag of (1) | 2.7 | 1.3 | 3.5 | 1.7 | |

low growth rates (almost zero) but prices recover, causing a rise in export values. Thus the lagged cycle prevails over the period 1820-1860.

The last question to be investigated is the relationship between domestic investment, in size and direction, and the supply of cotton exports. Table 6 shows the movement of both the rates of change of raw cotton exported and the movements in Rigbleman's building index, official land sales in the South, steamboat tonnage built on Western Rivers, and the percentage change in railroad mileage in operation in the South. We are appealing, then, to the size and regional direction of transporation and building investment[12] as the causative factor of export expansion. This suggestion is perhaps a bit trivial, since economic theory would most

---

12. The Rigbleman building index is not regional, it is true, but represents such activity for the nation as a whole.

certainly suggest a relationship of this kind, but the quantitative evidence is most enlightening. There has been no attempt, however, to determine whether price movements cause the flow of investment, or vice versa; only the evidence of correlation is presented.

Table 6 exhibits the dating of these domestic series. The direct correlation between our investment indices and cotton quantum expansion is very clear. There seems to be a consistent supply lag in almost all cases over the period as a whole, but there is little we can say about the relative size of the lags at peaks as compared to troughs. It does seem, however, that the building index and land sales have larger leads over cotton expansion than those of the two transportation investment indices. It should be added at this point that the inflow of foreign capital was very much a function of the state of the cotton market in the 1830's and 1840's. Perhaps more than at any other time in American history, the 1830's and 1840's reflect a very close correlation between the flow of foreign capital and the expansion of the export of primary products in the United States. Chapter VI delves into this question more deeply.

The supply response to price changes certainly assumes the dominating role in the analysis of ante-bellum balance-of-payments history. North would suggest even further that it plays the major part in determining the general pace of American internal development:

It is the central part of the argument with respect to long swings in prices and other economic activity that supply shifts in response to price changes proceeded irregularly, and, in conjunction with the speculative behavior which accompanied the latter phases of periods of accelerated growth, were important in the explanation of long swings in economic activity which characterized the United States development after 1815.[13]

Speculation certainly plays an important role in the cotton boom of the 1830's and even as late as the wheat boom in the seventies.

That the export sector should play an important role in the early stages of accelerated development has been implied in most of the contemporary literature.

---

13. North, *Economic Growth*, p. 2.

There are few exceptions to the essential initiating role of a successful export sector in the early stages of accelerated growth of
market economies. The reason is that the domestic market has
been small and scattered ... An expanding external market has
provided the means for an increase in the size of the domestic
market, growth in money income, and the spread of specialization
and division of labor.[14]

In the American case, sustained development owed much to
natural endowments. North argues that production possibilities,
so that the return on a number of goods were not too much less
than exports, made complementary growth and diversification
possible with changing factor proportions and external and internal demand. His thesis goes on to suggest that although the South
initiated the process of development through cotton, triangular
trade with the manufacturing North and the growing West
allowed the impressive growth of subsidiary industries.

It should by now be clear that the North thesis is an appealing
explanation of the patterns of American development in the ante-
bellum years. We have seen that the evidence briefly reviewed in
this chapter does not conflict with his thesis. However, the argument has certainly not been fully tested in this book or in North's
for that matter. Nothing has been done in this chapter or in
North's writings to adequately evaluate the importance of indigenous factors during the period 1820-1860 or to weigh the
relative significance of internal factors versus international devel-
opments in determining the trend and fluctuations in American
growth. Nevertheless, the hypothesis has a great deal of merit due
to its simplicity, if for no other reason, and we shall make further
use of it.

This same long movement in prices causing long swings in
supply response is exhibited, but to a much lesser extent, in the
grain industry. Perhaps more important as an export inter-
regionally than internationally, grain exports still play an important role in the trade balance during the fifties, sixties, and early
seventies. Quantum wheat exports hit a peak in 1862 and fall to a
trough in 1866 following the fall in wheat prices in the late 1850's
and early 1860's (see Table B-9). They then reveal a long period

---

14. *Ibid.*

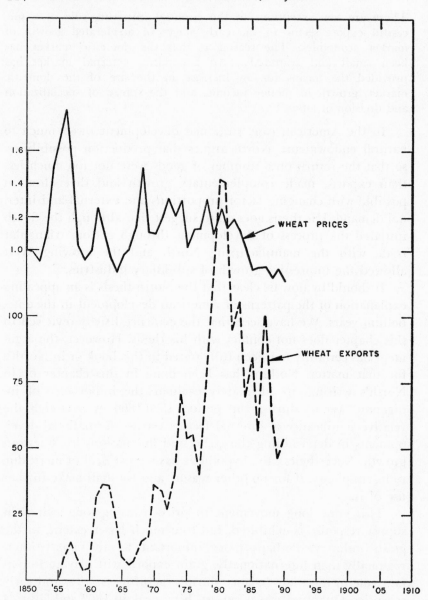

**Chart 8** United States Wheat Exports (in Millions of Bushels) and Wheat Price Index, 1850-1890

*Source:* Table A-9

of sustained expansion following the boom in prices in 1868, which is generally sustained until 1880 (see Chart 8). But even in the period of the 1850's, the flow of capital into the United States is used mainly in opening up the granary of the Midwest. Perhaps more than in the 1830's and 1840's, foreign capital is primarily interested in the securities offered by the transportation and communication sector; and this sector, especially in the 1850's, is very clearly related to the exploitation of a new primary product export, grain.

Even though grain exports equal the importance of cotton by 1870, agricultural products in general become less and less predominate in aggregate exports as the century progresses. In spite of the decline in relative importance of agricultural exports, even as late as the 1880's the flow of foreign capital is indirectly influenced, at least, by agricultural expansion and the rate of development of the railway network.

If some further speculation is allowed at this point, we may have underlined an interesting paradox. Prior to 1860 there are long swings in exports due to similar movements in the rate of development of American agricultural output. It appears that the long-swing mechanism (if it is indeed recurring) *may* have been initiated by the lagged response of supply to price. Once the mechanism began it was sustained throughout the nineteenth century, even after the United States had long passed into the stages of diversified economy and was relatively rich in capital and exporting manufactured products. After the 1860's exports no longer yield long swings—but it may have been ante-bellum long swings in export expansion which triggered the long-swing mechanism.[15]

---

15. There have been other contemporary economists who have thought it necessary to stress the importance of agricultural development and the export sector in American history: G. Murphy and A. Zellner, "Sequential Growth, the Labor-Safety-Valve Doctrine and Development of American Unionism," *Journal of Economic History*, XIX (September, 1959), 402-421; R. C. O. Matthews, *A Study in Trade Cycle History: 1833-1842* (Cambridge: Cambridge University Press, 1954); G. S. Callendar, "Early Transportation and Banking Enterprise of the States in Relation to the Growth of Corporations," *Quarterly Journal of Economics*, XVII (1903), 111-162; A. J. Youngson, *Possibilities of Economic Progress* (Cambridge: Cambridge University Press, 1959). We have already indicated some of North's writings on this subject. However, one other of his publications should be added to the small sample above: "Agriculture and Regional Economic Growth," *Proceedings of the American Farm Economic Association*, XLI (December, 1959), 943-951.

# III.

# IMPORTS AND THE LONG SWING

## Summary of Findings

We have seen thus far that exports do not exhibit consistent and systematic long swings from 1820 to 1913, and for that reason we treat them as unsystematic relative to our long-swing framework. Either exports are too dependent on variables outside the indigenous system (i.e., world prices, foreign demand and supply) or the effects of the domestic long swing upon export components are much too varied to produce a systematic pattern in aggregate exports directly *or* inversely related to domestic activity. This does not exclude the possibility, of course, that exports played an important role before the Civil War, if not by initiating the early Kuznets cycle at least by reflecting and supporting the domestic long swing.

Conceptually, the problem seems much simpler in the case of imports. If domestic price movements are correlated with real-income movements over the long swing, contradictory pressures will be exerted upon exports; a priori, this seems unlikely in the case of aggregate imports. On the contrary, not only will real growth stimulate import demand under normal conditions (i.e., where the income effect exceeds the rate of import substitution), but also price inflation will add to this increased demand for foreign goods with a movement out of relatively expensive domestic goods. Furthermore, in the case of exports, *marginal* export revenue and supply elasticities are important since the United States is to some degree a monopolist facing a limited market (i.e., cotton), while she is not likely to hold any monopsonist power during the greater part of the period 1820-1913. Theoretically, we should be able to treat foreign supply and world prices as given exogenously and unaffected by United States import demand; this a priori presumption will be challenged when we encounter the evidence in Chapter VI, but for the present the assumption will be retained. Thus, given external conditions, an increase in export supply does not necessarily imply an increase in export revenue, while an increase in import demand does imply an increase in import values. And, of course, the export of physical output, everything else equal, is a function of the *stock* of domestic capital, while imports are more a function of the *flow* of domestic investment and should be more sensitive to income movements and to the level of aggregate demand. Exports should be related to the *flow* of domestic investment only indirectly (and inversely) through domestic prices and availabilities. Finally, diversification tends to stabilize aggregate exports from the vagaries of foreign demand as well as from the multi-effect of domestic activity; imports, however, are more likely to reveal a consistency of movement since all the import components should be a direct function of domestic income. We should expect to find small leads and lags and variations in amplitudes among the import components, but a general sympathy of movement should exist among them. Aggregate imports should exhibit, therefore, a long swing with more clarity in both amplitude and periodicity than the aggregate export series.

In summary, *with a given supply,* exports will vary inversely with domestic demand, but positively with foreign demand (if exports are *not the cause* but the result of domestic long swings). Domestic demand may reveal Kuznets swings in the United States, but foreign demand will not, particularly since it is a compound of demand in a number of countries whose fluctuations are not synchronous. If domestic and foreign income movements were of equal importance, one would expect some inverse correlation. In addition, supplies are *not* constant. Our exports were heavily dominated by agricultural products and, therefore, by extension of acreage and by crop yields. In the pre–Civil War period and to a lesser extent in the 1860's and 1870's, agricultural expansion was linked to transport development and then to the domestic long swing. Later it was of less importance in total exports. Imports should vary directly with the domestic long swing with foreign supply responding flexibly to their demand, since our imports were chiefly manufactured goods and nonagricultural raw materials. Supposedly we held no monopsonistic position in the nineteenth century, and thus random fluctuations should be unimportant.

Aggregate imports do indeed reveal long swings of approximately twenty years in duration. The evidence of these movements is strikingly obvious in the annual import data (in current prices) without the use of trend removal or rates of change. The import series reveals five easily identifiable long swings from the 1820's to World War I. In the annual data, imports in current prices have the following long-swing chronology, from trough to trough: 1821-1843, 1843-1862, 1862-1878, 1878-1898, and 1898-1915. Generally, the amplitude of import movements over the long swing is far more excessive than that of exports. Even when exports move in the same fashion as imports over the long swing (ante-bellum), the trade balance is dominated by variation in import demand. Domestic upswings in Kuznets cycles during the nineteenth century are always characterized, therefore, by trade-balance and current-account deterioration, while sluggish growth tends to generate trade-balance surpluses or a progressive reduction in trade-balance deficits. Deflation of import values by an import price index, incidentally, does not interfere with the overall pattern of these long swings in imports. It is true, we shall see, that the amplitude of these swings in imports is reduced when deflated by import prices, but the effect of deflation on the dating of turning points is unimportant.

These five long swings in aggregate imports reveal considerable similarity to one another. In absolute values the import peak usually occurs late in the cycle. In rates of change, however, peaks occur very early in the cycle, are followed by a period of ten to

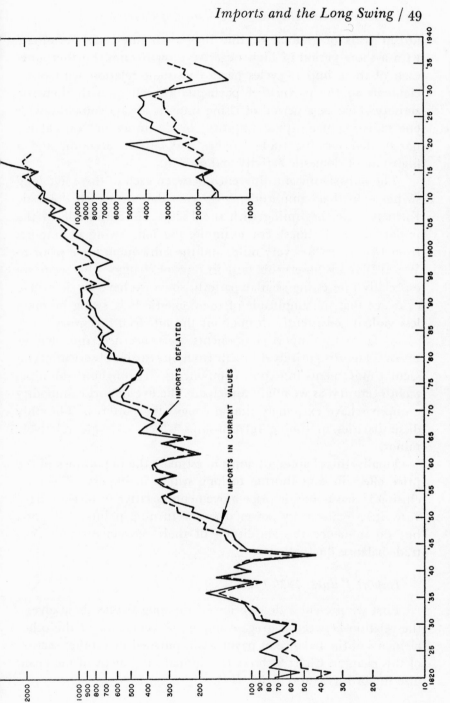

**Chart 9** United States Imports, in Current Prices and Deflated, 1820-1935 (in Millions of Dollars)

*Source:* Tables A-1 and A-5

fifteen years of gradual decline in growth rates, and terminate with a short period of high negative growth rates. Furthermore, each of these import cycles has a consistent relation with other elements in the balance of payments as well as with domestic activity. That is, a period of rising imports always coincides with one of rising net capital imports (or declining net capital exports), deteriorating trade balance and current account, and a high rate of domestic activity and growth.

The only significant difference between each of these five long swings is in their amplitude. It appears that with each domestic Kuznets cycle, beginning with the 1820's, the amplitude of the import series declines! For example, the long swing in imports from 1878 to 1898 is very mild, and the subsequent cycle prior to World War I is observable only in rates of change. This seems an especially interesting secular pattern, since we have no definitive evidence that the amplitude of the domestic long swing becomes less violent *consistently* throughout the nineteenth century.

As far as the import components are concerned, this chapter uncovers results entirely different from our earlier observations on secular movements in export components. Throughout the nineteenth century, as we might anticipate, the five import commodity groupings have extremely similar long-swing patterns. The only dissimilarities in timing relationships which arise are relatively minor.

Finally, this chapter attempts to estimate the importance of the price effect in contributing to long swings in imports. The conclusion is that domestic price movements, relative to foreign, have very little explanatory power over the turning points of imports but do influence the amplitude of their movements and thus trade-balance fluctuations.

### Import Values: 1820-1913

First we present a description of the long swings themselves—the relation between aggregate import movements and the other elements of the balance of payments is pursued in another section of this chapter. Chart 9 shows the annual movement of merchandise imports (see also Table B-1).

Imports fall from a peak in 1817, following the trade revival after the Jefferson embargo and the War of 1812, to a deep trough in the 1820's, terminating in 1822. The first long swing in aggregate imports then rises from that low to a peak in the panic year, 1837, and subsequently contracts to a trough in 1842, for a duration of twenty years. The amplitude of this secular movement

**Table 7** Comparative Amplitude Measurements for Imports and Exports[a]

| Year | Imports (current: smoothed) (millions of dollars) | $\|\Delta\|$ | Amplitude (M) $\Delta'$ | Per Year | $\Delta'$ | Amplitude (X) Per Year | $\|\Delta\|$ | Exports (current: smoothed) (millions of dollars) | Year |
|---|---|---|---|---|---|---|---|---|---|
| 1817 P | 111.9 | | | | | | | 80.5 | 1818 P |
| 1822 T | 70.7 | 41.2 | 0.368 | 0.074 | 0.198 | 0.050 | 15.9 | 64.6 | 1822 T |
| 1837 P | 149.2 | 78.5 | 1.110 | 0.074 | 0.785 | 0.049 | 50.7 | 115.3 | 1838 P |
| 1842 T | 102.0 | 47.2 | 0.316 | 0.063 | 0.126 | 0.021 | 14.5 | 100.8 | 1844 T |
| 1858 P | 334.3 | 232.3 | 2.277 | 0.142 | 1.924 | 0.137 | 193.9 | 294.7 | 1858 P |
| 1863 T | 263.1 | 71.2 | 0.213 | 0.043 | 0.332 | 0.066 | 97.8 | 196.9 | 1863 T |
| 1873 P | 595.8 | 332.7 | 1.265 | 0.127 | 3.195 | 0.163 | 629.1 | 826.0 | 1882 P |
| 1877 T | 476.0 | 119.8 | 0.201 | 0.050 | 0.115 | 0.029 | 94.8 | 731.2 | 1886 T |
| 1891 P | 842.3 | 366.3 | 0.770 | 0.055 | | | | | |
| 1896 T | 716.6 | 125.7 | 0.149 | 0.030 | | | | | |
| 1915 (T) | 2,174.5 | — | — | — | | | | | |
| 1927 P | 4,330.9 | 2,156.4 | 0.992 | 0.086 | | | | | |
| 1933 T | 1,838.3 | 2,492.6 | 0.576 | 0.096 | | | | | |

[a]Where $\Delta = (P - T)$ for peak to trough and trough to peak, and amplitude is measured for simplicity:

$$\Delta' = (P - T)/P \text{ for peak to trough.}$$
$$\Delta' = (P - T)/T \text{ for trough to peak.}$$

It is true that these amplitude measures are biased in that, if the absolute change were the same for expansions and contractions, the amplitude of expansions would appear greater than those for contractions. However, we are only interested in comparing import and export movements and not expansion of imports versus contraction of imports.

suggests a very sensitive response to income movements and a high marginal propensity to import. At no time, other than the depression of the 1930's, are the relative movements in depression more severe than in the 1820's and 1840's (Table 7 gives relative amplitude measurements). Perhaps much of this violence in import movement is due to the nature of triangular trade and the dependence of the export sector, the South, upon foreign imports to satisfy so much of its domestic need. The second long swing in our chronology begins its upswing from the trough in 1842. Aggregate imports then peak in 1858 before falling to a trough in 1863, for a duration of twenty-one years. This long swing is by no means war-induced although its sharp termination in 1862-1863 may be due to the Civil War itself. The war seems to have had more extensive effects upon exports in current prices than upon imports. The hostilities between North and South, as well as the ensuing blockade of the Southern ports certainly interfered with the triangular trade. The South's cotton exports, one-half of total United States exports, were severely interrupted, while imports into the industrial and more highly populated North were less sharply affected. Import values rise sharply in the early 1850's, but from 1853 to 1860 the rate of expansion slows down gradually and becomes negative in the late 1850's and early 1860's. The trough is not as extensive as that of the depressed forties, for imports increase abruptly during the later part of the war and after. This period clearly reflects a boom in American foreign trade, although some of the import expansion must be due to price inflation concomitant with the gold discoveries in the West. Nowhere in the nineteenth and twentieth centuries is there evidence of a more rapid expansion in imports (not necessarily *real* import demand) than over the span 1842-1858. This is complemented by a vigorous boom in exports, although aggregate exports do not expand as greatly as in the sixties and seventies.

The third swing in imports has a much shorter duration than the second. Imports rise sharply from the trough in 1863 to a peak in 1873 and then decline into the great depression of the seventies, which terminates in 1877, for a duration of fourteen years. (Remember that the dating itself is achieved by smoothing with a five-year moving average. The evidence of these long movements is derived from an examination of the unadjusted annual data.) Much of the relative mildness of import movements over the fourth long swing may be explained, at least in part, by secular price deflation, although it has not been proven that United States prices relative to those of the rest of the world fell during the upswing of this period.[1] Import values rise from the trough of 1877 to a peak in 1891 and fall to a trough in 1896, a duration of nineteen years. Not only is the amplitude of this swing less pronounced than in the preceding long swings, but there is an extensive period of unusually low growth rates in the mid-1880's. Later in this chapter it will become clear that this dip in the mid-1880's is also revealed in domestic activity but less seriously in net capital movements.

The progressive reduction in the severity of import long swings is evident in the amplitude measures exhibited in Table 7. This trend continues after the 1890's, for the next two decades reveal unique stability in import movements. From 1896, the terminal year for the cycle of the seventies and eighties, to 1915 imports in current prices do not move with the configuration we have discovered in past series. During these nineteen years, import values rise at somewhat rapid growth rates; the movements in rates of growth *do* reflect some of the characteristics we have identified in the other long swings. The *only* evidence of long swings, however, is in positive rates of change. The rate of growth of import values rises from a trough in 1896 to a peak in 1901 and gradually falls to a trough in 1913 (when a five-year moving average is applied to the annual rate of change we find a 10 per cent growth rate at the peak in 1901, 3 per cent in 1910, and 1 per cent at the trough in 1913). At first sight this would appear to be weak evidence of a long swing in import demand. However, from 1896 to 1913 import patterns seem fairly consistent with our knowledge of internal development, since this period is one of unusual domestic stability as well. The amplitude of these movements in rates of change is even further reduced when we apply a deflator to imports in current prices. We shall return, however, to an examination of the late 1890's and the pre–World War I years for a more extensive analysis.

We have established the existence of four long swings prior to World War I and a period from 1896 to 1915 revealing a cycle in rates of growth. Excluding the period 1896-1915, the average

---

1. Jeffrey G. Williamson, "Real Growth, Monetary Disturbances and the Transfer Process: The United States, 1879-1900," *Southern Economic Journal*, XXIX (January, 1963), 171-173.

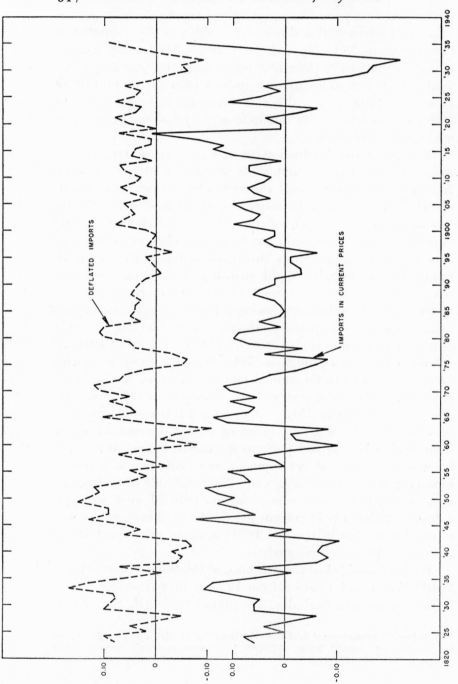

**Chart 10** United States Imports, in Current Prices and Deflated, 1823-1935 (in Percentage Rates of Change Smoothed by Five-Year Moving Average)

duration of these long swings in imports (in current prices and from trough to trough) is 18.5 years.

Each of these long swings has considerable similarity in configuration. In absolute values, the import peak in current values occurs late in the cycle. This is certainly to be expected, since the series is growing rapidly over the long-run course of economic development. But one interesting aspect of these movements can best be seen by glancing at Chart 10 where imports in *rates of change* are plotted after smoothing by a five-year moving average. In each case there is an exceedingly sharp increase in growth rates (from negative to high positive) very early in the cycle; on the average the peak is achieved within four or five years from the trough in negative rates of change. For the remaining ten to fifteen years of the swing, there is a gradual lessening in growth rates, terminating, of course, at a negative level. This configuration, in rates of change, is quite similar to movements in domestic series, and we might offer a tentative (and perhaps inadequate) explanation of it. The explanation itself describes domestic output movements; it applies to imports only in the sense that imports are a function of domestic income and output. The sharp and abrupt rise to very high growth rates in the early stages of the long swing reflects an extremely elastic factor supply and a fulfillment of this excess capacity and labor unemployment. Thus extremely high growth rates of 10 to 15 per cent over short periods are possible. The only limitation is aggregate demand and not the more classical resource limitation. At some point early in the cycle, a Hicksian capacity limitation occurs in resource use, and growth rates become restrained. The subsequent gradual fall in growth rates might, perhaps, be explained simply by an exponential approach to this ceiling (increasing at some constant rate dictated by the rate of capital formation and the rate of change in technology). It also could be explained by a movement into more capital intensive techniques (building and transportation investment) or by the inferiority of marginal resources employed.

An explanation of the general maintenance of imports at high rates of growth over a long span of the cycle may be found in the tendency of prices to rise when capacity is reached. It is true, however, that the period 1896-1913 is somewhat of an exception to our stylized model, although there is evidence of a Kuznets cycle in rates of change. It is also evident that both of these long swings in imports, 1877-1896 and 1896-1913, are less violent than any others in American nineteenth-century history. Although the swing from 1877 to 1896 can be explained in part by price movements, both of the Kuznets cycles after 1877 and prior to the European war may be explained by real factors: the domestic stability of the 1896-1913 period and the secular shift of comparative advantages

**Table 8** Balance-of-Payments Dating for Long Swings

| | Imports (current value) Smoothed | Imports (current value) Annual | Imports (deflated) Smoothed | Imports (deflated) Annual | Net Capital Inflow (current value) Smoothed | Net Capital Inflow (current value) Annual | | Trade Balance (current value) Smoothed | Trade Balance (current value) Annual |
|---|---|---|---|---|---|---|---|---|---|
| Peak   | 1817   | 1816   | —      | —      | 1817 | 1816 | Trough | 1817 | 1816 |
| Trough | 1822   | 1821   | 1822   | 1821   | 1825 | 1827 | Peak   | 1825 | 1830 |
| Peak   | 1837   | 1836   | 1837   | 1836   | 1837 | 1836 | Trough | 1837 | 1836 |
| Trough | 1842   | 1843   | 1842   | 1853   | 1842 | 1840 | Peak   | 1842 | 1843 |
| Peak   | 1858   | 1860   | 1859   | 1860   | 1852 | 1853 | Trough | 1855 | 1854 |
| Trough | 1863   | 1862   | 1863   | 1862   | 1858 | 1858 | Peak   | 1860 | 1862 |
| Peak   | 1873   | 1873   | 1874   | 1873   | 1871 | 1872 | Trough | 1871 | 1872 |
| Trough | 1877   | 1878   | 1877   | 1878   | 1879 | 1878 | Peak   | 1879 | 1879 |
| Peak   | 1891   | 1893   | 1895   | 1897   | 1889 | 1888 | Trough | 1888 | 1888 |
| Trough | 1896   | 1898   | 1896   | 1898   | 1900 | 1900 | Peak   | 1900 | 1901 |
| Peak   | —      | —      | —      | —      | 1911 | 1910 | Trough | 1908 | 1910 |
| Trough | (1915) | (1915) | (1915) | (1915) | 1917 | 1917 | Peak   | 1913 | 1919 |

reducing the share of the more violent component of imports, i.e., finished and semifinished manufactures.

Table 7 gives a measurement of amplitude for imports and exports in current prices. This at least gives us some feeling for the relative violence of import swings over the five long cycles. In four out of six cases from 1828 to 1877, imports have a more violent swing. This is the case even for both of the long swings prior to the Civil War, which are uniquely comparable to other balance-of-payments movements. The two exceptions are the fall to the trough of 1863 (and the war may account for this, since the fall in cotton revenue was extremely severe and was primarily war-induced while imports were less affected) and the rise to the import peak in the 1870's. The latter period is also an unusual one since exports in grain enjoyed a phenomenal boom with the extensive opening of the West. In general, however, imports tend to have more severe movements than exports. It is also generally true that, like imports, export movements become milder as the nineteenth century progresses—before the 1870's exports reveal much more severe movements, relative to import movements, than after.

These rough amplitude measurements show the relative mildness of the swing in imports from 1877 to 1896. There is no absolute change, of course, from peak to trough during the mild swing in rates of change, 1896-1915.

The general conformity of movements in import values to other elements of the balance of payments is evident from an examination of Table 8. There seems to be a systematic relationship among imports in current prices, net capital movements, and the trade balance. We have already noted in our discussion of export movements that imports seem to dominate the nineteenth-century trade balance. Exports apparently play only a minor role, randomly influencing the turning points of the merchandise trade balance. Furthermore, exports do not seem to affect the amplitude of the trade balance in any consistent manner. The merchandise trade balance, 1820-1845, is relatively mild in amplitude due to the conformity of import and export movements. It could be argued that in the earlier stages of United States development, the extreme sympathy of export and import movements to each other added stability to the foreign trade position during the growth process. This was caused primarily by the sensitivity of income movements to export conditions (due to the relative importance of the export trade in the domestic economy, a condition which is not satisfied over most of the nineteenth century).

More precisely, the evidence seems to indicate close conformity between the trade balance and imports, with the latter lagging, on the average, about 0.2 years (the two series are therefore practically synchronous). In the smoothed data and between 1817-1900, four turning points have imports lagging, three leading, and three synchronous.

One interesting aspect of the trade balance deserves em-

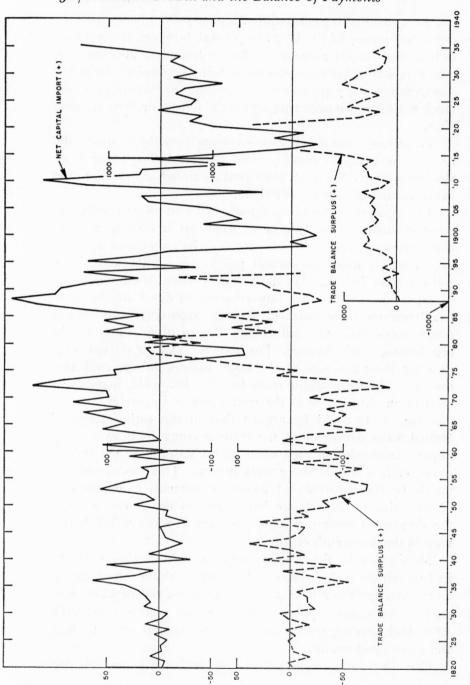

**Chart 11** United States Net Capital Imports and Merchandise Trade Balance, 1820-1935

phasis (for the time path of the trade balance 1820-1913 see Chart 11). Whereas imports in current prices and in absolute values do not exhibit any cyclic movement from 1896 to 1915, the trade balance does indeed exhibit a long swing rising from a trough in 1888 to a peak in 1900 and falling again to a trough in 1908 (and on to a peak with World War I). The trough in the trade balance in 1908 cannot be explained by movements in the absolute level of imports since they hardly peak in 1908. But the general fall in the trade balance from 1900 to 1908 and the subsequent rise to the war is paralleled by the *rates of change* in imports which fall from a peak in 1901 to a trough in 1913. It is also true that the amplitude of the trade balance is extremely mild from the import peak of 1901 to the trough of 1913 (which, of course, is consistent with the relatively mild movements in imports throughout the period).

Although the relationship between imports in current prices and net capital movements is described extensively in later sections of this chapter, it would be useful to briefly indicate the comparability between net capital inflow and import movements. In general, this long-swing configuration in imports and the trade balance is also exhibited by net capital flows over United States borders. Even by casual observation it does seem clear that net capital movements have much more violent relative amplitudes. A brief examination of Table 8 shows net capital imports generally leading commodity imports over the long swing as well.

The next step is to proceed to a disaggregation of imports into five commodity groupings: crude foodstuffs, manufactured foodstuffs, crude materials, semifinished manufactures, and finished manufactures, all of which are expressed in current prices in Table B-6. Over the period 1850-1913, export components exhibited very little conformity. This is not the case with the import components, however. The comparative dating of these five commodity import groups is given in Table 9 (including the dating for the World War I movements), and the movements in the unadjusted annual data are presented in Chart 12 (see Charts 13 and 14 for movements of components in rates of change). In general, the series seems to move together with surprisingly

minor discontinuities. Yet there are some comments of interest
that can be made about dissimilarities.

Crude foodstuffs lag current imports over the period 1850-
1900. Four of the six turning points lag and two are synchronous
with aggregate imports, for an average lag of 1.7 years. This is
certainly a relationship that we might have anticipated a priori,
since, as a general rule, food consumption seems to lag domestic
activity and exhibits milder fluctuations. Precisely the same
relationship is revealed in manufactured foodstuffs, though to

**Table 9** Dating for Import Components: Five Commodity Groups[a]

|  | Imports (current value) | Crude Materials | Crude Foodstuffs | Manufactured Foodstuffs | Semifinished Manufactures | Finished Manufactures |
|---|---|---|---|---|---|---|
| Peak | 1858 | 1862 | 1859 | 1859 | 1855 | 1855 |
| Trough | 1863 | 1863 | 1863 | 1863 | 1860 | 1863 |
| Peak | 1873 | 1873 | 1876 | 1873 | 1873 | 1873 |
| Trough | 1877 | 1877 | 1877 | 1877 | 1877 | 1877 |
| Peak | 1891 | 1891 | 1893 | 1892 | 1891 | 1891 |
| Trough | 1896 | 1896 | 1900 | 1900 | 1896 | 1896 |
| Peak | — | — | — | — | — | (1912) |
| Trough | — | — | — | — | — | (1914) |
| Peak | (1920) | (1918) | (1919) | (1921) | (1918) | — |
| Trough | (1921) | (1923) | (1923) | (1923) | (1920) | — |

[a]In absolute values after smoothing by 5-year moving average.

a lesser extent. Four of six turning points lag and two are synchronous, for an average lag of one year over the long swing.
Both crude foodstuffs and manufactured foodstuffs exhibit relatively mild amplitudes compared with the other three components of aggregate imports.

Secularly, crude material imports increase in relative importance until in the 1890's they become the leading import component, usurping the predominance of finished manufactures.
Somewhat surprisingly, crude material imports seem to be almost
synchronous with aggregate imports. Five of six turning points
are synchronous with and one lags aggregate imports for an average lag of 0.7 years. The relationship does not perceptibly
change with the secular increase in the importance of crude ma-

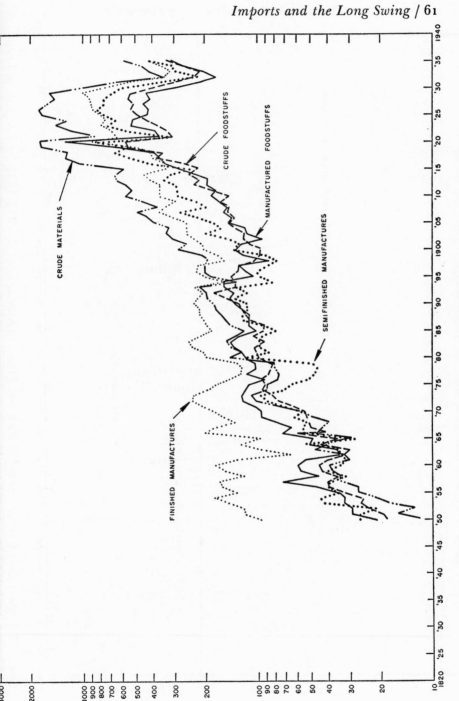

**Chart 12** Five Import Commodity Groups, 1850-1935 (in Millions of Dollars)

*Source:* Table A-6

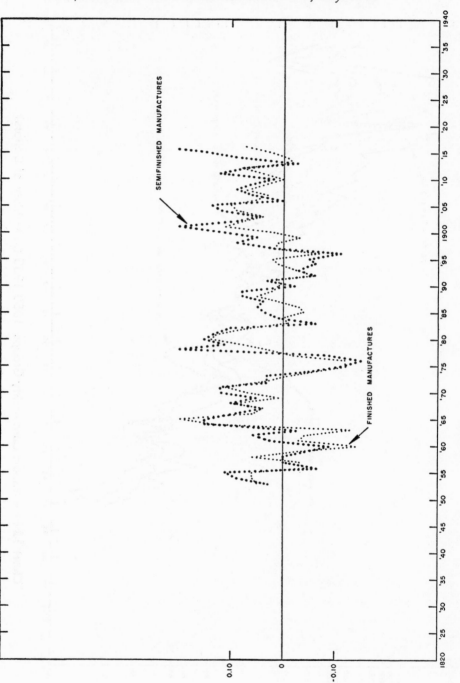

**Chart 13** Import Components: Semifinished and Finished Manufactures, 1853-1915 (in Percentage Rates of Change, Smoothed by a Five-Year Moving Average)

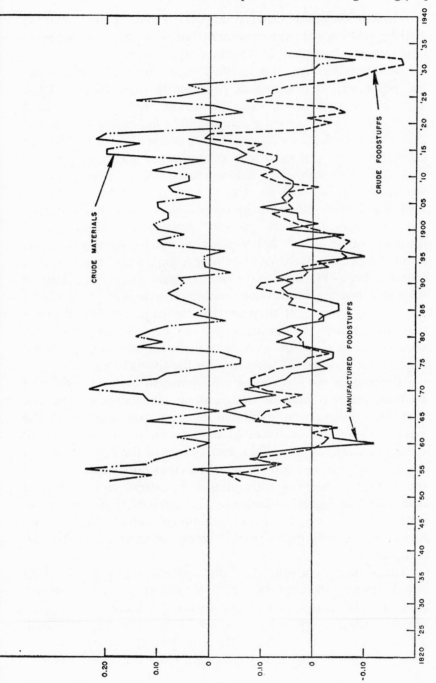

**Chart 14** Import Components: Crude Materials, Crude Foodstuffs, and Manufactured Foodstuffs, 1853-1933 (in Percentage Rates of Change, Smoothed by a Five-Year Moving Average)

terials, nor do crude material imports assume a more striking lead-lag relation with the structural change of the domestic economy over the latter half of the nineteenth century.

Both semifinished and finished manufactures seem to lead the other import components consistently from 1850 to 1900. This is not unexpected, since we would predict manufactured goods (both as intermediate inputs and as finished consumer and investment goods) to be more sensitive to fluctuations in domestic economic activity than strictly consumption goods of the foodstuff variety. Semifinished manufactures lead imports at two of six turning points and are synchronous in four for an average lead of one year. Since this group is more of an industrial input than manufactured goods (which lump together inputs for industrial output *as well as* consumption goods), we might expect semifinished manufactures to exhibit a longer lead than finished manufactures. Finished manufactures have an average lead of 0.5 years, but are synchronous with aggregate imports at five of six turning points. It may be that the apparent lag of crude materials, which one might expect to be sensitive to income movements in terms of leads, is entirely an inventory problem: crude materials may be more susceptible to stocking.

There does not seem to be any consistent behavior exhibited by these series at peak or trough alone. It is evident, however, that the configuration exhibited by aggregate imports in the rates of change is also revealed in the import components. All these series rise sharply in the early stages of the long swing and sustain high rates of growth which decline only gradually until the abrupt contraction precipitated by severe and protracted deficiencies in aggregate demand. The configuration of aggregate imports is not, then, a result of random coincidence in the movements of its components or due to the dominance of any one component.

Interestingly enough, the "dip" in the mid-eighties which is exhibited in the aggregate series is evident in the components as well. This period of low growth rates (negative in the mid-eighties, while a stylized model would reflect a period of high growth rates in the middle of the long swing) seems to be common to each of the series, although some are more seriously affected than others. Crude materials and crude foodstuffs do not reflect these movements as clearly as the remaining three; these two series rise rapidly from the trough of the mid-seventies and reveal a time shape similar to past swings. The "dip" itself is extremely mild in both series. The same seems to be true of semifinished manufactures, although the recession in the mid-1880's is a bit more severe in semifinished manufactures. Finished manufactures reach a peak in the early 1880's and remain stable over the decade until the mid-1890's. The movement in manufactures seems to explain a great deal about the relatively low growth rates in aggregate imports from the early to the late 1880's. Manufactured foodstuffs also exhibit a somewhat unique movement over this period: when smoothed by a five-year moving average, they have an extremely mild amplitude over the cycle 1877-1896. Just how much of this stability is due to price movements is not clear, but it is evident that the stability in manufactured foodstuffs helps explain the time shape of our aggregate import series. The explanation of the movements in manufactured foodstuffs itself, however, can be explained by exogenous price movements alone, which are most volatile in foodstuffs over this period (see Kreps' "agricultural import prices index,"[2] Chart 15).

*Deflated Imports: 1820-1913*

As in the case of exports, finding an adequate import price index to deflate aggregate imports is not an easy task. The series used is a collection of many sources and the adequacy of it cannot be left unquestioned, especially for the period 1820-1879. Some recent estimates are available for the period after 1879 which can be considered reasonably accurate for our purposes (see Table B-4). Arthur H. Cole's index of commodity import prices was used to cover the four decades 1820-1860.[3] This, as compiled

2. T. J. Kreps, "Import and Export Prices in the United States and the Terms of International Trade, 1880-1914," *Quarterly Journal of Economics*, XXXX (August, 1926), 708-720.

3. *Wholesale Commodity Prices in the United States, 1800-1860* (Cambridge, Mass.: Harvard University Press, 1938), pp. 148, 165, 167, 175, 178.

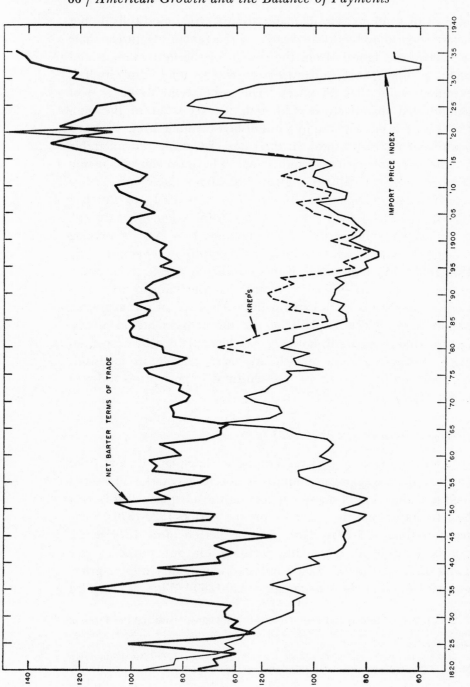

**Chart 15** United States Import Prices and Net Barter Terms of Trade, 1820-1935 (Composite Import Price Index: 1913 = 100; Kreps' Import Price Index: 1903-1913 = 100)

by North,[4] is an unweighted combination of price indices based upon commodities imported into Philadelphia, Charleston, and New Orleans. The Philadelphia series is unweighted while the Charleston and New Orleans are weighted. Just how much this biases the series toward Southern import trade is not known. (The majority of United States imports during most of this period were directed toward Northern ports. No figures on the relative compositions of those import bundles are available.) Nevertheless, the series has been adopted without adjustment.

For the period 1861-1878 we employ Simon's estimates which are constructed from the following sources: 1861-1865 is Mitchell's index constructed from ten series of import prices; 1866-1878 is from Graham's estimates.[5] For the period 1879-1900 Simon used Kreps' estimates without adjustment. But Kreps' series has been discarded in favor of a more recent and improved import price index compiled by Robert E. Lipsey.[6] This series has a distinct advantage over that of Kreps. Kreps' index is very heavily biased toward raw material and foodstuff imports, and, as a result, it overemphasizes the fall in prices to the mid-1880's, the rise to the early 1890's, and the subsequent fall to the late 1890's. Lipsey's price index reduces this bias with a more accurate weighting. Lipsey's index continues through 1923 and was utilized for the period without adjustment. (There are shipping tonnage figures available, but volume measures over periods as long as twenty years, with shifting import demand, would seem to be wholly inadequate. Lipsey, Kreps, and Graham are also of this opinion.)

---

4. Cole's estimates are aggregated in Douglass C. North, "The United States Balance of Payments, 1790-1860," *Trends in the American Economy in the Nineteenth Century* ("Studies in Income and Wealth," Vol. XXIV [Princeton, N. J.: Princeton University Press, 1960]), Table B-2, Col. 9, pp. 607-608 (this volume is hereafter cited as *Trends*).

5. Wesley C. Mitchell, *Gold Prices and Wages under the Greenback Standard* ("University of California Publications in Economics," Vol. I [Berkeley: University of California Press, 1908]), pp. 339-367; Frank D. Graham, "International Trade Under Depreciated Paper—the United States, 1862-1879," *Quarterly Journal of Economics*, XXXVI (February, 1922), 253. These figures are collected in Matthew Simon, "The United States Balance of Payments, 1861-1900," *Trends*, Table 7, Col. 1, p. 652.

6. Lipsey's revised estimates appear in *Price and Quantity Trends in the Foreign Trade of the United States*, National Bureau of Economic Research (Princeton, N. J.: Princeton University Press, 1963).

Just how accurate these figures are is not certain, especially in the pre-1879 era. But they should be helpful in shedding light on the hypothesis that these swings are "real" phenomena —related to domestic income and price movements—and not simply a reflection of external price movements. It is usually assumed that American business activity did not have very serious, if any, initiating effects upon world trade as a whole during the nineteenth century. But we may find that world price movements were coincident with United States business activity (and therefore, as we shall presently see, with aggregate imports) due to the transfer of foreign conditions *into* the United States. On the other hand, if British experience is any indication, an inverse relationship is possible since there is a great deal of evidence supporting inverse movement between United States and British building cycles. The former supposition would weaken our evidence of cyclic movement over these twenty-year periods and the latter strengthen such evidence of real movements. A third possibility is perhaps even more likely, in view of the evidence presented in Chapter VI. Although American and British building cycles were inversely related, the British export industry moved positively with American long swings. It is possible, therefore, that our import prices conformed to import values due to this positive correlation between British export prices and the domestic long swing in America.

In truth, there seems to be some consistent behavior between import turning points (in current prices) and those of the price index. Prior to 1860 the relationship is quite unclear: from 1820 to 1834 there is a secular fall in prices which moves without functional relationship to the long swing in import values; from 1828 to 1862 imports have very long leads at troughs while the lead-lag relation is unclear at peaks; but after 1862 imports in current prices conform extremely closely with import price movements, exhibiting what at first seem to be random leads and lags. Over the whole period covered in Table 10, there is an average *lag* of imports behind prices of 1.3 years. The result of this configuration of import prices (positively related to import demand) is to increase the amplitude of imports in current prices over most of the nineteenth and early twentieth centuries.

That is, when imports in current prices are deflated by import prices, the amplitude of import movements over the long swing is somewhat reduced. Only the period from 1820 to 1837, the peak in 1895, and the trough in 1863 are exceptions to this rule. It is apparent, therefore, that a portion of the amplitude of import values over the Kuznets cycle are due to import price movements alone. Prices are higher at every peak in import values than at the preceding trough and lower at every trough than at the preceding peak. Before examining deflated imports themselves (see Chart 9), it might be noted that the severity of the "dip" in imports in the mid-1880's *does* seem to be partially caused by the sharp fall in import prices from 1880 to 1886. But rather low growth rates over the eighties still persist. Generally, import prices did not contribute to the rise in imports from 1875

**Table 10** Lead-Lag Comparison of Imports and Import Prices

| Date of Turn in Annual Imports (current prices) | Lead (+) or Lag (—) of Import Prices at | |
|---|---|---|
| | Import Peak | Import Trough |
| P 1836 | —1 | |
| T 1843 | | —6 |
| P 1860 | +4 | |
| T 1862 | | 0 |
| P 1873 | +7 | |
| T 1878 | | +2 |
| P (1883) | +3 | |
| T (1885) | | 0 |
| P 1893 | +4 | |
| T 1898 | | 0 |

to 1892, but thereafter the cyclical movement in import values was strengthened by sympathetic import price movement.

Over the nineteenth and early twentieth centuries, this evidence suggests that external price movements regularly contributed to the long swings in import values (except 1820-1837 and 1875-1892). As far as timing goes, at first glance the series seem to reveal random leads and lags. A closer examination, however, discloses a fair degree of regularity if we examine peaks and troughs separately (see Table 10). Import prices lead import values 3.6 years at peaks and lag 0.8 years at troughs.

Any attempt to explain the apparent correlation must be preceded by some breakdown of import prices. Although some degree of consistency of international movements is possible (even in the face of the Anglo-American inverse building cycles), the United States did have profound effect upon world agricultural prices due to our swings in transportation investment and land expansion. But it does not seem very likely that agricultural products prices should have greatly influenced our own import prices (predominately manufactures and crude materials). It seems more sensible to search for some answers in British economic history. Since the United States was primarily a manufactured-goods importer over most of the century, British prices were likely to have been the main determinant of American import prices. The British export industry exhibits a long swing positively related to American import demand over this period, and the positive relationship between American imports and import prices may have its explanation here.

Chart 9 shows the movement of deflated imports from 1820 to 1913 (see also Table B-5). The only sharp differences between the current and deflated series are those revealed after the mid-1870's. The long swing from the mid-1870's to the mid-1880's resembles those swings of the past. The low rates of growth in the mid-1880's seem to have been due in part to "exogenous" import price movements. The extended depression of the 1890's in the import series is, however, much less severe. The low levels of import demand reflect low world prices rather than the results of domestic income movements, although the protracted depression in deflated aggregate imports is still quite clear. Another interesting change is that the war boom (1915-1920) was entirely a war-induced cycle in import prices and nothing more. In absolute values, imports rise from, say, 1900 to 1929 in the annual data with little evidence of a long swing. The rate of growth of deflated imports is uninterrupted up to 1914 in the annual data, but from 1914 to 1918 the growth rates are much lower. Since these are war years (there is no evidence of a slackening in growth rate prior to 1914) and since the "trough" 1914-1918 is much milder relative to other import cycles, no effort has been made to include it in the import chronology.

Here again, the stability of the series over the first fifteen years of the twentieth century is revealed.

The over-all effect of the deflation upon the dating of aggregate import turning points is insignificant (see Table 11); it only seriously changes the peak of imports from 1891 to 1895. The effect upon amplitude is given in Table 12.

*Imports and the Domestic Long Swing: Turning-Point Analysis*

So far we have made only casual reference to long swings in the rate of domestic expansion which, of course, should be the

**Table 11** Dating for Imports, Deflated and in Current Prices

|  | Imports (deflated) | | Imports (in current prices) | |
|---|---|---|---|---|
|  | Smoothed | Annual | Smoothed | Annual |
| Peak | — | — | 1817 | 1816 |
| Trough | 1822 | 1821 | 1822 | 1821 |
| Peak | 1837 | 1836 | 1837 | 1836 |
| Trough | 1842 | 1843 | 1842 | 1843 |
| Peak | 1859 | 1860 | 1858 | 1860 |
| Trough | 1863 | 1862 | 1863 | 1862 |
| Peak | 1874 | 1873 | 1873 | 1873 |
| Trough | 1877 | 1878 | 1877 | 1878 |
| Peak | 1895 | 1897 | 1891 | 1893 |
| Trough | 1896 | 1898 | 1896 | 1898 |
| Peak | (no cycle: only slackening of growth rates 1914-1918) | | (1920) | (1920) |
| Trough | — | — | (1921) | (1921) |

source of import, net capital, and trade-balance movements. The following two sections attempt to fill that gap by the use of two techniques. First, we have applied a less sophisticated lead-lag analysis to imports with reference only to long-swing turning points. Second, in the subsequent section we attempt to complement the turning-point analysis by a more extensive quantitative examination of lead-lag relationships using correlation analysis. Although net capital movements are briefly explored here, the remainder of this chapter is primarily devoted to import movements.

Finding a representative sample of indices to use as a measure of the rate of domestic expansion is somewhat difficult and, to some degree, arbitrary. Nevertheless, nine series have been chosen to represent American internal development over the long swing. The group includes indices of transportation development (mainly railroad building, with steamboat production to cover the earlier stages of the nineteenth century), building construction (both the Riggleman and Long indices of building activity), three output series (bituminous and anthracite coal production as well as the output of pig iron), public land sales,

**Table 12** Effects of Deflation on Amplitude of Imports[a]

|  | Imports (deflated: smoothed) | Amplitude Per Annum | Deflation Increase Amplitude (+) Decrease (—) | Imports (in current prices: smoothed) | Amplitude Per Annum |
|---|---|---|---|---|---|
| Peak | — | — |  | — | — |
| Trough | (1828) | — | + | (1828) | — |
| Peak | 1837 | 1.176 | 0.131 | + | 1837 | 0.892 | 0.099 |
| Trough | 1842 | 0.199 | 0.040 | — | 1842 | 0.316 | 0.063 |
| Peak | 1859 | 2.263 | 0.133 | — | 1858 | 2.277 | 0.142 |
| Trough | 1863 | 0.210 | 0.052 | + | 1863 | 0.213 | 0.043 |
| Peak | 1874 | 0.983 | 0.089 | — | 1873 | 1.265 | 0.127 |
| Trough | 1877 | 0.102 | 0.034 | — | 1877 | 0.201 | 0.050 |
| Peak | 1895 | 0.977 | 0.054 | 0 | 1891 | 0.770 | 0.055 |
| Trough | 1896 | 0.028 | 0.028 | — | 1896 | 0.149 | 0.030 |
| Peak | (1915) | 0.764 | 0.040 | — | 1927 | 4.904 | 0.158 |
|  | 1928 | 2.528 | 0.079 |  |  |  |  |

aFrom peak to trough, amplitude is measured as $(P-T)/P$. From trough to peak, it is measured as $(P-T)/T$.

and business incorporations. The main difficulty, imposed by the necessity of using such a small sample, is the historical length of the series available. It would have been more meaningful to use aggregative output and investment indices to measure the response of the balance of payments in general, and imports in particular, to the domestic long swing. In spite of this limitation, these series represent a rather broad sample of American business activity, even though they reveal more violent swings than more general income-output measures. They also have the advantage of extensive coverage. Each is composed of one homogeneous commodity and covers the greater part of the nineteenth century. Thus they are continuous and more susceptible to time-series analysis.

It is not the purpose of this chapter or any other to present an extensive examination of, or explanation or argument for, the long swing in United States internal development (including the question whether these swings are self-generating or purely episodic). Self-generating or not, it is clear that the international sector must play a role in satisfying varying import requirements. We have therefore depended upon evidence of long swings in United States development published by Simon Kuznets, Arthur Burns, Brinley Thomas, and especially research presently being pursued by Moses Abramovitz. For these reasons, our examination of these domestic series may seem cursory, since in this book we are far more interested in the relation between the balance of payments and domestic series than the movements in the domestic series themselves.

All these domestic series reveal long swings, similar to those discovered in the balance-of-payments components, from ten to twenty years in duration. These long swings are visually more obvious in the series related to the investment flows (certainly not an unexpected result, especially with respect to transportation-building investment). The indices of building activity (Riggleman), railway mileage added, steamboat tonnage built on Western rivers, and public land sales all reveal sharply delineated long swings from 1820 to 1913. Swings in the output series are less blatantly obvious to the naked eye since long swings in output are more in evidence in rates of change, except during protracted troughs. This is quite consistent with the research done by Kuznets, Abramovitz, and Burns.[7] The long swing is more clearly isolated when the trend is removed from these output series, as in the case of bituminous coal.

Finally, it also should be made clear that Abramovitz's dating and analysis is primarily in terms of rates of development, since

---

7. See, for instance, Moses Abramovitz, "Resource and Output Trends in the United States since 1870," *American Economic Review* (Supplement), XLVI (May, 1956), 5-23; and his statement in *Hearings before the Joint Economic Committee of the Congress of the United States*, 86th Cong., 1st Sess., 1959.

**Table 13** Dating of Net Capital Movements, Imports, and Domestic Activity over the Long Swing
**Table 13.1**

| | Imports (current value: smoothed) | Imports (deflated: smoothed) | Net Capital Inflow (current value: smoothed) | Riggleman Building Index | Long Building Index | Pig Iron Production | Anthracite Coal Production | Railway Mileage Added | Bituminous Coal Output | Steamboats Built on Western Rivers | Business Incorporations | Public Land Sales |
|---|---|---|---|---|---|---|---|---|---|---|---|---|
| Peak | 1817 | | 1817 | | | | | | | 1818 | 1815 | |
| Trough | 1822 | 1822 | 1825 | | | | | | | 1822 | 1821 | 1823 |
| Peak | 1837 | 1837 | 1837 | 1836 | | | 1837 | 1840 | | 1839 | 1837 | 1837 |
| Trough | 1842 | 1842 | 1842 | 1843 | | | 1840 | 1845 | | 1841 | 1842 | 1843 |
| Peak | 1858 | 1859 | 1852 | 1853 | | | 1856 | 1851 | 1848 | 1855 | 1852 | 1855 |
| Trough | 1863 | 1863 | 1858 | 1864 | 1859 | 1860 | 1860 | 1863 | 1852 | 1861 | 1860 | (1860)d |
| Peak | 1873 | 1874 | 1871 | 1871 | 1871 | 1873 | 1873 | 1871 | 1859 | 1870 | 1872 | — |
| Trough | 1877 | 1877 | 1879 | 1878 | 1880 | 1876 | 1876 | 1876 | 1873 | 1875 | 1877 | — |
| Peak | 1891 | 1895 | 1889 | 1890 | 1888 | 1891 | 1894 | 1881c | 1878 | | 1893 | 1886 |
| Trough | 1896 | 1896 | 1900 | 1900 | 1900 | 1894 | 1898 | 1896 | 1883c | | 1895 | 1896 |
| Peak | (a) | — | 1911 | 1909 | 1911 | 1917 | 1917 | 1905 | 1896 | | 1921 | 1909 |
| Trough | (1915) | — | 1917 | 1918 | 1918b | 1921 | 1922 | 1922 | (1905) | | 1923 | 1917 |

aIn rates of change, the series peaks in 1901 and troughs in 1913.
bExcluding war years, 1915-1916.
cBoth these series exhibit severe recessions in the mid-1880's.
dLast year in series with series falling up to 1860.

he is concerned with an explanation for resource and income-output trends. The analysis here is in terms of absolute levels (simply because the fluctuations are more severe in the international accounts).

Table 13 gives the dating of the turning points of these series, but before proceeding with a lead-lag analysis a further qualification is necessary. The balance-of-payments figures are not entirely comparable with the domestic series in terms of dating. Both the import and export figures (and thus the trade balance

**Table 13.2**

| | Imports (current value) Lead (+), Lag (—) Composite of Nine Indices of Domestic Activity | Net Capital Movements Lead (+), Lag (—) Composite of Nine Indices of Domestic Activity |
|---|---|---|
| Peak | —0.5 | —0.5 |
| Trough | 0 | —3.0 |
| Peak | +0.7 | +0.7 |
| Trough | +1.1 | +1.1 |
| Peak | —4.6 | +1.4 |
| Trough | —2.3 | +2.7 |
| Peak | —1.3 | +0.7 |
| Trough | 0 | —2.0 |
| Peak | —2.8 | —0.8 |
| Trough | +0.9 | —3.1 |
| Peak | — | +0.8 |
| Trough | — | +3.1 |
| Average at Peaks | —1.7 | +0.4 |
| Average at Troughs | —0.1 | —0.2 |
| Average | —0.9 | +0.1 |

and net capital movements) were reported on a fiscal basis rather than on a calendar year basis. Prior to 1843 the fiscal year ended September 30 and from 1843 to 1915 the fiscal year ended June 30. Thus from 1843 to 1915 there is a manufactured lag of one-half year of the balance-of-payments components behind the domestic series. We cannot, therefore, demand too much precision from our conclusions of lead-lag analysis, although relative lead-lag comparison should not be impaired.

In all cases imports lag behind these domestic series. Their largest average lag at both peak and trough is behind railway mileage added, bituminous coal production, and public land sales in that order; the smallest average lags are found with the Riggleman and Long indices and anthracite coal production. Excluding the fifth long swing in imports, which is reflected only in rates of change, imports in current prices have an average lag of 0.9 years behind the composite of the domestic series.

In general, imports are more responsive (reveal shorter lags) to domestic movements at troughs than at peaks. The average lag is 1.7 years at peaks and 0.1 years at troughs. Since imports are measured on a fiscal basis from June to June (over the greater part of the period under analysis), then imports in current prices may well be almost synchronous with domestic activity at troughs but lag from one to two years at peaks. At peaks, four of five import turning points lag domestic activity, while at troughs only one out of five lags.

It would indeed seem that imports exhibit a positive correlation with domestic activity and that these long swings found in the balance of payments have their source in domestic fluctuations which reveal similar long cyclic movements of from ten to twenty years in duration.[8] From 1820 to 1913 our preliminary findings show imports moving in sympathy with domestic activity: rising in periods of protracted domestic boom and high growth rates and falling in periods of extended recession, depression, and very sluggish rates of expansion. This is not unexpected since we usually treat imports, in long- and short-period analysis, mainly as a function of income (or domestic activity, as we have approximated it here).

In this connection, the relation between the timing of our domestic series and those of income may be ambiguous, and we should be wary of the implication that these results apply to an income-output lag analysis. In spite of the fact that Kuznets' income estimates do not go back farther than 1869, which compels us to choose such industry investment and output series that are available, a valid national income series probably would not

8. This is not meant to imply that external conditions play no role, but only that domestic conditions dominate import movements over the Kuznets cycle. Chapter IV will demonstrate, however, that external conditions do indeed play a major supporting role in causing an observed long swing in net capital movements.

display long swings in absolute levels (Kuznets' estimates do not). The peaks and troughs in rates of change in income occur, for reasons that should be obvious, much earlier than peaks and troughs in the absolute levels of our domestic series. The point here is that although the above results are interesting and informative in themselves, they do not clearly imply that imports tend to turn a little later than *income*. A general production index would be a more adequate measure of the movements in industrial output. Indeed, in the more extensive analysis using

**Table 14** Comparative Dating of Imports and Economic Activity

| Rates of Change | (1) Economic Activity or Gross National Product[a] | (2) Industrial and Commercial Production[a] | (3) Imports in Constant Prices | (4) Lead (+) or Lag (—) of (3) over (1) |
|---|---|---|---|---|
| Peak | 1834 | | 1833 | +1 |
| Trough | 1840 | | 1842 | —2 |
| Peak | 1846 | | 1849 | —3 |
| Trough | 1858 | | 1863 | —5 |
| Peak | 1864.25 | 1864.25 | 1871 | —7 |
| Trough | 1874.25 | 1874.25 | 1876 | —2 |
| Peak | 1881 | 1881 | 1881 | 0 |
| Trough | 1886.50 | 1884 | 1885 | +1 |
| Peak | 1889.75 | 1888 | 1888 | +2 |
| Trough | 1892.25 | 1892.25 | 1896 | —4 |
| Peak | 1899 | 1899 | 1901 | —2 |
| Trough | 1911 | 1906.75 | 1913[b] | —2 |
| Peak | 1914.50 | 1913.25 | 1918 | —4 |

[a]Taken from Abramovitz's statement in *Hearings before the Joint Economic Committee of the Congress of the United States,* Tables 9 and 16, pp. 411 and 466. [b]A minor trough; not negative.

regression technique, we do rely on the Frickey index of manufacturing production.

Our suspicions are reduced when we compare Abramovitz's chronology of peaks and troughs with our import series. His dating estimates are for economic activity in general and for industrial and commercial production in particular, but in terms of rates of change. Imports in rates of change exhibit an over-all lag behind Abramovitz's dates (see Table 14). Imports in constant prices lead in three cases, lag in nine, and are synchronous in one, for an average lag of approximately 2.1 years.

Earlier in this study we commented upon the somewhat un-usual nature of import movements from 1877 to 1915. The cycle from 1877 to 1896 in imports has a relatively mild amplitude; the import values series reveals a double peak. Imports rise rapidly to the early 1880's, but they exhibit an extended period of low growth rates with a mild trough in 1885 before rising to a second peak in 1891. This long swing in imports has many similarities with domestic series. Railway mileage added has a double peak in 1882 and 1888 with an intermediate trough in 1885. Riggleman's building index rises rapidly to about 1881-1883, and then a period of relatively low growth rates follows before the peak in 1890. The pig iron series falls to an inter-mediate trough in 1884-1885 after peaking in 1882. And both the bituminous coal output and public land sales series are double peaked: bituminous coal attaining an early major peak in 1883 and falling to a trough in 1886; public land sales peak in 1884 and 1888 with an intermediate trough in 1885-1886. It is clear, then, that although the long swing in imports from 1877 to 1896 is relatively mild with low growth rates in the mid-eighties, the same kind of configuration is exhibited in the domestic series.

From 1896 to 1915 imports do not exhibit a long swing in absolute values (only a swing in rates of change). Except for the extremely sharp fall from 1916 to 1918, Riggleman's index also exhibits a comparatively mild amplitude over its swing 1900-1916. Railway mileage added rises sharply to an early peak in 1905 and falls gradually until 1913. The bituminous coal series also has a very mild swing over this period. This helps, in part, to suggest an explanation for the mild amplitude over this long swing since these series lack a terminating trough which is characteristic of past historical experience. It certainly seems reasonable to implicate the war boom as an explanation for the United States import boom 1916-1920—the boom itself is in terms of prices. Therefore, it may also explain the *lack* of evi-dence of an import trough prior to or during the war. Most of these domestic series, and especially the investment series *includ-ing* net capital movements, trough in the middle of the war: net capital movements trough in 1917, Riggleman's and Long's building indices in 1918, and public land sales in 1917. As with the import series, the remaining domestic series trough at the conclusion of the war: pig iron troughs in 1921, anthracite coal production in 1922, railway mileage added in 1922, and business incorporations in 1923.

There are many other similarities between domestic movements and the long swings in imports. We might mention one more. The relative shortness of the long cycle 1863-1877 (and its sharp amplitude) is also revealed in the Riggleman index of building activity, railroad building, and public land sales.

Although this exercise has given us some flavor of the relationships, the lead-lag analysis only involves the turning points of these series. What remains to be done is a more extensive analysis of the relationship between imports and domestic activity using simple correlation techniques. The import analysis follows while a similar and more adequate examination of the relationship between net capital movements and the domestic long swing must wait until Chapter IV.

## *Imports and the Domestic Long Swing: Regression Analysis*

Four series were used in this lag analysis on aggregate imports: two investment series, the Riggleman building index and Poor's estimates of railway mileage added (see Tables B-10, B-13); an output index of a particular industry, bituminous coal (see Table B-12); and a more general index of industrial production for the second half of the nineteenth century, the Frickey index of manufacturing production (see Table B-11). Since the Frickey index goes back only as far as 1860, it was considered worthwhile to divide the analysis into periods. The regressions were run in three separate periods, allowing an overlap between these time spans: 1830-1870, 1860-1900, and 1890-1914.

The major problem was to choose an appropriate method for adjusting the annual data prior to the regression analysis. The annual data turned out to be inadequate for our purposes since, as might be expected, over a period of forty years the secular trend of growth far overshadowed the importance of the long swing. When a simple regression was calculated between, say, the Frickey index and the annual import data, the correlation coefficients were so spuriously high that any lag analysis was hardly meaningful. The first step, therefore, was to remove the trend from the import data as well as from the domestic series representing our independent variables. Following Frickey and Kuznets, the trend removal used was that which allows for a retardation in the rate of growth.[9] The second problem arose using this trendless annual data (in terms of percentage deviation of actual from predicted values). The short-run movements now assumed such relative importance as to produce correlation coefficients which were too low. The final step then was to apply a five-year moving average to both the import and domestic series.

The regressions themselves were applied to both deflated imports and imports in current prices, but the emphasis was put on the deflated series in an effort to isolate, as much as possible, domestic income effects upon import demand. No deflation of the domestic series was necessary, of course, since all were real output series or indices of real output. The results of the regressions are compiled in Tables 15 and 16.

Before examining the results explicitly two general comments should be made. First, the initial impression is that there is general consistency between the results here and those of the more casual turning-point analysis. In all cases, the best fit appears to be with imports lagging behind the domestic series from one to four years. The second comment is in the form of a repeated word of caution. Imports, from 1842 to 1915, are in terms of fiscal years ending June 30 and thus may have a "manufactured" half-year lag.

First, let us turn to a comparison of results between current and deflated imports. For forty years of the nineteenth century, 1830-1870, current and deflated imports have similar lags. From 1830 to 1870 current imports $(M_C)$ lag the Riggleman building index by one or two years; this is also true of deflated imports $(M_D)$ over the same time span. However, from 1860 to 1914 the comparative lags are somewhat different. Using the Frickey manufacturing index, 1860-1900, the best lag of $M_C$ is one year behind the

---

9. $\text{Log } y = \alpha_0 + \alpha_1 t + \alpha_2 t^2$.

**Table 15** Lag Analysis of Deflated Imports on Domestic Series, 1830-1914[a]

| | Number Years Lag | $\hat{\beta}_1$ | r=Correlation Coefficients |
|---|---|---|---|
| | **1830-1870** | | |
| (1) Riggleman Building Index | 0 | 0.4787 | r = 0.872 |
| (1830-1870) | 1[b] | 0.5205 | r = 0.951[b] |
| | 2 | 0.5133 | r = 0.937 |
| | 3 | 0.4685 | r = 0.857 |
| (2) Railroad Mileage Added | 0 | 0.3095 | r = 0.753 |
| (1830-1870) | 1[b] | 0.3248 | r = 0.790[b] |
| | 2 | 0.3008 | r = 0.734 |
| (3) Bituminous Coal Output | 2 | 1.4205 | r = 0.511 |
| (1845-1870) | 3 | 1.7906 | r = 0.647 |
| | 4[b] | 2.0156 | r = 0.739[b] |
| | **1860-1900** | | |
| (1) Frickey Index | 0 | 0.9336 | r = 0.582 |
| (1860-1900) | 1 | 1.2800 | r = 0.782 |
| | 2[b] | 1.3315 | r = 0.822[b] |
| | 3 | 1.1788 | r = 0.744 |
| (2) Riggleman Building Index | 0 | 0.2289 | r = 0.652 |
| (1860-1900) | 1[b] | 0.2447 | r = 0.683[b] |
| | 2 | 0.2091 | r = 0.589 |
| (3) Railroad Mileage Added | 0 | 0.0971 | r = 0.517 |
| (1860-1900) | 1 | 0.1553 | r = 0.809 |
| | 2[b] | 0.1783 | r = 0.938[b] |
| | 3 | 0.1721 | r = 0.927 |
| (4) Bituminous Coal Output | 0 | 0.7703 | r = 0.733 |
| (1860-1900) | 1[b] | 0.9198 | r = 0.858[b] |
| | 2 | 0.8440 | r = 0.795 |
| | **1890-1914** | | |
| (1) Frickey Index | 2 | 0.9639 | r = 0.676 |
| (1890-1914) | 3 | 1.0199 | r = 0.715 |
| | 4[b] | 0.7186 | r = 0.752[b] |
| | 5 | 0.8122 | r = 0.567 |
| (2) Riggleman Building Index | 0 | 0.4154 | r = 0.789 |
| (1890-1914) | 1[b] | 0.4370 | r = 0.871[b] |
| | 2 | 0.4075 | r = 0.840 |
| (3) Railroad Mileage Added | 2 | 0.1789 | r = 0.800 |
| (1890-1914) | 3[b] | 0.1924 | r = 0.903[b] |
| | 4[b] | 0.1856 | r = 0.901[b] |
| (4) Bituminous Coal Output | 2 | 0.9090 | r = 0.811 |
| (1890-1914) | 3 | 0.9722 | r = 0.884 |
| | 4[b] | 0.9284 | r = 0.897[b] |
| | 5 | 0.8984 | r = 0.798 |

[a] Where $\hat{\beta}_1$ is the estimated coefficient of the independent variable explaining imports.

[b] Best fit occurs at this lag although no tests for significance were undertaken to determine a more realistic and statistically rigorous range of "best lags."

Frickey index while $M_D$ lags by two years. This result—$M_D$ exhibiting a larger lag over the latter half of the nineteenth century—lends further support to our earlier conclusion that import prices lead aggregate imports. It is not surprising that import prices are positively correlated with aggregate imports since the British export industry also undergoes long swings during the latter half of the nineteenth century, and these reveal a positive correlation with American domestic long swings. The results are equally informative from 1890 to 1914: $M_C$ lags the Frickey index by two or three years while $M_D$ reveals a lag of four years.

$M_D$, 1830-1870, lags the Riggleman index by one year, railroad

**Table 16** Lag Analysis of Current Imports on Domestic Series, 1830-1914

| | No. Years Lag | $\hat{\beta}_1$ | r=Correlation Coefficients |
|---|---|---|---|
| Riggleman Building Index | 0 | 0.7651 | r = 0.886 |
| (1832-1870) | 1[a] | 0.8399 | r = 0.953[a] |
| | 2[a] | 0.8543 | r = 0.948[a] |
| Frickey Index | 0 | 1.3256 | r = 0.596 |
| (1860-1900) | 1[a] | 1.5299 | r = 0.659[a] |
| | 2 | 1.3857 | r = 0.593 |
| Frickey Index | 2[a] | 1.6845 | r = 0.768[a] |
| (1890-1914) | 3[a] | 1.6801 | r = 0.765[a] |
| | 4 | 1.5396 | r = 0.695 |

[a]Best fit occurs at this lag (see Table 15, footnote b).

mileage added by one year, and bituminous coal output by four years. In the period 1860-1900 the lag behind the Riggleman index is again one year, whereas it increases to two years behind the railroad index and is only one year behind bituminous coal production. One explanation for the secular increase in the lag of $M_D$ behind the railroad index is the increasing importance of railroad investment activity in setting the pace of development over the long swing. In the earlier portion (1830-1850) it was a young industry which was slow to fall victim to movements in aggregate demand on the downswing. One might then expect to see $M_D$ lagging further behind railway expansion during the century as the railways began to play a more important role in setting the pace of American development.

Although these regressions that were run on the Riggleman index, railroad construction, and bituminous coal output are certainly informative in themselves, they should not be interpreted literally as general income-output relationships. The Frickey manufacturing index should better serve as an income variable. For nearly half a century (1860-1900), $M_D$ lags behind the index of manufacturing production by two years—a result consistent with our conclusion derived from turning-point analysis. In the immediate prewar period (1890-1914) it is, however, much larger: $M_D$ lags by four years. Although part of this period (1900-1914) is one of unusual long-run economic stability, it still remains unclear why deflated imports do not begin a fall to a trough some years before the war. This would give it the time shape consistent with other long swings. The lag of deflated imports behind domestic series, at any rate, is certainly longer than in any other period prior to the World War I.[10]

## Imports and the Price Effect

After pursuing an investigation into the income effect upon imports, this section examines briefly the importance of the "price effect." Under a flexible paper standard, 1862-1878, the relative movements in general price levels should not play an important role except in partially determining the level of the foreign exchange rate. But under the gold standard, 1820-1861 and 1879-1913, the movements in relative prices (domestic relative to foreign) ought to help us explain the true shape of import demand movements. Either domestic price movements may help to explain import value turning points by themselves, or they may suggest some explanation for the general lag of imports behind

---

10. It is sometimes suggested that the mildness of the long swing in imports from 1890 to 1914 is explained in part by the economic stability of the period. This assertion is left somewhat in doubt after examining the size of the $\beta_1$ *coefficients*. The coefficients are reasonably close to unity in both output series from 1890 to the war. In contrast, from 1860 to 1900 the values for $\beta_1$ are mostly greater than unity and reflect the relative violence of import movements compared to the index for manufacturing production over the domestic long swing. This is even more apparent for the earlier portion of that century (1845-1870) where import movements exhibit far more violent amplitudes than bituminous coal output ($1.4 < \beta_1 < 2.0$).

movements in domestic activity (the general conclusion reached in earlier sections). This may be possible since price movements seem to lag output changes, especially at peaks, due to their relative downward inflexibility. This second suggestion is quite attractive since our lead-lag analysis shows imports lagging domestic activity at peaks from one to two years, while they are almost synchronous at troughs. Thus, if prices remain high or are rising after the peak in output, there may be a shift into cheaper foreign goods in excess of or equal to the negative income effect so as to produce such a lag. Finally, perhaps a great deal of the difference in amplitude from one import cycle to the next can be explained by the change in domestic prices.

For the analysis which follows, we have settled on two price indices: the Warren-Pearson "all commodity" wholesale price index and the Warren-Pearson "30 basic commodities" wholesale price index.[11] Whether either of these price measures differs substantially from the price level of commodities competing with foreign goods is not considered here. We can only hope that any differences do not interfere with the applicability of our general conclusions. A second difficulty arises when we recognize that it is not domestic prices alone which determine the price effect but the movements in domestic prices *relative* to foreign prices. As an attempted solution to this problem we have taken the ratio of both Warren-Pearson indices to our import price index. When referring to the movements in prices, then, we are referring to relative prices and to movements in those ratios (see Chart 16).

Is there any relationship between the amplitude of deflated imports and the relative movements in prices? Even if the correlation is positive, of course, we cannot be sure that the larger amplitude of deflated imports is not due to the variations in real income alone. Over the eighty years 1820-1900 and from trough to peak, deflated imports have their greatest amplitude in the upswing of the 1850's, the 1830's, and the late 1870's and 1880's, in that order—eliminating 1862-1878 (see Table 12). This is certainly consistent with our price movements. The greatest relative price

---

11. U. S. Bureau of the Census, *Historical Statistics of the United States, 1789-1945* (Washington, D. C.: U. S. Government Printing Office, 1949), L 2, L 3, pp. 231-232.

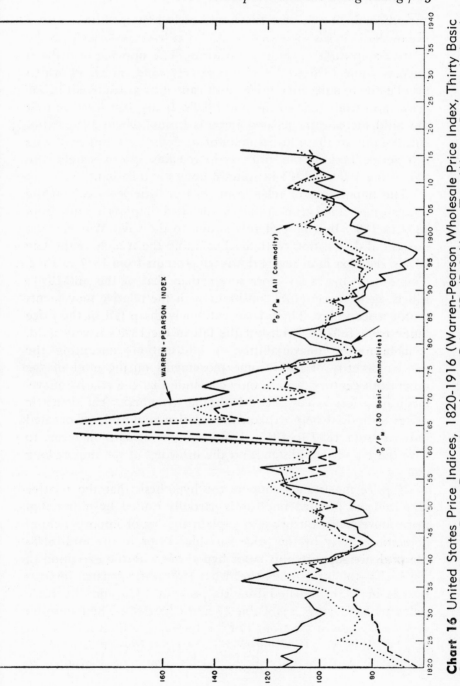

**Chart 15** United States Price Indices, 1820-1916 (Warren-Pearson Wholesale Price Index, Thirty Basic Commodities; Relative Price: Domestic ÷ Import Prices [$P_D/P_M$] Using Two Warren-Pearson Indices)

*Source:* See Text

rise occurs during the late 1840's and early 1850's, while the price rise of the 1830's is somewhat less. This at least conforms with the relative amplitude of the two upswings. The upswing of deflated imports from 1876 to 1895 is relatively mild, much of which may be due to a negative price effect caused by a steady fall in the price ratio from 1882 to the mid-1890's. It may also be true that the mild increase in deflated imports from 1896 to 1915 is not entirely due to the unusual amount of domestic stability during this period because our price ratio remains approximately constant from 1900 to 1915 in spite of domestic inflation.

The importance of relative prices is a little less clear on the downswings. The greatest fall in deflated imports occurs from 1859 to 1863, but most of this is due to the Civil War and the exogenous destruction of trade. Excluding the trough of the late 1870's, the next most severe downswing occurs from 1837 to 1842. This downswing is far more severe than that of the mid-1890's which, again, is certainly consistent with the relative movements in our price index. There is an extremely sharp fall in the price index from 1837 to 1842, but the fall in the 1890's is very mild.

Due to the unavailability of information concerning the relative severity of real-income movements during most of the nineteenth century, we can only conclude that the relative movement in prices is consistent with the hypothesis that domestic prices do indeed help explain the relative amplitude of deflated imports from 1820 to 1915. However, this conclusion seems to have more positive substance on the upswings of the import long cycle.

If price movements support the hypothesis that the relative amplitude of deflated imports is partially caused by differential price movements, can we also explain the lag of imports behind domestic activity by the price variable? Prior to the mid-1850's the evidence supports this latter hypothesis with the exception of the 1820's—the price index rises from 1820 while deflated imports trough in 1821. Deflated imports peak in 1836 and the price index peaks in 1837 (see Table 17 and Chart 16). The two series are synchronous at the trough of the 1840's since both reach a low in 1843. However, the long lag of aggregate imports behind indices of domestic activity in the 1850's cannot be attributed to price movements. The price index peaks in 1854 and continues to fall until 1860, whereas deflated imports do not peak until 1860. And while deflated imports fall to a trough in 1862, the price index rises sharply from 1861 to 1862.

The evidence is no more illuminating for the long swing in deflated imports, 1878-1898. Imports in constant prices rise from the trough of 1877 to a peak in the mid-1890's, but the price index rises from a trough in 1878 to a peak in 1882 and falls to 1894. When deflated imports rise from the trough of 1898, they lag four years behind the upswing in this price index.

During the nineteenth century, then, only three cases (1837,

**Table 17** Turning-Point Comparison of Domestic Prices and Deflated Imports

| | (1)<br>Warren-Pearson "All Commodity" U.S. Price Index ÷ Import Price Index<br>(annual data) | (2)<br>Warren-Pearson "30 Basic Commodity" U.S. Price Index ÷ Import Price Index<br>(annual data) | (3)<br>(1) Prices Lead (+) or Lag (—) Imports (4) | (4)<br>Deflated Imports<br>(annual data) |
|---|---|---|---|---|
| Trough | 1820 | 1820 | + 1 | 1821 |
| Peak | 1837 | 1837 | — 1 | 1836 |
| Trough | 1843 | 1843 | 0 | 1843 |
| Peak | 1854 | 1854 | + 6 | 1860 |
| Trough | 1860 | 1860 | + 2 | 1862 |
| Peak | 1864 | 1864 | + 9 | 1873 |
| Trough | 1878 | 1878 | 0 | 1878 |
| Peak | 1882 | 1882 | +15 | 1897 |
| Trough | 1894 | 1894 | + 4 | 1898 |

1843, 1878) support the hypothesis. We must conclude that in spite of the obvious importance of relative price movements in aggravating the long swing in deflated imports (relative price movements precipitate a shift which is in excess of the income effect, into imports on the upswing and out of imports on the downswing), prices do not appear to be of importance in influencing turning points.[12] In order to give positive support for our hypothe-

---

12. Furthermore a multiple regression was run using both the price index and the Frickey index over the period 1879-1914. The coefficient of the price variable was not significant under any reasonable set of lag conditions.

sis that the lag of imports behind domestic activity could be as-
cribed to relative price movements, either our price index would
conform in timing or lag behind it. But in five out of eight cases in
the nineteenth century (excluding the period 1862-1878) the price
index *leads* import peaks and troughs: 1821, 1860, 1862, 1897,
1898. The only possible conclusion is that prices have no initiating
effect upon imports but do serve as an important influence on the
amplitude of their movements and thus on the movements of the
trade balance.

# IV.

# A QUANTITATIVE AND QUALITATIVE HISTORY OF AMERICAN NINETEENTH-CENTURY CAPITAL MOVEMENTS

*An Over-all View of Net Capital Movements: 1820-1913*

Initially we advance the apparently reasonable hypothesis that capital movements were, mainly, independent of aggregate imports. By independent we mean that nineteenth-century capital flows had a causal relationship to domestic activity and were not simply short-term loans used to finance trade or long-term loans of the "tied" sort. It is clear, under these assumptions, that net capital movements and imports must be *statistically* related since both were a function of domestic activity.

Presumably, the motivation of private capital movements in the nineteenth century, or in any other, was to search out investments yielding high rates of return. Given that a secular net capital importer reveals sizeable fluctuations in its pace of development, we surely should expect similar fluctuations in its rate of capital import to help finance that development. To the extent that rates of return on American securities vary with the long swing, increasing on the upswing and falling on the downswing, we would predict that the rate of net capital import would increase on the upswing and decline on the downswing of a Kuznets cycle. Net capital imports should be positively correlated, therefore, with long swings in commodity imports.

Furthermore, net capital movements should typically undergo more violent amplitude and lead import demand at both peaks and troughs. Domestic investment, which long-term capital presumably helps finance, has much more violent fluctuation over the long swing than either consumption or income, of which import demand is a function. To continue this very elementary exposition, investment tends to lead both consumption and income, and thus net capital import turning points should lead commodity import turning points. Finally, net capital imports should produce even greater amplitude and leads given that foreigners may have been more sensitive to shifting risks and rates of return.

There are other sound reasons for predicting secular patterns of this sort. The transportation-communication sector displays perhaps more violent fluctuations in its rate of development than any other sector. Indeed, some students of American development have identified the transportation and building sector as the prime mover of the long swing. If foreigners are mainly interested in the securities offered by this sector, considerable secular variations in net capital movements are to be expected since the rate of new issues, expected returns, and prices of these securities are likely to reveal extremely violent fluctuations as well. There is also evidence that transportation investment leads general net capital formation over the long swing, especially at peaks; clearly, then, it would also lead general income-output movements. Another reason for suspecting more violent movements in net capital flows than in import movements arises with the knowledge that British building cycles move inversely to American over the latter half of the nineteenth century. Thus the supply push of foreign investment out of British domestic outlets may further aggravate long swings in American net capital imports. Finally, movements in the money market are likely to influence the amplitude of net capital flows over the long swing. Given only three markets, rapid growth on the upswing of the cycle may tend to generate excess demand for both money and goods and an excess supply of securities. The greater the excess demand for money left unsatisfied by internal production of gold or variations in the reserve ratio, the greater the rise in interest rates (all else given), and thus the greater the attractiveness of American securities to foreigners.

In this investigation, capital movements over United States borders shall be considered as a fortuitous pool of foreign exchange resources that allows the satisfaction both of import demand, a necessary input for the development process, and of an excess demand for money, which allows rapid development to proceed without price deflation or an insufficiency in aggregate demand. This pool of resources was a necessary concomitant for growth in spite of the obvious fact that the United States historically needed very small marginal doses of foreign inputs, especially during the most dynamic periods of post-bellum growth. A major loss in gold or foreign exchange is incompatible with growth, a fact that is painfully clear to contemporary developing nations. Under nineteenth-century gold-standard conditions, a major loss of gold might have severely retarded rapid growth on the upswing of a Kuznets cycle.

What does the historical pattern of net capital flows look like? Over the period 1820-1913 there are five extremely prominent long swings in American net capital movements. Prior to 1895 the United States was a debtor nation in the early stages of rapid development, and thus net capital movements fluctuated in rates of positive inflow with outflow occurring only at deep and protracted troughs (see Chart 11). With 1896 and after, however, the United States rapidly achieved a young creditor position and net capital movements fluctuated in rates of positive outflow (or negative inflow) with the peak of 1908-1912 as the single exception.

The first period of significant capital inflow into the American economy followed the Napoleonic era (1800-1814) when net capital movements fluctuated about zero with no evidence of long swings (see Chart 11 and Table B-1). Although this period of inflow (1814-1820) was relatively short, it was nevertheless substantial since its peak in 1816 ($58 million) was almost equal to that of 1836, two decades later. Net capital movements fell from that peak in 1816 to a trough in the mid-1820's.

The first long swing (these turning-point dates are for smoothed data) rose very sharply from a trough in 1825 to a peak in 1837 and fell to a trough in 1842, for a duration of seventeen years from trough to trough. This long swing has an extreme amplitude in the annual data. A relatively insignificant capital outflow of about $6.8 million occurred in 1825, while in 1836 it attained a peak annual *inflow* of $62.2 million and a maximum outflow in the trough of the forties of $30.8 million. From the extended depression of the 1840's, the second long swing in the smoothed net capital movements data produced a peak inflow in 1852 before declining to a trough in 1858 for a duration of sixteen years. The amplitude of this cycle is less pronounced, at least in relation to its terminal point in 1858. Unfortunately, it is impossible to isolate the effects of the war. Nevertheless, in the annual data net capital imports contracted sharply from an inflow of $55.6 million in 1853 to a net outflow of $23.1 million in 1858. The next long swing reflects an intensive period of capital inflow into the United States during and after the Civil War. After the late 1850's capital flowed into the young American economy at increasing rates up to 1871 (in the smoothed data), subsequently declined, and reached an extended trough in 1879. According to the annual data, we imported $243 million at the peak while at the trough an *outflow* of about $162 million was recorded. The duration of this war and postwar cycle was twenty-one years trough to trough.

The fourth long swing also covers a period of extensive capital inflow. Net capital imports reached a peak in 1889 and then underwent a tremendous decline to a protracted trough in 1900, for a duration of twenty-one years. After this swing the United States never again attained a position of significant capital inflow. Although America was still an average debtor in 1900, she was a consistent marginal creditor beginning as early as the mid-1890's. The next long cycle is mainly in the form of net capital exports. On the upswing, net exports of capital contracted rapidly and by 1906 net imports began again. In spite of the interruption of the depression of 1907-1908, net capital imports rose to very high levels in 1910 (1911 in the smoothed data) and then fell away and were succeeded by the heavy capital exports of World War I. The trough in 1900 produced an outflow of approximately $296 million, the peak inflow in 1910 amounted to about $229 million, and the 1917 trough attained an outflow of $2,983 million!

We have, then, five full long swings from peak to peak and trough to trough from 1817 to 1917. From peak to peak, these five long swings have an average duration of 18.8 years; from trough to trough, an average of 18.4 years. This may be compared with the average duration of the import cycle of 18.5 years from trough to trough.

**Table 18** Lead-Lag Comparison of Imports and Net Capital Movements

|  | Imports (current prices: smoothed) | Net Capital Movements, K (inflow: smoothed) | K: Lead (+) or Lag (—) | |
|---|---|---|---|---|
|  |  |  | Annual Data | Smoothed Data |
| Peak | 1817 | 1817 | 0 | 0 |
| Trough | 1822 | 1825 | —6 | —3 |
| Peak | 1837 | 1837 | 0 | 0 |
| Trough | 1842 | 1842 | +3 | 0 |
| Peak | 1858 | 1852 | +7 | +6 |
| Trough | 1863 | 1858 | +4 | +5 |
| Peak | 1873 | 1871 | +1 | +2 |
| Trough | 1877 | 1879 | 0 | —2 |
| Peak | 1891 | 1889 | +5 | +2 |
| Trough | 1896 | 1900 | —2 | —4 |
| Peak | — | 1911 | — | — |
| Trough | (1922) | 1917 | — | (+5) |
|  |  | Average: | +1.2 | +1.0 |

Further comparison with import movements should be pursued at this point. In all cases but two, net capital flows (annual data) lead or are synchronous with imports in current prices: 1817, 1837, and 1878 are synchronous; in 1821 and 1898 imports lead (see Table 18). The average lead of net capital movements over the period is 1.2 years in the annual and one year in the smoothed data. If we eliminate the "trough" of imports in 1922, there is a lead of 0.6 years.

Whether or not this implies that net capital movements are more sensitive to domestic activity (in a lead-lag relationship) is deferred to later in this chapter when we examine the domestic series. But it does seem clear that capital movements do not respond to satisfy import demand but rather move "independently," leading imports of merchandise over the long swing.

Unfortunately, it is almost impossible to derive a comparable measurement for the time shape of capital movements to allow amplitude comparison with import movements. Since they fluctuate around zero (from negative to positive), we can apply neither rates of change nor relative amplitude measurement to net capital movements. But there are some comparative observations that can be made. First, the time path of capital movements is more like that of aggregate imports in *rates of change* than of absolute levels of aggregate imports (compare Charts 10 and 11). This may simply reflect the importance of the transportation sector as a leading industry in the growth process.

But we also find that capital movements do not necessarily fall from a peak coincident with the peak in the rates of change of imports. Capital movements seem to fall from a peak coincident with the termination of a fairly long period of high and somewhat stable growth rate. The rates of change of imports begin falling *sharply* to a trough in 1834, 1852, 1871, 1888, and 1905, and capital movements peak in 1837, 1852, 1871, 1889, and 1911. Using these rough measures, imports in rates of change *lead* capital movements with an average of two years. Admittedly, the turning-point measurement here is much less precise and should be treated accordingly.

Second, we can say something about the *absolute* measures of the amplitude of imports and capital movements. The absolute share of net capital movements in satisfying import demand would be a useful measure of the relative importance of capital movements for maintaining stability in the balance of payments over the development process or, put another way, in financing the necessary external inputs (in excess of export revenue) concomitant with the growth process. In order to measure this effect over the long period from trough to peak of the cycle, the yearly increments have been summed over the initial low level at the trough. This gives us an aggregate measure of the total *increase* in import demand from trough to peak over the long swing. From

1828 to 1837, 48 per cent of the increase in import demand over time is satisfied by increases in the inflow of capital (or reductions in the rate of capital outflow); 1842-1858, 22 per cent; 1863-1873, 33 per cent; 1877-1891, 48 per cent; and 1915-1927, 23 per cent. The remainder, of course, is satisfied by export expansion and by the flow of specie (which is most important, it seems, from 1842 to 1858). The measurements above underlie the importance of capital movements in United States balance of payments. Although the level of net capital flows may be low when averaged over the Kuznets cycle (and most certainly relative to imports), its amplitude is quite large. Large enough, it seems, for its absolute changes to account for from one-quarter to one-half of the changes in imports from trough to peak over the long swing.

Using the same measure of amplitude relative to import movements, capital movements have even more violent changes from peak to trough of the long swing. The absolute changes in the decrease of net capital inflow (or increase in net capital outflow) are in *excess* of the absolute fall in merchandise imports. From 1837 to 1842 the decrease in net capital inflow is 114 per cent of the fall in imports; in 1873-1877, 167 per cent; and in 1891-1896, 145 per cent. On the average, then, the absolute changes in net capital movements are about 1.5 times that of merchandise imports. The peak-to-trough movement from 1858 to 1863 is not included here since net capital movements lead to such an extent that they are rising while imports are falling. Then on the up-swing of the long cycle, capital movements account for as large a part as one-quarter to one-half of import changes and on the downswing for as much as 1.5 times import changes. Clearly then, the movements in net capital flows are extremely volatile and important in the process of United States development. And it may be that on the downswing the "excess" movement in capital import compared with imports of goods and services prevents the decline in imports of goods and services from contributing to the liquidity of United States banks and business.

We have already noted that net capital movements over United States borders exhibit a substantial and persistent lead over the long swing in commodity imports. Net capital movements produced much more severe long swings throughout the nineteenth century as well. There is one aspect of these movements left to be introduced. How *do* net capital movements behave relative to domestic activity?

The average lead of net capital inflows is 0.1 years over the composite of domestic activity presented in Chapter III (which may, in reality, be somewhat greater due to the nature of official reporting on a fiscal basis). But again, as in the case of imports, we find more synchronism at troughs than at peaks: there is an average lag at troughs of 0.2 years while there is a lead of 0.4 years at peaks. Thus the rate of capital inflow tends to be synchronous with domestic activity at troughs and to lead by about a year at peaks (see Table 13).

Finally, a casual examination of the pattern of domestic investment components appears to suggest potential explanations for unique characteristics of individual long swings in net capital movements. The abrupt and relatively violent swing from 1825 to 1842 is true also of indices of building activity and public land sales. The long and protracted depression of the 1840's in net capital imports (and commodity imports) is repeated in the building indices. The double peaked nature of the railroad boom in the 1880's and 1890's is echoed in the net capital movements series: in the annual data net capital movements rise to a minor peak around 1882, then remain approximately constant from 1883 to 1885 before climbing to a major peak in 1888. Incidentally, it is interesting to note that the boom in net capital inflow in the 1880's and 1890's marks the end of an extensive period of net foreign capital flowing to the United States. This period is also the secular peak in railroad investment since the next peak in railroad investment in the first decade of the twentieth century is far below that of the 1880's, and the series continues its secular decline thereafter.

## The Nature and Direction of Net Capital Movements: A Summary

After even a cursory examination of the meager stock of literature on the nature and direction of nineteenth-century American net capital movements, it is impossible to be left unimpressed by the striking importance of the transportation industry as an absorbent of foreign funds. Although empirical confirmation of any hypothesis concerning the first half of the nineteenth century is more difficult, the major role of the transportation sector in absorbing external funds remains outstandingly clear. Whereas after 1868 the railroads with their phenomenal growth and heavy capital requirements were far and away the chief attraction for foreign long-term capital and the dominant source of an excess supply of domestic securities, prior to the Civil War it seems to have been early railroad development and a combination of canal building, port and harbor expansion, and highway construction. The non-railroad investments were fostered mainly by state and local bond issues. Thus, over the nineteenth century as a whole, it is the transportation-communication sector which mainly concerns the foreign investor, and this dominance persists even into the first fifteen years of the twentieth century, although to a lesser extent.

A condition existed in the period 1820-1913 which is painfully lacking among contemporary developing nations. During the course of these long swings in the rate of growth of domestic output, there was a concomitant and violent swing in the rate of development of the transportation sector. As suggested earlier in this chapter, long swings in the rate of output growth and in the rate of expansion of the transportation industry also seemed to be accompanied by varying excess supplies of securities generated by the transportation sector. Fortunately, America was able to offer in increasing amounts securities which were attractive to foreign investors during periods of rapid growth and rising trade-balance deficits. The United States was able to continue long periods of rapid growth, with its ensuing excess demand on the goods and money market and excess supply in the securities market, since these markets were cleared in a very important way—via the balance of payments—without severe bottlenecks in the goods market or price deflation due to excess demand in the money market.

Not only does the history of foreign capital movements into the United States provide a distinction according to the types of securities offered by the transportation sector pre– and post–Civil War, but also their time dimension presents us with another delineation. Short-term capital seems to be extremely important prior to and during the 1840's. This is much less true later in the century. We shall see that this distinction may be due to the nature of the export bundle as well as to the liquidity of the early American economy.

This brings us to a third meaningful distinction between these historical periods of capital import. During the first half of the century, foreign investment—mainly British capital—was largely motivated by the desire to facilitate the export market to insure Europe's supply of raw material inputs. In the first long secular swing (1830's and 1840's) it is cotton: long-term capital moves as if to insure an increasing supply of cotton in the future and short-term capital to facilitate the export of that year's crop. In the second long swing (1840's and 1850's) it is less cotton and more an expansion of the Western granary. After the 1850's, although the relative interest in the railroads increases, it is no longer necessarily the facilitation of a future export stream which dictates the movement of foreign capital but, as North has said, the effects of "residentiary activity"[1] and a broader base of economic growth.

The following discussion will tend to substantiate the statement that the trade in goods dictates movements in capital, but hardly through import movements. The relation of net capital movements to the export market in both the long and short run is a tenuous one indeed. That is, from 1820 to 1860 (or at least until 1850) the export sector appears to play a major role in dictating the general level of domestic activity and the rate of development. The inflow of foreign capital is intimately tied to the state of the export market, not only due to the importance of the cotton market in influencing the rate of development, but also directly related to Southern security issues that facilitated an expanding export supply. In the decades during and after the Civil War, the state of the grain market had an important influence on the rate of railroad development—and most of the net inflow of long-term capital flowed into the railroad industry. After the 1880's and 1890's, the intimate relation between the export

1. Douglass C. North, *The Economic Growth of the United States, 1790-1860* (Englewood Cliffs, N. J.: Prentice-Hall, Inc., 1961), pp. 1-14.

market and the flow of foreign capital over United States borders disappears entirely (as does the importance of agriculture in American development).

The purpose of the following sections on capital movements is threefold. First, we attempt an explanation for the movements in foreign capital over these violent long swings prior to 1870 where quantitative analysis is almost impossible. Second, we try to isolate the industrial direction of this capital inflow into American business which, of course, the aggregate estimates do not tell us. This is important not only to understand better the nature of American securities offered and their differing degrees of attractiveness to foreign investors over the long swing, but also as an indispensable aid to choosing the explanatory variables of domestic demand for foreign funds in quantitative tests (1840-1860 and 1870-1914) which appear in the subsequent sections. And third, we would also like to know more about the sources of that capital inflow so as to include the likely importance of supply conditions for foreign capital movements across the Alantic.

To repeat, much of the remaining analysis in this chapter is devoted to the earlier portion of the nineteenth century simply because of our lack of knowledge about it and the difficulty of quantitative test. But it is also true that there is a great deal that is unique about this early phase of American development and needs clarification.

In the course of the following discussion about the qualitative nature of American capital imports, the reader may refer to Chart 11 or to Table B-1 where the quantitative estimates are exhibited.

### The First Long Swing: 1825-1842

The first large inflow of foreign capital into the United States occurred during the 1830's. The net movement of capital into the American states after the War of 1812 was not insignificant, to be sure, but it is not until 1830 that a large sustained net import occurred. Indeed, so large was the inflow of foreign funds in the decade 1830-1839 that North says of it, "Relative to the size of the economy it was probably the most significant inflow of capital during the nineteenth century."[2] Even when we compare peak years of inflow, that of the 1830's exceeds the peak in the mid-1850's though the latter may have been prematurely inhibited by the Crimean War as well as by an excess supply of real-money balances.

There can be little doubt that the majority of foreign funds was directed into the purchase of state and local bond issues. We know, for example, that even as late as 1853, after the vigorous beginnings of the first railroad boom, as much as 68 per cent of foreign long-term holdings were in the form of state and local bonds issued for internal improvements (see Table B-2). That the percentage should still be that high after the disastrous period of defaults and repudiations on state debt in the forties certainly implies that the relative magnitude of foreign investment in state and local bonds was even greater in the thirties than in 1853.

Furthermore, while the source is considered less reliable, George Paish estimated that by the early 1850's public securities issued to English investors were about 85 per cent of total American issues to English investors.[3]

The Erie Canal was the first major state enterprise financed by foreign funds. From 1817 to 1825 $7 million worth of New York bonds issued to finance this spectacular state-owned and state-constructed venture passed into English hands. Within ten years the total profits accumulated paid off obligations at a premium before maturity. It is historically clear that New York benefited from the ensuing trade with the Western states. But perhaps more important, the lucrative example of this enterprise set a precedent for future state issues. Philadelphia and Baltimore were clamoring for state enterprise and foreign capital to construct canals to the interior, with Washington, D. C., and Richmond quickly recognizing this competition. Maryland gave bonds and guarantees to private companies for both the Chesapeake and Ohio Canal and the Baltimore and Ohio Railroad. Europe was eager

---

2. Douglass C. North, "The United States Balance of Payments, 1790-1860," *Trends in the American Economy in the Nineteenth Century* ("Studies in Income and Wealth," Vol. XXIV [Princeton, N. J.: Princeton University Press, 1960]), p. 585 (this volume is hereafter cited as *Trends*).

3. Quoted in Albert H. Imlah, *Economic Elements in the Pax Britannica* (Cambridge, Mass.: Harvard University Press, 1958), p. 68.

to acquire these bonds, and several London houses, acting through agencies in New York, bought up entire state issues for resale in England.[4] "In the Middle West state canal systems on a comprehensive scale, supported by federal land grants, were planned in Ohio, Indiana, Illinois, Michigan and Kentucky."[5]

Only the Pennsylvania coal routes, the Schuylkill Coal and Navigation Company, the Philadelphia and Reading Railroad, with some short railroads in New England and central New York, ventured to proceed with neither guarantee nor bonds from a paternal legislature. Before 1836 over 90 million dollars had been invested in canals and railways in the North, of which more than half was a charge upon public credit. The bulk of this capital had been procured from England.[6]

In the South the forces of expansion were different, but the states still acted as financial intermediaries just as they did in the North. Capital was desired mainly for cotton expansion. By 1824 Louisiana initiated the state land bank, the prominent recipient of foreign investment in the South throughout the thirties and forties, which issued bonds in the East and in London to secure *working* capital. Soon, ". . . Florida, Arkansas, Missouri, Illinois, and Indiana came to boast of state owned banks, all deeply concerned in the land business. And loans for most of these undertakings directly or indirectly were sought in London."[7]

It is true that some of the state debt was held at home, but the largest part was in foreign portfolios. The Pennsylvania state debt, as a case in point, amounted to more than $34 million in June, 1842, of which more than $23.7 million were held abroad. Alabama's debt amounted to $11.5 million, of which more than $6 million were made payable in London. Finally, New York state had a debt of $26 million (July, 1845), of which $10.8 million were held abroad.[8]

4. Cleona Lewis, *America's Stake in International Investments* (Washington, D. C.: The Brookings Institution, 1938), p. 17.
5. Leland Jenks, *The Migration of British Capital to 1875* (New York: Alfred A. Knopf, 1927), p. 74.
6. *Ibid.*, p. 75
7. *Ibid.*, pp. 75-76.
8. Lewis, *America's Stake,* p. 20. Madden estimates that of a total of $191 million in state bonds issued by 1860 (most were issued prior to 1850) $73 million,

**Table 19** Objects of State Debts up to 1838, by States[a]

| | Banks | Canals | Railways | Roads | Misc. | Total |
|---|---|---|---|---|---|---|
| Alabama | $ 7,800,000 | | $ 3,000,000 | | | $ 10,800,000 |
| Arkansas | 3,000,000 | | | | | 3,000,000 |
| Illinois | 3,000,000 | $ 900,000 | 7,400,000 | | $ 300,000 | 11,600,000 |
| Indiana | 1,390,000 | 6,750,000 | 2,600,000 | $1,150,000 | | 11,890,000 |
| Kentucky | 2,000,000 | 2,619,000 | 350,000 | 2,400,000 | | 7,369,000 |
| Louisiana | 22,950,000 | 50,000 | 50,000 | | 235,000 | 23,285,000 |
| Maine | | | | | 554,976 | 554,976 |
| Maryland | | 5,700,000 | 5,500,000 | | 292,980 | 11,492,980 |
| Massachusetts | | | 4,290,000 | | | 4,290,000 |
| Michigan | | 2,500,000 | 2,620,000 | | 220,000 | 5,340,000 |
| Mississippi | 7,000,000 | | | | | 7,000,000 |
| Missouri | 2,500,000 | | | | | 2,500,000 |
| New York | | 13,316,674 | 3,787,700 | | 1,158,032 | 18,262,406 |
| Ohio | | 6,101,000 | | | | 6,101,000 |
| Pennsylvania | | 16,579,527 | 4,964,484 | 2,595,902 | 3,166,787 | 27,306,700 |
| South Carolina | | 1,550,000 | 2,000,000 | | 2,203,770 | 5,753,770 |
| Tennessee | 3,000,000 | 300,000 | 3,730,000 | 118,166 | | 7,148,166 |
| Virginia | | 3,835,350 | 2,128,900 | 354,800 | 343,139 | 6,662,189 |
| Total | $52,640,000 | $60,201,551 | $42,871,084 | $6,618,868 | $8,474,684 | $170,356,187 |

[a] E. L. Bogart, *The Economic History of the United States* (2nd ed.; New York: Longmans, Green, and Company, 1913), p. 195.

But if the outstanding portion of foreign investment in the American states from 1830 to 1839 was in the form of state and local bonds, it is also evident that, as between the North and South, the types of state-owned and state-sponsored enterprises financed by external funds were quite different. Whereas the investment in the Northeast and Northwest was mainly for social enterprise and an expansion of the existing transportation-communications network (to facilitate triangular trade and an immediate market in the South for the West's foodstuffs as well as a future market for the West's products across the Atlantic), the

**Table 20** Objects of State Debts up to 1838, by Areas[a]
(Regions as Percentages of Totals)

|  | Banks | Canals | Railways | Roads | Canals, Railways, Roads |
|---|---|---|---|---|---|
| South | 0.88 | 0.10 | 0.25 | 0.07 | 0.14 |
| Northeast | 0.00 | 0.59 | 0.45 | 0.39 | 0.51 |
| Northwest | 0.12 | 0.31 | 0.30 | 0.54 | 0.35 |

[a]Derived from Table 19.

investment of foreign funds in the South was mainly of a shorter term sort. Either these funds were used to facilitate the immediate production of the South's cotton for European consumption through state land banks, or they were even shorter term loans, American bills, financing the marketing period between production and sale.

Table 19 and Table 20 give a summary of the expenditure out of state debts and relative shares according to regions and types of expenditures in 1838. Of the state debts, which do not include expenditures out of municipal bond issues devoted almost entirely to internal improvement, about one-third was to finance the land banks and the remainder was devoted to investments in transportation and communication. But perhaps more interesting is the type of expenditure by region. The South accounts for 88 per cent of

or 32 per cent, were held abroad (John J. Madden, "British Investment in the United States, 1860-1880," Conference on Research in Income and Wealth [New York: National Bureau of Economic Research, 1957; mimeographed], p. 25).

the total state expenditure out of debt issue into the banks. Investment in transportation improvements, canal building, the railways, and the roads is almost entirely in the North. Fourteen per cent of the aggregate was directed toward the cotton and sugar producing states while 51 per cent is attributable to the Northeast and 35 per cent to the Northwest.

From the early 20's until its demise in 1841, the Bank of the United States took an active part in supplying these credit needs of the South. With a stockholder's list which showed foreign ownership ranging from something like 10 percent in 1822 to slightly more than 24 percent in 1832 and 56 percent in 1841, and with the prestige of the government back of it, the Bank had direct access to foreign sources of capital. The planters, however, in search of credit in as favorable terms as possible, called into being a variety of locally controlled banks, the greater number of which were financed by the respective states.[9]

Within a decade (1834), every new slave state in the South ... had established one or more banks ... to provide capital for producing and marketing cotton and sugar of the region. All or nearly all of their capital was supplied by the sale of state bonds, and directly or indirectly most of them sought loans in London.[10]

The private southern economy, even in the boom years of the mid-thirties, did not have access to long-term capital. Almost all of its foreign sources were to support the state banks. The South's chief sources of loanable funds, then, "were the commercial banks and mercantile houses that were limited by the character of their business to short-time advances."[11] Even the Bank of the United States, which was later to attempt to encourage the flow of short-term capital from Europe after the 1837 panic and which was an important source of funds for the South, did not supply anything other than more liquid loans.[12]

This apparent difference between the final expenditure out of state and local debts, financed by foreign capital, certainly should not imply independent economic development between

9. Lewis, *America's Stake*, pp. 14-15.
10. *Ibid.*, p. 15.
11. Milton S. Heath, "Public Railroad Construction and the Development of Private Enterprise in the South before 1861," *Journal of Economic History* (Supplement), IX (1949), 48.
12. Thomas Berry, *Western Prices Before 1861: A Study of the Cincinnati Market* (Cambridge, Mass.: Harvard University Press, 1943), pp. 410-411.

the two regions. The South opened up an extremely lucrative field for the employment of labor and capital, and the economic advantage went primarily to the revival and extension of the slave system. Its effect upon the Northern states and especially the Northwest was nevertheless important. It was the initial expansion of the South which gave the Northeast and Northwest their first important market and supplied a requisite for their economic development.[13] The great expansion of the Northwest for the purpose of supplying an international economy was yet to come. Perhaps this "residentiary activity" in the North supported by foreign funds was a necessary condition for a future expansion of external trade. It is suspected that R. C. O. Matthews would stress the interdependence between the North and South, and the dominance of the latter even more strongly.

The central position occupied by cotton in the boom of the mid-1830's in the South was inevitable in view of its dominance in the Southern agricultural economy. Should we go further and say that cotton was the progenitor of the entire boom throughout the country or even its mainstay during the whole of its course?[14]

In spite of the evidence that a good share, and perhaps the majority, of net *long-term* capital imports was flowing into the North, cotton does seem to be king. The movements in external capital were certainly very sensitive to the state of the cotton export market. In early 1837 the fall in cotton prices (25 per cent in February and March) finally exceed the rise in bales produced, and export revenues begin to fall. Whether an earlier bad turn in cotton prices (1835) caused a downward readjustment of foreign investors' expectations or whether the fall in export revenue directly interfered with the payments of interest, European purchases of American securities did come to a pause. Lewis believes, as we do, that it was the latter. British houses specializing in American securities were badly hit since a large share of American payments on commercial debts and for interest and dividends

---

13. G. S. Callendar, "Early Transportation and Banking Enterprise of the States in Relation to the Growth of Corporations," *Quarterly Journal of Economics*, XVII (1903), 125.

14. R. C. O. Matthews, *A Study in Trade Cycle History: 1833-1842* (Cambridge: Cambridge University Press, 1954), p. 51.

payable abroad was provided by the export revenue from cotton.[15] That is, plantation owners or cotton brokers might have found themselves unable to pay their debts to the Southern land banks, and the banks in turn would have been unable to pay interest on foreign security holdings. Or it may have been that Southern states found it impossible to pay interest on their debts due to a sharp decline in their tax revenue. It seems likely that foreign investors, especially British investors, were less impressed by the movements in cotton prices than by their more painful lagging fall in cotton export revenues. American cotton prices began to fall late in 1835 and the English in 1836, but net capital imports rose to a peak in 1836 which was double their 1835 level.

The effect upon the movement of capital of the panic of 1837 and the ensuing deep depression of the 1840's was tremendous. In spite of the efforts of Nicholas Biddle to stem the tide, the inflow of capital was sharply curtailed after 1839 and ceased with the depression of the forties. During the early 1840's the borrowing states found it impossible to meet their interest and dividend payments. Nine states stopped interest payments in 1841 and 1842, while Michigan and Mississippi repudiated their debt outright. Indiana, Illinois, Louisiana, Arkansas, Pennsylvania, and Maryland professed inability to pay. This rash of repudiations and defaults on state and local debts was a crushing blow to European bondholders, and it prompted Rothschild to make his much-quoted reply to an American agent in 1842: "You may tell your government that you have seen the man who is at the head of the finances of Europe, and that he has told you that they cannot borrow a dollar, not a dollar,"[16] Jenks' estimate of British investments in the United States by 1838, $174 million, amounted to one-quarter of total English investments abroad and "almost the whole was in default or repudiated by 1842."[17]

Before leaving this section and our description of the nature and direction of net capital imports in the late 1820's, the thirties, and early 1840's, there are two further questions that should be examined. First, why did foreign funds find their way into Ameri-

---

15. Lewis, *America's Stake,* p. 25.
16. Jenks, *Migration,* p. 106.
17. Imlah, *Economic Elements,* p. 137.

can issues of state and local bonds in such enormous amounts, relative to American standards, during the cotton-dominated boom from 1825 to the late 1830's? The question of a "supply push" from abroad is important enough to deserve special attention and is reserved for later sections of this chapter. There is strong evidence of an inverse correlation between the levels of domestic investment opportunity in Great Britain and the United States after 1870. But whether this may also help explain the fortuitous timing of the supply of foreign funds into the American economy during the boom of the 1830's is questionable.

It is true, however, that the canals in Great Britain had been extremely lucrative investments and the British expansion of their canal network preceded that of the United States. Great Britain had also the advantage of experience in early railroad building, although the first great mania was yet to come in the 1840's. The British investor, then, was not only familiar with the types of investments in internal improvements which were being financed by state and local bond issues in the United States from the Erie Canal to the late thirties, but he was also familiar with the unusual success which these privately financed enterprises had had in England. The financial success of the early American canals served as a buttress to his confidence in the profits to be derived from internal improvements projects.

But this does not explain why foreign investors did not seem to be interested in private securities. One answer may simply be that, although numerous canal and railway companies were in existence in the thirties, industrial companies did not become common until the sixties.[18] England was at this time far ahead of America in the application of the joint-stock principle. Even so, "it is not surprising that the stocks of no American manufacturing concern were publicly on sale in London, for scarcely any British industries were financed in that manner, or indeed bore the aspect of joint-stock enterprise at all."[19] By 1850 some of the states had corporate laws of one kind or another on the books, although they were much more limited in scope than the British Companies

18. C. K. Hobson, *The Export of Capital* (New York: Macmillan Co., 1914), p. 113.

19. Jenks, *Migration*, p. 77.

Act of 1862 that was taken as a model by the United States and by other countries as well.[20]

Why not, then, buy bond issues from private enterprise? In the 1830's the English investor was ignorant of investment conditions in the United States. Under those conditions, even bond holdings might be too risky. This, perhaps, is one of the more important explanations of the enormous flow of foreign funds into public bond issues. The guarantee and backing of the state and local governments was an extremely attractive attribute of American bonds to the European, especially the British, investor. The early retirement of the Federal debt prior to the secular boom of the late twenties and thirties did much to enhance their attractiveness in the eyes of the foreign investor. What they did not seem to realize, and what was to cause them so much pain in the disastrous forties, was that the states had sovereign power and were beyond any court of law and outside Federal jurisdiction. Thus, in view of their ignorance of the risk premium attached to American bonds, the state and local government guarantee was as attractive as the high interest rates offered. But even domestically the securities market was extremely immature. The securities exchanges attempting to channel the flow of domestic savings into the most efficient investment projects were very inadequate. Government security issues, mostly on the state and local level, were necessary to bridge the gap between savers and investors.[21] Another attractive explanation of British interest in state bond issues used to finance improvements in transportation is that this sector was simply generating a tremendous excess supply of securities. Americans were more interested, it seems, in reinvestment in local enterprise. This explanation is more fully discussed later.

It may also be true that the English merchant (who was also the holder of surplus funds for foreign investment) was not unaware of the importance of maintaining and expanding the supply of raw cotton input for the English textile industry. Nor is

---

20. Lewis, *America's Stake*, p. 70.

21. For an elegant, and more abstract, discussion of financial immaturity see John G. Gurley and Edward S. Shaw, *Money in a Theory of Finance* (Washington, D. C.: The Brookings Institution, 1960), especially Chapter IV, pp. 92-131.

it surprising that English merchant bankers "whose principle business was to export British manufactures to the United States should not display zeal to develop in that country industries which could be competitive."[22] Surely the British investor's portfolio selection must have been influenced by these two factors, and the explanation of the shorter term investments in the exploitation of cotton exports should become even more clear. This tie between the trade in goods and the flow of capital between the United States and Europe does not disappear entirely with the cotton boom of the thirties.

A second question still remains unanswered. Why did the United States find it necessary to issue state and local bonds for the development of internal improvements, while in England and in America before 1840 it was primarily private enterprise which developed the transportation network with a minimum of public interference? Furthermore, why was it necessary to sell these long-term bond issues to foreign investors rather than at home?

Transportation investment is not a marginal capital expenditure but a "lumpy" one yielding high social returns. As early as 1830 the United States was woefully lacking in the financial intermediaries necessary to consolidate enough private savings to finance these large ventures (even if the savings *had been* available domestically). As we have mentioned earlier in this chapter, even the new state banks established during the thirties in the South and Northwest were lenders of short-term and more liquid funds. This also seems true of the Bank of the United States. At the beginning of the nineteenth century,

Not only was the price of capital high, but domestic financial intermediaries were limited to three banking institutions in Philadelphia, New York, and Boston, which catered to the existing internal and foreign trade of the country. While Great Britain continued to provide merchantile credit which facilitated our foreign trade, there were no organized international financial intermediaries to span the Atlantic and provide a partial substitute for a domestic long-term capital market.[23]

---

22. Jenks, *Migration*, p. 77.
23. North, *Economic Growth*, p. 23.

North's discussion of the financing of the canals cites a typical case:

These canals entailed large scale capital expenditures and necessitated state government participation and underwriting, since both the limitations of private saving and the primative state of financial intermediaries made private undertakings on such a scale impossible. In many cases banks provided the initial capital, but it was the flotation in England of the securities of the states which provided most of the funds.[24]

If the state became a temporary substitute for private financial intermediaries prior to the 1840's and early 1850's, why did these debt issues financing internal improvements find their way to Europe? Indeed, why did so many promoters go directly to London to float these securities? Apparently the American businessman did not have an externally investible surplus either due to a lack of savings or because investors were more attracted by local projects with which they were familiar. Private returns may also have been too low on such investments. Thus the foreign inflow of capital freed private individuals from the responsibility of financing an increase in the transportation network where social returns may have considerably exceeded private ones.

It may very well be that foreign capital during the first long swing was a necessary precondition for investment in transportation and economic development. Whereas in later periods the inflow of capital seemed to respond to the existing rate of development over the long swing, in the 1820's, 1830's, and 1840's there is evidence that an acceleration in the pace of United States development had to wait for an external supply of funds before it could proceed, due to the fact that the institutions needed to finance large investment projects simply did not exist.[25] Even more important, it may be that the pool of savings in the United States was inadequate to finance such "lumpy" investments, and in this case as well, foreign investment was a precondition for

---

24. *Ibid.*, p. 196. See also Berry, *Western Prices*, Chapter XIII, for an excellent discussion of the lack of financial intermediaries in the Midwest from 1823 to 1835.
25. R. C. O. Matthews, *The Business Cycle* (Chicago: University of Chicago Press, 1959), p. 188.

rapid economic development during this first long swing, which ended in the depression years of the 1840's.

## The Second Long Swing: 1843-1858

Most economic historians who have examined net capital movements into the United States during the late forties and the decade of the fifties consider this period the first to bring a really substantial inflow of long-term capital. We have found it somewhat difficult to reconcile the qualitative discussions of this era of American economic history that imply the net inflow of foreign capital during the early 1850's was a far more substantial contribution to American development than that of the more speculative and shorter term inflow of the 1830's. In actuality, the peak net inflow of foreign capital in 1853 was *less* than that of 1836 (see Chart 11). Since this apparent contradiction is discussed in Chapter V in relation to gold flows, we will examine it only briefly here. It may be that gold substituted for short-term capital. Although long-term capital may have been greater than the inflow of the 1830's, the lack of short-term capital inflow resulted in an aggregate net import in 1853 less than that of the late 1830's. There is another unusual aspect of this long swing in net capital imports that is not characteristic of American experience prior to and after the decade of the 1850's. Although the other components of the balance of payments and of the domestic series peak late in the 1850's, net capital inflow exhibits an unusually long lead and reaches its peak in 1853. The question here is whether this also implies a long lead over domestic development as well. It is necessary first to attempt an explanation of these two aspects of aggregate movements before disaggregating net flows to determine the direction which foreign capital takes into the domestic system.

The explanation of the early peak in 1853, four years before the panic of 1857 (in the annual data imports peak in 1860, exports in 1860, but the trade balance in 1854), may perhaps be the easiest task. One possible explanation is the Crimean War of 1853-1856, which created a serious disturbance to the flow of capital from Great Britain to the United States. Although this autonomous interruption did not seem to interfere too seriously with the movement of long-term investment in the United States, short-term funds were withdrawn en masse by British investors to finance that war.

Then came the period of the Crimean War, 1853-1856, when Europe withdrew a large part of the short-term capital loaned here and liquidated some securities. But even during this period and the panic year of 1857 there was some new foreign lending to the railways.[26]

After rising from low levels in 1849, net capital imports increase sharply to a peak in 1853. The years 1854 and 1855 see an abrupt reduction in the rate of inflow that is primarily due to the Crimean War and the resultant withdrawal of short-term loans from the United States. This hypothesis seems consistent with the movements of net capital after that autonomous shock: 1855, 1856, and 1857 are years prior to the panic during which net imports capital stabilizes at a constant level about equal to that of the early 1850's.

There is also an endogenous explanation for this "lead" of net capital movements. In the quantitative test for the period 1844-1860 in the next section, an excellent explanation of net capital movements is derived by the inclusion of British and American stock prices. This would seem to suggest that qualitative descriptions, as well as the one above, tend to exaggerate the importance of the Crimean War in disturbing the inflow of capital four years before the panic of 1857. Nor does it seem likely that the severe reduction in the inflow of capital from Great Britain in 1853 *caused* the fall in American railroad stock prices since that series peaks in 1852. Nevertheless, from 1853 to 1855 railroad stock prices do not fall greatly but remain more or less constant after the serious decline in 1852-1853.

There is another sound reason to suspect the importance that we initially attached to the Crimean hostilities. We may be misinterpreting the nature of that domestic long swing. Abramovitz feels that 1853 is a pivotal year, that after 1853 there is a general retardation in the pace of development and recoveries from business cycles are generally less vigorous. Although the more dramatic panic is delayed until 1857, the long-swing down-

---

26. Lewis, *America's Stake*, p. 30.

turn occurs much earlier. This is consistent with the evidence that the trade balance peaks in 1853. Perhaps the problem is really the lag of imports and exports behind domestic movements rather than net capital movements leading the movements in goods.

The interruption of the Crimean War may help explain the relatively low levels of net capital movements compared to the 1830's (the general price level in 1853 is higher or equal to that of 1836), but there are other explanations as well.

The 1850's started like the 1830's with relatively modest capital imports following initial domestic expansion, gradually accelerating as expansion became a boom. This time the railroad boom in the West attracted foreign investors, not states securities for canals or banking facilities. But in the 1850's the Crimean War interrupted the capital inflow so that it had subsided long before the panic of 1857, and California's gold production and the export of this gold was sufficient in itself to balance large import surpluses. Clearly the volume of capital imports in the 1850's was not nearly as large, relatively, as it had been in the 1830's.[27]

Gold, then, is the second explanation. In the quotation above, North does not explicitly describe the *process* by which gold is substituted for short-term capital. It is not enough to say the United States did not "need" greater capital imports since excessive gold supplies were available to help pay for a deficit on the current account and were "sufficient" to "balance large import surpluses." This does not seem to explain the dynamics of equilibrium adjustment in the balance of payments. It does, however, seem clear that net capital movements in the aggregate (mainly due to *short-term* capital adjustment) yielded to the outflow of gold. The usual specie-flow mechanism, however, does not appear to be the cause of the excessive outflow of gold. The trade-balance deficit does not have an unusually large amplitude over the long swing in the late forties and the fifties. Rather, it seems that aggregate net capital movements are lower than we might have expected (indeed, net capital imports amounted to $62.2 million in the 1836 peak and only $55.6 million in the 1853 peak). Besides the serious interruption of the Crimean War, these low levels must be explained by a host of complex

---

27. North, *Trends,* p. 858.

variables. Two explanations, however, are most prominent. First, foreign investors, and British investors in particular, were hesitant to invest in American securities due to the memory of the defaults of the 1840's, less than a decade before. Second, there were other regions competing for British long-term capital during the fifties. Thus, net *long-term* capital imports were not sufficient to finance the trade-balance deficit. Domestic gold production and the ensuing excess supply of real-money balances, however, substituted for (or generated) the "deficiency" in net capital, allowing domestic economic expansion to continue of its own accord without creating serious disequilibrium in the balance of payments and interfering with monetary expansion.

In discussing the directions which this long-term inflow took during the second long swing, we might first examine the atmosphere in which it took place. Incorporation was still in its infancy, and it was not until the late 1860's and early 1870's that it was to assume importance.

The principal [incorporation] made rapid progress through the American codes. And in 1850, incorporation by special legislative act had almost disappeared from the American commonwealth and in many of them had become unconstitutional. The scarcity of capital, the uncertainty of standards of honor among people who engaged in business and sought capital from others, and the whole-souled order with which the American people ... assimilated the spirit of capitalism, combined to make the United States the great field for the growth of corporate action in business and industry.[28]

As early as 1853, however, almost 10 per cent of foreign long-term holdings (excluding federal debt) were in corporate stocks, although half of this was attributable to the railroads (see Table B-2).

The depressed forties, with its great rash of defaults and repudiations by the states, had a tremendous effect upon both creditors and debtors. Although all but three states resumed dividend payments, the states profited by earlier experience and

... decided to leave to private initiative the prodigious task of 'winning the West,' and likewise the South and East. They put their

---

28. Jenks, *Migration*, p. 235.

resolution on record by writing into their constitutions provisions prohibiting the use of state funds or credit for internal improvement . . . it was the railways, rather than the states, that were now taking the lead in borrowing abroad.[29]

By 1853 only 68 per cent of foreign long-term investments were still in state and local bonds, an impressive decline if Paish's figure of 85 per cent for 1836 is reasonably accurate. This figure falls to 60 per cent in 1866 and abruptly to 25 per cent in 1868 during the period of reconstruction.[30] Clearly, the 1850's seem to reflect a period of transition in which the responsibilities of transportation development and expansion are passed from public to private hands. And most of this private initiative was relegated to the railroads to finance their first boom: in 1853 one-quarter of foreign holdings of American securities was in the railroads, only half a decade after the initiation of the boom in 1848-1849.

Most of the long-term capital which found its way into the United States railway expansion came from Great Britain. As with the canals in the thirties (and fortunately for American interests), the British investor was already experienced in railroad financing by the late 1840's. The British railway boom ended with the panic of 1847,[31] and the stage was set for foreign financing of the American railroad expansion.

There was indeed a demand for capital in the railroad industry. Railroad mileage added in the United States, perhaps an inadequate measure of railroad demand for funds, reached a trough in 1843 and recovered gradually to moderate levels in 1848-1849. With the gold discoveries the westward expansion became dynamic, and railroad mileage added tripled from 1848 to 1849,[32] continuing its rapid extension into the late fifties in

---

29. Lewis, *America's Stake*, p. 30.

30. These percentage figures are given in Table B-2 and refer to foreign long-term investment excluding federal debt issues in an attempt to eliminate the overt effects of the Civil War.

31. During the 1840's, about 4,500 miles of railroad track were added to the British network, the peak occurring early in the decade.

32. Earlier it was suggested that the rate of expansion of the transportation network (1825-1842) may well have been conditioned by the willingness of foreign investors, mainly British, to purchase such securities as were issued by the states to finance transportation improvement. It seems less likely that this situation applied

116 / *American Growth and the Balance of Payments*

spite of a temporary slackening after the outbreak of the Crimean War (see Table 21). The circumstances were ideal by 1849: the railroads were anxious to expand their network in the West and the British and European investor was quite willing to lend.

Following the depression of the early forties, English investors' interest in American railway securities was slow to develop. For that matter, until 1848 or 1849 consistent net *outflows* were typical of the decade. American railway securities had not yet

**Table 21** Railroad Mileage Completed, 1843-1861[a]

| Year | Railroad Mileage Completed | Year | Railroad Mileage Completed |
|------|------|------|------|
| 1843 | 159 | 1853 | 2,452 |
| 1844 | 192 | 1854 | 1,360 |
| 1845 | 256 | 1855 | 1,654 |
| 1846 | 297 | 1856 | 3,642 |
| 1847 | 668 | 1857 | 2,487 |
| 1848 | 398 | 1858 | 2,465 |
| 1849 | 1,369 | 1859 | 1,821 |
| 1850 | 1,656 | 1860 | 1,837 |
| 1851 | 1,961 | 1861 | 660 |
| 1852 | 1,926 | | |

[a] H. V. and H. W. Poor, *Poor's Manual of the Railroads of the United States, 1912* (New York: H. V. and H. W. Poor, 1912), Appendix B, Table B-13.

been tested in world markets: the charter of America's oldest road dated back only to 1827, and the first loan issued in London to finance railroad construction was for the Baltimore and Ohio in 1836, only a decade prior to the beginnings of active foreign interest in Amercan railroads. Moreover, British investors were still smarting from their losses sustained by the defaults and repudiation of the states. "However, with the discovery of gold in

to the late 1840's and the decade of the 1850's. The railroad boom began, apparently, in 1848-1849 without the help of foreign capital. In 1849 there was still a net outflow of capital from the American states. Similarly the rate of railway mileage added continues to increase up until 1856 while, as has been shown, net capital imports peak in 1853. It may be that the general level of railroad expansion during the 1850's was influenced by the average of net capital imports and the foreign purchases of railroad bonds and stocks, but the timing of that long swing in railroad development is not likely to have been influenced by foreign investment.

California and the attendant railway building boom, America was rediscovered as a land of opportunity for foreign capital."[33]

In spite of the interruptions of the Crimean War, long-term capital mainly from Great Britain continued to flow into the American railways. Lewis estimates that the value of British holdings in long-term securities was approximately $300 million in 1852 and $500 million in 1857.[34]

... British capital flowed steadily into American railroad securities. The equipment of the New England lines in the 'forties, and of the railways in the Middle and South Atlantic States and States east of the Mississippi during the 'fifties, was largely supplied from Great Britain, and paid for by the issue of bonds; and the aggregate value of British holdings at the beginning of the Civil War was immense.[35]

With the panic of 1857 the inflow of capital halted abruptly, and a large outflow occurred in 1858. It was not until the outcome of the Civil War was no longer in doubt that capital began again to flow into the United States.

When the American railroad network was being extended during the 1840's, mainly financed by domestic funds, the geographic direction of railroad expansion was predominantly into the urban and growing industrial Northeast with the Midwest playing an important secondary role. In the decade 1840-1849 New England accounted for 37.6 per cent of railroad mileage added, the Middle Atlantic and "old" Midwest—Ohio, Michigan, and Indiana—for 35.8 per cent, and the Southern cotton producing states for only 24.2 per cent. With the boom, however, the direction of railroad expansion changed drastically into an enormous extension of the transportation network in the Midwestern granary. The Midwest and the Middle Atlantic states easily dominated the railroad boom during the decade of the 1850's: from 1850 to 1859, 65 per cent of all railroad mileage added occurred in these two regions (see Chart 17 and Table 22).[36] The production of grains exhibits a fantastic growth dur-

---

33. Lewis, *America's Stake*, p. 36.
34. *Ibid.*
35. Hobson, *Export of Capital*, pp. 115-116.
36. These two regions include Illinois, Iowa, Wisconsin, Missouri, Minnesota,

ing this boom in Midwest railroad expansion (financed by foreign—mainly British—capital). From 1851 to 1857 the total value of grain exports increased by approximately nine times while wheat exports in bushels increased fourteen times. This does not mean, however, that the Midwestern granary replaced the Southern states' cotton export as the predominant source of foreign credits on the current account. On the contrary, cotton was still far and away the main source of export revenue: crude foodstuffs, from 1850 to 1857, increased their share from 5 per cent to 11 per cent in total export revenues; crude and

**Table 22** Regional Distribution of Railroad Expansion, 1840-1879[a]

| Year | New England | Middle Atlantic and Old Midwest[b] | South | New Midwest[c] | Louisiana and Arkansas Ind. Terr. | West |
|------|-------------|-------------------------------------|-------|----------------|------------------------------------|------|
| 1840-1849 | 37.6% | 35.8% | 24.2% | 1.9% | 0.5% | — |
| 1850-1859 | 6.9 | 42.2 | 27.0 | 22.9 | 0.5 | 0.5% |
| 1860-1869 | 2.9 | 30.3 | 17.9 | 27.4 | 1.1 | 20.4 |
| 1870-1879 | 4.4 | 27.7 | 10.1 | 32.2 | 1.3 | 24.3 |

[a]Miles added, region relative to total United States. U. S. Bureau of the Census, *Tenth Census of the United States:* Vol. IV, *Transportation* (Washington, D. C.: U. S. Government Printing Office, 1883), Tables A and B, pp. 289-290.

[b]Michigan, Indiana, Ohio, New York, Pennsylvania, Maryland, Delaware, and New Jersey.

[c]Illinois, Iowa, Wisconsin, Missouri, and Minnesota.

manufactured foodstuffs combined had a less spectacular increase from 20 per cent to 28 per cent of that total.

But if cotton was still the main source of export revenue in the late 1850's, it was no longer the main progenitor of the boom and certainly was much less important influencing the rate of net capital inflow. It had, in fact, assumed a supporting role. From 1840 to 1849, 24.2 per cent of railroad mileage added was devoted to the South and from 1850 to 1859, 27 per cent. The Midwest was no longer dependent upon trade with the South, primarily because of extension of the transportation network

Michigan, Indiana, Ohio, New York, Pennsylvania, Maryland, Delaware, and New Jersey.

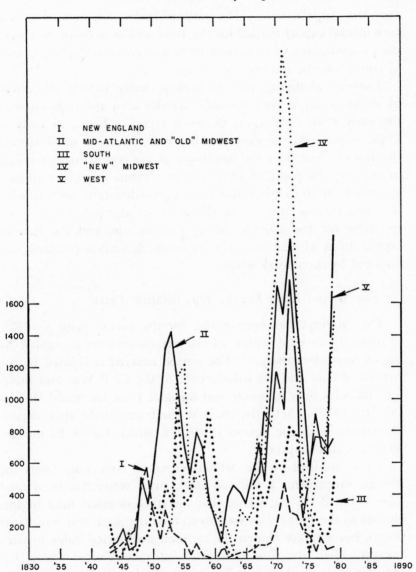

I     NEW ENGLAND
II    MID-ATLANTIC AND "OLD" MIDWEST
III   SOUTH
IV    "NEW" MIDWEST
V     WEST

**Chart 17** Railroad Mileage Added by Regions, 1843-1879 (in Miles)

*Source:* Table 22

over the Appalachians. The railroad expansion created a new agricultural export market for the West and in so doing destroyed the predominance of triangular trade and reduced the importance of cotton on the national economy.

Cotton's changing role is perhaps more clearly illustrated by its long lags behind domestic activity after the depression of the early 1840's. Whereas domestic recovery began as early as 1843, cotton revenue does not begin its recovery until late in the forties. Nor does the condition of the cotton market reflect in any way the panic of 1857; cotton revenue enjoys its greatest expansion at the end of the 1850's. Northeastern industrialization and the opening up of the West are the prime factors responsible for the growth during that decade, and the flow of capital from abroad into the railroads is only secondarily influenced by the cotton states.

### The Second Long Swing: Quantitative Tests

One attempt has been made, for the period prior to 1870, to quantify an explanation of the net movements of capital by use of regression analysis. The period covered is limited by the paucity of data and the interference of the Civil War and therefore includes only a decade and one-half from the mid-1840's to the late 1850's. Actually, the test itself was made after experimentations with the period 1870-1914, which follow in the last section of this chapter.

As a measure of the attractiveness of American assets for foreign investment, a railroad stock price series has been used (see Table B-17). It is true that the stock of assets held by foreigners in the mid-1850's was predominantly state and municipal bonds, but we have chosen the railroad stock price index for two reasons. First, the *flow* of capital into the United States, beginning with 1849 and ending with the late fifties, was conditioned by assets offered by the rails more importantly than the stock of foreign holdings indicates in 1853. For this reason it hardly seems spurious to use a railroad stock price index as an explanatory variable for the pull of foreign funds into the American system. Second, it seems likely that the conditions which might have dictated the relative movements in the attractiveness of state and municipal bonds over the long swing also applied to railroad stock issues. Both were used to finance transportation development. Consequently, this series seemed to be the most adequate available for our purposes. It would have been more desirable to use bond prices or yields, since this was the dominant form of security issue purchased by foreigners, but an adequate bond price series was not available.

**Table 23** United States Net Capital Imports, Railroad Stock Prices, and British Share Prices, 1844-1860

| Year | $\dot{K}$ (smoothed; millions of dollars) | Railroad Stock Prices Index[a] (trend removed: smoothed) | British Share Price Index[b] (trend removed: smoothed) |
|---|---|---|---|
| 1844 | —10.3 | 58.3 | 107.8 |
| 1845 | — 3.1 | 67.3 | 109.2 |
| 1846 | — 7.7 | 70.0 | 103.7 |
| 1847 | — 5.7 | 70.7 | 95.0 |
| 1848 | — 6.3 | 71.4 | 87.5 |
| 1849 | 9.5 | 72.7 | 84.6 |
| 1850 | 11.2 | 79.2 | 84.9 |
| 1851 | 17.5 | 88.1 | 86.3 |
| 1852 | 26.4 | 95.1 | 88.8 |
| 1853 | 35.6 | 93.5 | 90.2 |
| 1854 | 34.2 | 84.7 | 92.0 |
| 1855 | 19.1 | 74.4 | 93.7 |
| 1856 | 12.8 | 66.1 | 94.9 |
| 1857 | 1.0 | 59.5 | 95.1 |
| 1858 | 6.1 | 52.0 | 96.6 |
| 1859 | — 1.9 | 51.7 | 99.1 |
| 1860 | 39.0 | 51.5 | 101.6 |

[a]Derived from Table B-17.
[b]Derived from Table B-25.

As a measure of the varying degree of supply push of foreign funds into American rails, we used Brinley Thomas' index of British share prices,[37] since the overwhelming source of foreign capital for the American states prior to 1860 was the United Kingdom (see Table B-25). Both the English and American

37. *Migration and Economic Growth* (Cambridge: Cambridge University Press, 1954), Table 99, p. 289.

series have had their secular trends removed so that we are dealing only with their movements with respect to the long swing.

If we use only American railroad stock prices as an explanatory variable, the results for 1840-1860 are significant: with no lag, $\overline{R}^2 = 0.486$, and with net capital movements lagging behind railroad stock prices one year, $\overline{R}^2 = 0.769$.[38] Railroad stock prices leading certainly makes good sense, since foreign investors need time to gain such information and to assimilate it. It also seems likely that foreign investors should reveal some caution after a serious depression at the termination of a long swing in order to be relatively sure about future long-run trends. They may, incidentally, be less hesitant in selling their holdings on the downturn.

The results are much better, of course, when we add another variable. Again using the period 1844-1860, $\overline{R}^2 = 0.512$ when neither the British nor the American series is leading, and the best fit, $\overline{R}^2 = 0.910$, seems to occur when American railroad stock prices lead net capital imports by one year and English share prices by two years:

$$\dot{K}^t = 46.82 + 0.6787\ P^{t-1}_{US} - 0.9231\ P^{t-2}_{GB};\ \overline{R}^2 = 0.910.$$
$$(0.1152) \qquad\qquad (0.1780)$$

By using a British share price index to approximately quantify the push of British funds out of domestic industry to search for more attractive investment opportunities, and an American index of railroad stock prices representing the varying degree of pull with changing attractiveness of United States assets offered abroad, we find an excellent explanation of the long swing in the net flow of capital over United States borders. The sign of $P_{GB}$, British share prices, is negative—the lower the attractiveness of British investment at home, the greater the push of foreign investment abroad—while the sign of $P_{US}$, American rail stock prices, is positive—the higher the attractiveness of American investment, the larger the foreign capital influx. The exogenous incident of the Crimean War loses much of its importance as an explanation

---

38. $\overline{R}^2$ is the coefficient of determination corrected by the number of observations.

of the *movements* of net capital over the long swing, although it may still explain the relatively low levels of net capital inflow during the 1850's.

That American stock prices should lead by one year was not unexpected (it is also true of the period 1870-1914), but can we make use of the conclusion that the British series reveals an even longer lead over net capital imports into the United States? If we could be sure that both $P_{US}$ and $P_{GB}$ were adequate measures of the relative profitability of investment, one could say that the *timing* of United States development of its transportation network was not dependent upon British capital export. This implication seems applicable since British capital exports do indeed lead American capital imports as the timing of share and stock prices suggests: from 1844 to 1860, British share prices lead United States stock prices by at least two years. Capital export from Great Britain came first in the late 1840's; the United States had only to compete with other countries for the outflow of British investment already occurring for the four years 1846-1849. It seems more likely that in the long swing of the 1830's and 1840's the timing of transportation expansion was heavily conditioned indeed by the flow of British investment. This is not evident in the 1840's and 1850's, however fortunate the United States may have been to desire capital in increasing amounts when British investors had already, for a number of years, turned away from domestic and into foreign investments.

The apparent power which these two price variables seem to have in explaining the flow of net capital movements into the United States is at the same time somewhat surprising. First, we have chosen price variables which should primarily dictate the flow of long-term capital, while the flow of capital which we are actually explaining is the series of long- and short-term capital. Does not the movement of short-term capital deviate at all from long-term movements over this period? It may be that this period is one in which gold reduces short-term capital to unimportance and that it is only in later periods that short-term capital movements interfere with the relation between aggregate net capital flows and long-term price variables. A second, and perhaps more serious, question is why conditions in other countries do not seem to play a very important role in influencing the net flow of capital over United States borders. That is, a large share of British investment was directed into other nations—South America, India, Australia, Europe, and in later years Canada—and should not conditions there have seriously interfered with the correlation? It is true that the correlations are much poorer in later periods (1870-1915) when a smaller share of British investment is devoted to American business. But even then, although the average share of British investment going to the United States is relatively small and declining secularly, the marginal share is fairly large over the long swing.

### The Third Long Swing: 1858-1879

The third long swing in net capital inflow can be divided easily into two distinct and quite separate parts. The division occurs abruptly in 1869. For seven years, 1863-1869, the purchase of Union bonds by foreigners is overwhelming and eclipses without question the very small movements of private assets over United States borders. With 1869 a new era of foreign investment in private American assets begins: from 1869 to 1914 the net flow of capital is dominated entirely by the movement of foreign funds into the American railroads.

Although the net inflow of capital recovers temporarily in 1859 and 1861, the early years of the Civil War (1862-1863) reflect an uncertainty on the part of the foreign investors concerning not only the results of the war but also its effects upon future American economic development. Hobson overstates the true condition of the foreign market for American securities, if Simon's estimates are at all accurate,[39] but his description is informative:

Foreign investment in the United States during the greater part of this period was sharply curtailed. For the outbreak of war was fol-

---

39. Commenting on the derived series of the accumulating balance of indebtedness, Simon states: "A close relationship exists between the derived figure of $495,200,000 as of June 30, 1863 and the $500 millions estimate of the Secretary of the Treasury for that year" (Matthew Simon, "The United States Balance of Payments, 1861-1900," *Trends*, p. 706). This would suggest that Simon's estimates for 1860-1863 are reasonable and that the United States could have hardly exhibited, as Hobson asserts, a clean national ledger in respect to foreign indebtedness.

lowed by a panic among foreign investors and an extensive transference of securities hitherto held abroad. The judgment of the English and French investors was affected by prejudice in favor of the Confederate states, preying upon ignorance as to the inherent strength of the North, and a belief, perhaps, that whatever the result of the war, America would be crippled for many years to come. Every kind of security, national, State, and corporate, was suddenly flung back upon the American market for sale at almost any sacrifice; and by 1863 the United States was said to exhibit a clean national ledger in respect to foreign indebtedness. Nor could English or French investors be persuaded to subscribe to the Union loans, although a Confederate loan of £3,000,000 was subscribed . . .[40]

Somewhere after 1863, however, when the issue of the war was no longer in doubt, there began an extended period of foreign purchases of national war and reconstruction bonds. The victories of the Northern armies at Gettysburg and Vicksburg must have highly recommended the Union bonds to the European investor. Nevertheless, the *public* sales abroad during the war were relatively small since Jay Cooke, the financier handling the sale of war bonds for the North, opposed their sale abroad. Two direct sales were made in 1863, however: $10 million to a German account and $10 million more to an English account.[41] After 1863 a flood of government securities reached Europe. The major portion of American foreign indebtedness, in fact, was in the form of federal securities originally issued in America but transferred abroad by private individuals. In 1866, 58 per cent of foreign long-term investment in the United States was in federal bonds. In 1868 it had risen to a peak share of 75 per cent, and in 1869 it still remained high at 72 per cent (see Table B-2).

The Treasury issued two kinds of long-term bonds, registered and coupon, the latter being transferable without recourse to the Treasury. Since the coupon bonds could be shifted among persons and countries with the least effort and cost, they were particularly suitable for foreign investors. Thus, by the mid-1870's, after the flood of new government issues had stopped, practically all registered bonds were held in America and the

---

40. Hobson, *Export of Capital*, p. 132.
41. Lewis, *America's Stake*, pp. 53-54.

greater part of the coupons were held abroad (65 per cent in 1875).[42]

Interestingly enough, although British investors did become important lenders to both the American federal government and the railroads after 1869, they were not important purchasers of federal bonds from 1863 to 1869. The Germans and Dutch began purchasing substantial amounts of five-twenties late in 1863, and by 1865 over $150 million of federal securities had been sold abroad. However, "the evidence suggests that British purchases amounted to a very small part of this sum," despite the large amounts placed in Europe.[43] Between 1865 and early 1869, an

**Table 24** Percentage of Federal Coupon Bonds Held Abroad, 1866-1878[a]

| Year | Outstanding Coupon Bonds (millions of dollars) | Estimated Federal Bonds Abroad (millions of dollars) | Percentage of Coupon Bonds Held Abroad |
|---|---|---|---|
| 1866 | 695 | 255 | 37 |
| 1870 | 1,160 | 518 | 45 |
| 1875 | 967 | 623 | 65 |
| 1878 | 821 | 308 | 38 |

aMadden, "British Investment . . . ," p. 32.

additional $300 million in federal bonds were sent to Europe, but the evidence "still suggests that the greater part was bought by Continental investors."[44]

In March, 1865, no less than $250 million of federal bond issues were held in Germany and Holland, while an additional $70 million were held in other European securities. The adoption of a constitutional amendment abolishing slavery was greeted in Germany and Holland with great enthusiasm, and the price of Northern bonds was bid up 8 to 10 per cent above New York quotations.[45]

---

42. Madden, "British Investment . . . ," pp. 31-32.
43. *Ibid.*, p. 33.
44. *Ibid.*
45. Lewis, *America's Stake,* pp. 54-55.

After 1869, however, there is an abrupt change in the nature of net capital movements into the United States. Not only does Great Britain suddenly reassume its position as major lender to the United States, but also there is a gradual shift out of federal securities and into railroad issues. Most foreign investors, including British, immediately transferred their capital into railroad securities when the federal bonds came due. But if there was a shift out of federal debt and into railroad securities within the existing stock of debt held by foreigners, there was also a

**Table 25** American Securities Issued Publicly in the United Kingdom, 1869-1880[a]
(In Millions of Pounds Sterling)

| Year | Rails[b] | Oils and Mines | Banks, Industrials, Real Estate | Government State | Government Municipal | Totals |
|------|------|------|------|------|------|------|
| 1869 | 1.0 | 0.05 | — | 0.2 | — | 1.2 |
| 1870 | 3.2 | 0.4 | — | 0.8 | — | 4.4 |
| 1871 | 6.4 | 3.4 | — | 1.1 | — | 10.9 |
| 1872 | 13.8 | 1.0 | 1.8 | 0.7 | 1.7 | 19.0 |
| 1873 | 15.3 | 0.7 | 0.6 | 0.1 | 1.0 | 17.7 |
| 1874 | 17.6 | — | — | — | 0.8 | 18.4 |
| 1875 | 5.7 | — | 1.6 | 0.3 | 0.7 | 8.3 |
| 1876 | 2.7 | — | — | — | — | 2.7 |
| 1877 | 0.3 | — | — | — | — | 0.3 |
| 1878 | 0.2 | — | — | — | — | 0.2 |
| 1879 | — | — | — | — | — | — |
| 1880 | 0.6 | 0.5 | — | — | — | 1.1 |

[a]Madden, "British Investment . . . ," Table 8, p. 28.
[b]Excludes railroad shares issued in London.

tremendous increase in the rate of capital inflow from 1868 to 1872 stimulated by the boom in railroad expansion.

Certainly the large majority of foreign investment in private American securities was in the railroads. But English investment, at least, in oils, mines, banks, industrials, and real estate was not insignificant. British investment in the oils and mines is particularly interesting. As with the railroads, this type of investment did not become popular until very late in the sixties, after maturity of the federal bonds. Madden's figures do not reveal it, but a great deal of the investment in the development of American mines and wells was of a direct nature. In Great Britain "at least sixty-seven companies were registered with the Board of Trade from 1870 through 1873 to carry on mining or milling" in the West, exclusive of the Pacific Coast.[46] It is also worth special note that the direct investment in the mines was not independent of railroad development and, thus, the flow of foreign capital into rail development. The surge of British capital investment in the early seventies flowed into those mining regions served by the rails. For instance, Idaho, Montana, Arizona,

**Table 26** Anglo-American Mining Companies and Their Nominal Capital Registered with the Board of Trade, 1869-1880[a] (In Thousands of Pounds Sterling)

| Year | Total Nominal Capital |
|---|---|
| 1869 | 390 |
| 1870 | 1,500 |
| 1871 | 4,550 |
| 1872 | 1,286 |
| 1873 | 1,587 |
| 1874 | 1,942 |
| 1875 | 152 |
| 1876 | — |
| 1877 | 269 |
| 1878 | 723 |
| 1879 | 60 |
| 1880 | 1,290 |

[a]Spence, *British Investment,* Appendix II, p. 261.

and New Mexico accounted for only seven of the eighty-three western joint-stock companies formed in Great Britain between 1860 and 1873.[47] Direct British investment in American railroads, however, was never really extensive between 1860 and 1880.

After 1869 and until World War I, by far the major attraction for foreign funds were the securities offered by the railroads.

---

46. Clark C. Spence, *British Investments and the American Mining Frontier, 1860-1901,* American Historical Association (Ithaca, N. Y.: Cornell University Press, 1958), p. 5.
47. *Ibid.,* p. 9.

By 1868-1869, 62 per cent of all *nonfederal* assets held abroad were in the form of railroad securities, and the peak level of federal bonds held abroad relative to total assets held by foreigners was 75 per cent in 1868. Madden's figures on the flow of capital into the United States from Great Britain reveal more about the post-1870 period, although his data are less representative of total foreign investment in the United States because British investors were slow to purchase federal issues prior to 1870; this was not true of Dutch and German investors, of course.

The long swing in railroad mileage added, 1860-1880, was a fantastic one in spite of, and relatively brief due to, the interruption of the war. From 1866 to 1871 Poor's estimates for railway mileage added increase almost fivefold. The peak in 1871 was equaled or exceeded in only four years between 1871 and 1900. Thus, although relatively short, the life of this long swing

**Table 27** Estimated Nominal Value of British Holdings of American Securities, 1860-1880[a]
(In Millions of Pounds Sterling)

| Year | Federal | Railroad | State and Municipal | Other | Total |
|------|---------|----------|---------------------|-------|-------|
| 1860 | 3  | 20  | 11 | 1  | 35  |
| 1863 | 3  | 15  | 7  | 1  | 26  |
| 1870 | 34 | 38  | 10 | 2  | 84  |
| 1874 | 86 | 99  | 15 | 9  | 209 |
| 1876 | 92 | 106 | 16 | 11 | 225 |
| 1880 | 25 | 96  | 15 | 11 | 147 |

[a]Madden, "British Investment...," Table 8, p. 43.

in railroad development was certainly spectacular. The regional direction of railroad development was predominantly the "new" Midwest and the far West, although a large share was devoted still to the Middle Atlantic states. The share of the Middle Atlantic states fell from 30.3 per cent to 27.7 per cent between the decades 1860-1869 and 1870-1879, the share of the "new" Midwest increased from 27.4 per cent to 32.2 per cent, and the far West increased in importance from 20.4 per cent to 24.3 per cent (see

Table 22). The expansion of the railroad network was predominantly, and increasingly so, in the West.

Foreign investment in the United States paralleled this boom in railroad development. Europe continued to purchase railroad bonds and, to a lesser extent, stocks until the crash in the autumn of 1873. In 1876, even after numerous failures and after considerable withdrawals, Hobson estimates that European holdings of

**Table 28** Net Capital Movements and Related Domestic Variables, 1860-1880

| Year | Net Capital Movements into U.S. (Simon)[a] (millions of dollars) | American RR Loans Issued Publicly in U. K.[b] (millions of Pounds Sterling) | Poor's Mileage Added[c] | Ulmer's Net Capital Expenditure in Rails[d] (millions of dollars) | American RR Loans Issued Publicly in U.S.[e] (millions of dollars) |
|---|---|---|---|---|---|
| 1860 | — 7.3 | 0.2 | 1,837 | | 2.8 |
| 1861 | 104.4 | — | 660 | | 10.6 |
| 1862 | — 1.1 | — | 834 | | 18.4 |
| 1863 | 12.6 | — | 1,050 | | 31.9 |
| 1864 | 110.6 | 3.4 | 738 | | 26.5 |
| 1865 | 68.7 | 0.8 | 1,177 | | 33.8 |
| 1866 | 94.4 | 0.3 | 1,716 | | 83.3 |
| 1867 | 145.6 | 0.2 | 2,249 | | 61.1 |
| 1868 | 72.7 | 3.3 | 2,979 | | 141.3 |
| 1869 | 169.2 | 2.0 | 4,615 | | 213.6 |
| 1870 | 99.4 | 4.5 | 6,078 | 324 | 246.2 |
| 1871 | 100.9 | 10.5 | P 7,379 | P 358 | P 274.9 |
| 1872 | P 242.8 | P 18.1 | 5,870 | 306 | 158.9 |
| 1873 | 182.9 | 17.0 | 4,097 | 181 | 195.0 |
| 1874 | 82.2 | 17.7 | 2,117 | 68 | 136.4 |
| 1875 | 86.9 | 5.7 | T 1,711 | T 27 | 87.5 |
| 1876 | 1.8 | 2.7 | 2,712 | 29 | T 71.2 |
| 1877 | — 57.3 | 0.3 | 2,274 | 46 | 72.0 |
| 1878 | T —161.9 | 0.2 | 2,265 | 47 | 130.2 |
| 1879 | —160.2 | T — | 4,809 | 57 | 189.6 |
| 1880 | 29.4 | 0.6 | 6,711 | 204 | 263.4 |

[a]Table B-1.

[b]Madden, "British Investment . . . ," Table 1, p. 5. Includes loans part of which were issued on the Continent and in the United States but excludes conversions.

[c]Appendix C, Table B-13.

[d]Appendix B, Table B-14.

[e]Madden, "British Investment . . . ," Table 3, p. 7. Includes loans which were issued on the Continent or in the United Kinglom but excludes conversions wherever possible.

American railway securities amounted to $375 million as against $243 million in 1869.[48] As reflected in the estimates of net capital imports themselves, the panic and ensuing depression were serious. After the crisis in the fall of 1873 and numerous defaults, hundreds of millions of dollars of American railroad securities were thrown upon the New York and Philadelphia markets and sold at enormous sacrifices. With the mid-1870's, "the only European investors who are supposed to have purchased more American securities than they sold [were] the Swiss investors through Geneva."[49] As a result, there is a net outflow of capital from the United States which continues until the net inflow of 1880.

**Table 29** American Railroad Securities Issued in London as a Percentage of All Railroad Bonds Issued[a]

| Years | Total American Loans | Amount Issued in London | Percentage Issued in |
|---|---|---|---|
| | (millions of Pounds Sterling) | | London |
| 1860-1867 | 55 | 5.4 | 10 |
| 1868-1870 | 123 | 9.8 | 8 |
| 1871-1874 | 157 | 63.3 | 40 |
| 1875-1880 | 167 | 9.5 | 6 |

a Madden, "British Investment . . .," p. 8. These figures refer to *new* issues of securities. The net flow of capital can, of course, be new issues as well as old.

Beginning in 1869 and terminating with the first year of net capital outflow in 1877, the importance of foreign capital was substantial not only in the balance of payments but also as a contributor to capital formation. The share of net foreign investment in domestic net capital formation varied between 9 per cent and 27 per cent from 1869 to 1875, for an average of 15.5 per cent. This was certainly larger than in any other period between the Civil War and World War I (see Table 33). Even when we

48. Hobson, *Export of Capital*, p. 140. Quoted from W. Z. Ripley, *New York Journal of Commerce*, December 6, 1911 (no page given).

49. Hobson, *Export of Capital*, p. 139. Quoted from Nathaniel T. Bacon, *Yale Review*, November, 1900, p. 278.

compare American railroad securities issued in London (a great deal smaller than net British investment in the railways) with all American railroad bonds issued, the importance of the British investor is impressive (see Table 29).

The estimated figures for American railroad loans issued in the United Kingdom and Simon's estimates of net capital movements over United States borders lag perceptibly behind domestic series representing the pace of railroad development (see Table 28). At the peak in 1871 both these series (and presumably British foreign investment dictates the movements in total United States net capital imports) lag one year behind Poor's railway mileage added, Ulmer's estimate of net capital formation in the rails, and Madden's estimate of American rail securities issued in the United States. The lag at the trough is even greater (three to four years). This lag at both peaks and troughs cannot be explained by ignorance on the part of the foreign investor nor upon lack of sufficient communication as to the state of the American bond market. The large lag at the trough *can* be explained in part by the caution of foreign investors in purchasing securities after a serious depression in order to be relatively sure about future trends and the "safety" of bond holdings. The Germans and Dutch reduced their net investment in American securities, including the rails, before the English, and as early as 1874 the German and Dutch investor began to sell their holdings on a large scale while the British continued to increase their investments until the end of 1876.[50]

The explanation for the unusually long lag of British attitudes in excess of our expectations derived from earlier examinations lies not in a peculiar reaction of the British investor to domestic movements in the United States, but rather in the regional direction that his investment in the rails took. It seems that English capital from 1869 to 1880 was predominantly concerned with financing railroad expansion in the East, not the West. British investment was of a conservative nature, directed into the established companies which British capital founded in the 1850's and, in general, into the developed regions of the American states. Madden's research, summarized in Table 30, underlines the

50. Madden, "British Investment . . . ," p. 37.

nature of British investment in the railroads during a period of Western boom. The net flow of English capital into the United States was then primarily into New England, the Middle Atlantic, and the "old" Midwest, where the risks were at a minimum. But if British investments were in the established roads of the East, they freed American, Dutch, and German capital to concentrate on the expansion of the Western railroad network and its risky, high-yield, land-grant bonds.[51]

This gives us an excellent explanation of the unusually long lag in net capital movements, in general, and British investment, in particular, from 1869 to 1880. Railroad mileage added in the

**Table 30** Percentage Distribution of Publicly Issued Rail Bonds, 1860-1880[a]

|  | Developed Regions | Developing Regions | Underdeveloped Regions |
|---|---|---|---|
| All American Issues | 32% | 24% | 42% |
| Issued in U. K. and Continent | 58 | 21 | 21 |
| Issued Solely in U. K. | 69 | 22 | 9 |
| Total Issued in U. K. | 64 | 23 | 13 |

[a] Madden, "British Investment . . . ," p. 53.

New England and Middle Atlantic states lags substantially behind the South and the Western regions in the trough of the mid-1870's. While railroad development in the West accelerates rapidly again from 1875 (or at the latest 1878), New England mileage added falls secularly to 1879. In the Middle Atlantic there is only a minor recovery in 1876, followed by a constant rate of mileage

---

51. "Further proof of the essentially conservative nature of British investment can be seen from the fact that most new rail issuing houses whose reputations were based on the knowledge that they never issued speculative bonds. Thus, Barings, J. S. Morgan, and McCalmert & Company, alone issued £34 m. of bonds and six such companies, Barings, Morgan, McCalmert, Morton & Rose, R. Benson & Co., and the London agents of the Pennsylvania Railroad were responsible for two-thirds of all bonds issued in Britain (£50 m.)." *Ibid.*, pp. 55-56.

added until 1879 (see Chart 17). Earlier in the century, New England railroad building would have played a more rigorous role as a leading region, and thus the lags in our 1844-1860 regressions are smaller.

It would seem that, as in the forties and fifties, the long-swing turning points of the sixties and seventies reflect demand pull rather than supply push of foreign capital into the railways. This seems to be a reasonable conclusion since British investment in American railroad securities and net capital imports into America both lag behind United States railway mileage added, estimates of net capital investments in the railroads, and total American securities issued. This is not to say that the *amplitude* of the long swing in net capital imports may not have depended in a very important way upon the inverse nature of the investment opportunities in the lending country. But in no case is there similarity with the 1830's and 1840's for which one can construct an argument that the timing of United States development was conditioned in part by the supply of foreign funds.

Nor does the post–Civil War period reveal a conscious movement on the part of British investment to facilitate the export of agricultural or raw material goods. This is true of cotton in the 1830's and 1840's and of cotton and especially grain in the 1850's, but the great grain boom in the 1870's is certainly not directly the doing of British railway investment. On the contrary, British investment was concentrated in the developed and urbanized regions of the East and not the granary of the West. It is true, of course, that large British investment in the East freed American, Dutch, and German capital to extend the network of the West and facilitate the great grain export boom which followed, but British capital was in no important way directly involved.

Nevertheless, the railroad boom in the East was concomitant with expansion in the West. So again during periods of rapid economic development and worsening in the trade balance, the pace of economic development also generated an excess supply of American securities which appealed to foreign investors and helped achieve relative stability in United States balance of payments.

*The Fourth and Fifth Long Swings: 1879-1900, 1901-1917*

The quantity and quality of the historical data necessary for our analysis of the ante-bellum period is much more satisfactory. A more adequate measure of the supply conditions for foreign investment in the United States is available: for example, the Cairncross series of British home investment, which begins in 1871 (see Table B-24). The quality of American estimates of demand conditions improves as well with such estimates as Ulmer's net capital expenditure in the railways (see Table B-14), which begins in 1870,[52] and various bond and stock yield indices. For these reasons, the next section attempts a more rigorous explanation of net capital movements into the United States from the later part of the decade of the 1870's to World War I than we were able to formulate concerning the long swings from 1825 to 1870. This section is devoted mainly to the determination of the variables that should give a good explanation of the long swing in the net flow of foreign capital. The historical description is less extensive than that which we have presented for 1825-1870.

From the termination of reconstruction in the South to the outbreak of the World War I, long-term foreign investment was directed primarily into the railroads. Indeed, contemporary descriptions of foreign interests in United States development rarely mention any other attractions for investment from across the Atlantic during the two long swings 1879-1900 and 1901-1917. Table B-2 reveals that 62 per cent of foreign long-term investments in the United States in 1868 were in securities issued by the railroad industry. (That is, 62 per cent of *private* issues were railroad securities of some type. Federal bonds were still the dominant assets held abroad.) Approximately 23 per cent of this figure found its way into corporate stocks issued by the railroads, while 39 per cent went into railroad bond issues. Again in 1869 the railroads absorb the lion's share of foreign funds in private issues with the same figure of 62 per cent, 29 per cent of which is in

---

52. Melville Ulmer, *Capital in Transportation, Communication and Public Utilities: Its Formation and Financing*, National Bureau of Economic Research (Princeton, N. J.: Princeton University Press, 1960), Table C-1, pp. 256-257.

stocks and 33 per cent in bonds. By 1914 this percentage share has not declined seriously despite the relative decline in the railroads as a prime mover of economic development. Prior to the outbreak of the war in Europe, 57 per cent of foreign long-term investments in the United States were in bonds and stocks issued by the rails, but the relative importance of bonds seems to have increased, with 41 per cent in bonds and only 16 per cent in stocks. Clearly, then, for the half century 1870-1915 about three-fifths of the *stock* of private assets held abroad were in the railroads. Thus, the secular *flow* of foreign investment into American railroad issues over the period 1870-1915 was approximately 60 per cent of total private American securities purchased by foreigners, a very large share indeed. The relative importance of the railroads is even more

**Table 31** Distribution of American Securities in the British Portfolio, 1864-1880[a]
(Millions of Pounds Sterling)

| Years | Federal Securities | Railroad Securities | State and Municipal Securities | Other Securities | Total Securities |
|-------|--------------------|--------------------|--------------------------------|------------------|------------------|
| 1864-1870 | 27 | 15 | 2 | 1 | 45 |
|  | (60%) | (34%) | (4%) | (2%) |  |
| 1871-1874 | 54 | 51 | 5 | 7 | 117 |
|  | (46%) | (44%) | (4%) | (6%) |  |
| 1875-1876 | 6 | 7 | 1 | 2 | 16 |
|  | (38%) | (44%) | (6%) | (12%) |  |
| 1877-1880 | — | 1 | — | 2 | 3 |
|  |  | (33%) |  | (67%) |  |

[a]Madden, "British Investment . . . ," Table 9, p. 44.

impressive if we compare the share of railroad issues in total private *and* public issues held abroad. In 1868-1869, due to the importance of Union bond issues, 16 to 17 per cent of foreign long-term investment was in railroad bond and stock issues. In 1914, however, 57 per cent was in the rails—the ratio of the *flow* of foreign investment into the rails to the total flow to foreign investment into the United States was almost 70 per cent! In the analysis that follows, we have good reason to treat demand for net foreign long-term investment as emanating almost entirely from conditions in the railroad industry. This does not seem to be an unwarranted simplification in view of the discussion above.

Goldsmith's estimates of the importance of railroad securities in foreign portfolios of American issues are somewhat higher.[53] Using his figures, approximately 60 per cent of foreign-held American assets were in railroad securities of some kind in 1900. In 1912 the share increases to 63 per cent, reflecting perhaps the relative severity in amplitude of net investment in the rails or of railroad bond and stock prices compared to other industrial demands for foreign funds over the long swing. (By 1914 Goldsmith's estimate of that share had fallen to 61 per cent. This is somewhat higher than the figure of 57 per cent in Table B-2).

The conclusion that the major security exports from the United States after the Civil War was railroad stocks and bonds is also supported by Madden's research (see Table 31). British investors were inclined more toward the rails than the average investor. From 1871 to 1874, 44 per cent of their total holdings of private *and* public American security issues and 81 per cent of total *nonfederal* issues were in railroad securities of some kind. By 1880, however, with gradual disappearance of federal bonds, 65 per cent of total British holdings of American securities (public and private) were railroad issues.[54] Somewhat less credible is Madden's estimate of the proportion of railroad bonds to nonfederal loans issued publicly on the continent. This amounts to an enormous 88 per cent over the period 1869-1872.[55] In spite of this rather unlikely estimation, the conclusion about relative importance of the railroads as an issuer of debt to foreigners gains further support.

Cleona Lewis has also recorded estimates indicating the direction of net foreign investment into the United States, which are not included in Table B-2. Using her figures, in 1899, 58 per cent of Dutch holdings in American securities were railroad stocks or bonds.[56] The German portfolio of American securities in 1914 is weighted less heavily with the rails which are 46 per cent of total holdings.[57] However, as late as 1908 British investors, our most

---

53. Raymond W. Goldsmith, *A Study of Saving in the United States* (Princeton, N. J.: Princeton University Press, 1955), Vol. I, Table K-6, p. 1089.
54. Madden, "British Investment . . . ," Table 8, p. 43.
55. *Ibid.*, Table 11, p. 49.
56. Lewis, *America's Stake*, p. 526. Taken from Bacon, *Yale Review*, pp. 265-285.
57. Lewis, *America's Stake*, p. 537.

important creditors, chose to hold 85 per cent of their American holdings in the form of rail issues.[58]

It also seems reasonable to assume that the *fluctuation* of net capital movements *over the long swing* was predominantly conditioned by the movements in the rate of railroad expansion and activity, given our evidence concerning secular trends from 1870 to 1915. We know, for instance, that the relative amplitude of investment in the railroads is severe compared to other industries and compared to total net investment as a whole. If this is true, there is no reason to expect that the long swing in net capital flow

**Table 32** Average Share of Railroad Net Investment in Total Net Capital Formation, 1870-1915[a]

| Years | |
|---|---|
| 1870-1874 | 0.34% |
| 1875-1879 | 0.04 |
| 1880-1884 | 0.17 |
| 1885-1889 | 0.10 |
| 1890-1894 | 0.10 |
| 1895-1899 | neg. |
| 1900-1904 | 0.02 |
| 1905-1909 | 0.10 |
| 1910-1914 | 0.12 |

a Net capital formation estimates are from Simon Kuznets, "Technical Tables Underlying Series in *Supplement to Summary Volume on Capital Formation and Financing*," (New York: National Bureau of Economic Research, 1956; mimeographed), Table T-8, Col. 3, pp. T-15, 16, and are in current prices. Net capital expenditure in the railroads is taken from Ulmer, *Capital*, Table C-1, Col. 7, pp. 256-257.

over periods of twenty years is dominated by other sectoral demands for foreign capital when we have evidence that the *trend* movements (1870-1914) of net capital flow are dominated by foreign interests in the rails. On the contrary, over the period 1860-1880 the relative amplitude of British foreign investment in the American rails exceeds that of total British investment in American business. This is reflected in Madden's estimates (Table

58. *Ibid.*, p. 531. Taken from Sir George Paish, "Trade Balance of the United States," *Miscellaneous Articles*, Report of the National Monetary Commission (Washington, D. C.: U. S. Government Printing Office, 1910), Vol. XX, p. 174.

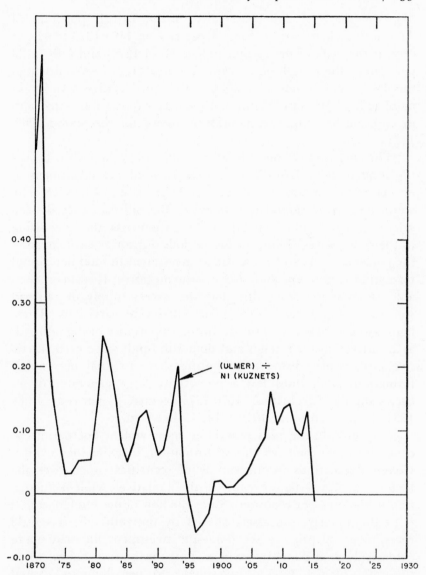

**Chart 18** Relative Amplitude of Investment in United States Railroads, 1870-1915 (Investment in Railroads [Ulmer] ÷ Total Net Investment [Kuznets])

*Source:* Table 32

31): the share of American rails in the British portfolio of American securities rises from 34 per cent in 1864-1870 to 44 per cent at the peak of net capital inflow (1871-1874) and falls to 33 per cent in the trough of net capital inflow (1877-1880), although the last figure is not very significant. The relative severity in amplitude of the rate of railroad security exports was noted also in Goldsmiths' estimates, mentioned above, for the period 1900-1912.

The amplitude of net capital expenditure in the railroads over the long swings (1870-1915) relative to total net investment as estimated by Kuznets can be seen in Table 32 and Chart 18. The amplitude of net capital investment in the railroads exceeds considerably that of total net capital formation over the long swing in these two series. Thus, during periods of protracted depression the percentage share of net railroad investment in total net capital formation is very low and at one point negative. It seems reasonable to conclude from this that the excess supply of railroad securities should also reveal relatively severe variations. These figures also clearly reveal the declining importance of the railroads as an attraction for foreign and domestic funds since each successive peak is at a lower contributing share to total net capital formation (and, thus, less a potentially large generator of an excess supply of securities): 1870-1874 averages 34 per cent; 1880-1884, 17 per cent; and 1910-1914, 12 per cent.

Not only do the rails reveal the most violent fluctuations as contributors to total net capital formation, but also they exhibit violent fluctuations in the supply of securities issued over the long swing (or perhaps *because of* their relatively violent fluctuation in the pace of expansion). Since the flow of net foreign capital is predominantly into assets offered by the railroads, it should occasion no surprise to see domestic investment fluctuate more extensively than domestic savings. This can be seen below, when the ratio of net foreign investment to net domestic capital formation fluctuates rather decisively with the Kuznets cycle. Net foreign investment rises to its peak contribution during secular booms, when the rails are also at their peak share in net capital formation, and falls to its minimum contribution (an outlet for domestic savings) during protracted contractions (see

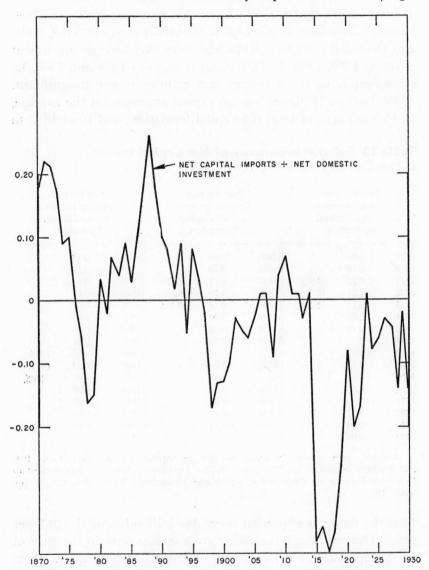

NET CAPITAL IMPORTS ÷ NET DOMESTIC INVESTMENT

**Chart 19** Relative Amplitude of United States Net Capital Movements, 1870-1930 (Net Capital Movements ÷ Total Net Investment [Kuznets])

*Source:* Table 33

Table 33 and Chart 19). The series that estimates the share of net foreign investment in net capital formation peaks in 1869, 1888, and 1910 and troughs in 1878 and 1898. Net foreign investment peaks in 1872, 1888, and 1910 and troughs in 1878 and 1900. Its contribution in the seventies and eighties is not insignificant. From 1869 to 1876, net foreign capital amounts, on the average, to 15.5 per cent of total net capital formation, and from 1882 to

**Table 33** Relative Importance of Net Capital Imports in Net Capital Formation, 1869-1914[a]

| Net Foreign Capital Imports ÷ Net Capital Formation | | | Net Foreign Capital Imports ÷ Net Capital Formation | | | Net Foreign Capital Imports ÷ Net Capital Formation | | |
|---|---|---|---|---|---|---|---|---|
| 1869 | 0.27 | | 1885 | 0.03 | | 1900 | —0.13 | |
| 1870 | 0.18 | | 1886 | 0.10 | | 1901 | —0.10 | |
| 1871 | 0.22 | 1869- | 1887 | 0.17 | 1882- | 1902 | —0.03 | |
| 1872 | 0.21 | 1876: | 1888 | 0.26 | 1893: | 1903 | —0.05 | |
| 1873 | 0.17 | 15.5% | 1889 | 0.18 | 10.3% | 1904 | —0.06 | |
| 1874 | 0.09 | | 1890 | 0.10 | | 1905 | —0.03 | |
| 1875 | 0.10 | | 1891 | 0.08 | | 1906 | 0.01 | |
| 1876 | 0 | | 1892 | 0.02 | | 1907 | 0.01 | |
| 1877 | —0.06 | | 1893 | 0.09 | | 1908 | —0.09 | 1906- |
| 1878 | —0.16 | | 1894 | —0.05 | | 1909 | 0.04 | 1912: |
| 1879 | —0.15 | | 1895 | 0.08 | | 1910 | 0.07 | 2.5% |
| 1880 | 0.03 | | 1896 | 0.03 | | 1911 | 0.01 | |
| 1881 | —0.02 | | 897 | —0.02 | | 1912 | 0.01 | |
| 1882 | 0.07 | | 1898 | —0.17 | | 1913 | —0.03 | |
| 1883 | 0.04 | | 1899 | —0.13 | | 1914 | 0.01 | |
| 1884 | 0.09 | | | | | | | |

[a]Derived from Simon-Goldsmith net foreign capital import series, Table B-1, and Kuznets' estimates in "Technical Tables Underlying Series in *Supplement to Summary Volume on Capital Formation and Financing*," Table T-8, Col. 3, pp. T-15, 16.

1893 the figure is somewhat lower but still substantial (10.3 per cent). Thus, although the 1880's are a secular peak in the level of net foreign capital movements over United States borders, these movements decline in the 1870's from a higher level in terms of contribution to net capital formation.

The inflow of foreign capital is not, it seems, an insignificant proportion of total domestic net capital formation, although it is of much minor importance as a component of aggregate demand than in nineteenth-century Great Britain. The predominance of railroad stocks and bonds in foreign holdings of American securities would also seem to explain the violent amplitude of net capital import fluctuations from 1870 to 1915.[59]

It remains necessary to find support for the hypothesis, derived from a reading of qualitative histories of United States capital imports of the nineteenth century, that the main source of these foreign funds was Great Britain. Although the proportion of British capital exports to the United States was small relative to total British exports, an average of 15 per cent from 1860 to 1880,[60] Great Britain was an extremely important source of funds for the United States.

Although most scholars take for granted the overwhelming importance of British capital in total United States net capital imports, there are very few quantitative estimates of their importance after the Civil War and prior to the turn of the century. Again Madden's research sheds a great deal of light on our problem. Using his estimates of British and Continental holdings for selected years from 1860 to 1880, we have constructed the estimates exhibited in Table 34. The ratio of British to the sum of British and Continental holdings of American securities varies substantially from a low of 44 per cent in 1870 to a high of 73 per cent in 1860. The average "share" of British holdings of American securities in the postwar period, 1870-1880, is approximately 60 per cent. However, when we compare British holdings of American securities with Simon's estimate of the United States net ac-

---

59. It should be made clear again that net foreign investment does not necessarily take the form only of new issues of American securities. But surely the attractiveness of new and old issues move together over the long swing. Thus when there is an excess supply of new issues, the attributes of the new offers attractive to foreign investors should also be true of the stock of past issues.

60. Madden, "British Investment . . . ," Table 10, p. 46. This does not preclude the possibility that American capital imports from Great Britain had much larger amplitude than other sources of demand for British capital. We may find, therefore, that although the average share (over ten to twenty years) of capital exported to America compared to total British exports was relatively small, the marginal propensity may have been large enough to have had major influence over the level and timing of total British net exports of capital. For example, the figure is as high as 40 per cent in 1871-1874 and falls to zero in 1875-1876. (If indeed the *changes* in total British capital exports were not controlled in an important way by American conditions—although the average share going to America was small—then conditions in other countries would have to be included in our regression analysis below. The point is pursued further in Chapter VI.)

cumulating balance of indebtedness, the figures are much lower. If we discard the war years estimates, 1860 and 1863, the directions of movement of the British contributing share in both column 4 and column 5 are the same; there seems to be a somewhat constant difference of 10 per cent between the two series. Averaged over the span 1870-1880, the British contribution to total net capital imports into the United States lies somewhere between 50 and 60 per cent—a large share indeed.

Our next estimates occur fully twenty years later.[61] It was

**Table 34** Relative Importance of British Capital in Total Net Capital Imports, 1860-1880

| Year | (1) Estimated Nominal Value of Continental Holdings of U.S. Securities[a] (millions of dollars) | (2) Estimated Nominal Value of U. K. Holdings of U. S. Securities[a] (millions of dollars) | (3) (1) + (2) | (4) (2) ÷ Simon's Estimate of U. S. Net Capital Balance (percentage) | (5) (2) ÷ (3) (percentage) |
|---|---|---|---|---|---|
| 1860 | 65 | 175 | 240 | 47 | 73 |
| 1863 | 70 | 130 | 200 | 28 | 65 |
| 1870 | 540 | 420 | 960 | 35 | 44 |
| 1874 | 580 | 1045 | 1625 | 57 | 64 |
| 1876 | 480 | 1125 | 1605 | 59 | 70 |
| 1880 | 440 | 735 | 1175 | 48 | 63 |
| Average 1870-1880 | | | | 50 | 60 |

aColumn (1) from Madden, "British Investment . . . ," Table 12, p. 50. Column (2) derived from *ibid.*, Table 8, p. 43.

perhaps somewhat extravagantly estimated in 1899 that 79 per cent of American securities held abroad were in British hands, 8 per cent were held by the Dutch, 6 per cent by the Germans, and 7 per cent by the rest of the world. By 1908 the British share in American foreign obligations had declined somewhat (reflecting, perhaps, Bacon's exaggerations in his 1899 estimates) to 58 per cent, Germany held 17 per cent, the Dutch 13 per cent, and

61. Both Lewis and Hobson refer to the same figures but give different primary sources. Lewis, *America's Stake*, p. 524, refers to Bacon, *Yale Review*, pp. 265-285. Hobson, *Export of Capital*, p. 154, refers to Ripley, *Journal of Commerce* (n.p.).

the rest of the world 12 per cent.[62] Finally, for 1914 Lewis estimates that the British share was as high as 60 per cent, Germany 13 per cent, and the Netherlands 9 per cent.[63]

These quantitative estimates of the relative importance of British capital as an American source of foreign funds confirm and support the qualitative descriptions of the movements of capital over United States borders during the half century 1870-1914.[64] Over this period, British investors contributed somewhere between 55 and 60 per cent of total net foreign investment in American business. With this knowledge, surely we must find that domestic investment opportunities for British capital had an important impact on the movement of foreign capital into the United States.

## The Fourth and Fifth Long Swings: Quantitative Tests

This section attempts to quantify an explanation for the long swings in net capital imports after 1870. As we did with the regression analysis for the period 1844-1860, we have tried to isolate adequate measures of the demand pull for foreign funds into the United States and of the supply push at the sources of American net capital imports. Our examination above clearly points to the railroad industry as the source of demand pull and to Great Britain, primarily, as the source of supply push.

Before passing on to the tests themselves, we should emphasize again a point discussed earlier in this chapter. In spite of the evidence that an extremely large share of American long-term capital imports had its source in Great Britain (1870-1915), there is no reason, a priori, to include conditions in British business as the only initiator of "supply push." The evidence for such a statement lies simply in the fact that a relatively small share of British capital exports went to the United States.[65] Thus, should we not

62. Paish, "Trade Balance . . . ," p. 174 as quoted in Lewis, *America's Stake*, p. 530.

63. Lewis, *America's Stake*, p. 546.

64. The implied importance of British capital can be seen, for example, in the words of Jenks, Cairncross, Thomas, and Hobson.

65. A. K. Cairncross, *Home and Foreign Investment, 1870-1913* (Cambridge: Cambridge University Press, 1953), Table 41, p. 183, estimates that about 25 per cent went to the United States in 1870, 23 per cent in 1885, and that the share falls secularly until World War I.

include conditions in other countries receiving capital from Great Britain in order to derive an adequate explanation of United States net capital imports? There are two related reasons for suspecting that conditions outside the United States and Great Britain are relatively unimportant in explaining the long wave in the flow of capital over United States borders. First, although the average share of British capital exports going to American enterprise is only 25 per cent in 1870 and 23 per cent in 1885, it is the largest share. Using Cairncross' figures again, in 1885, 20 per cent was going to India, 18 per cent to Australasia, 9 per cent to Canada, 12 per cent to South America, and 13 per cent to Europe.

**Table 35** British Capital Exports to the United States Compared to Total British Capital Exports, 1860-1880[a]

| Years | (1) Total British Capital Exported to the United States (millions of pounds sterling) | Δ (1) | (2) Total British Capital Exported to All Countries (millions of pounds sterling) | Δ (2) |
|---|---|---|---|---|
| 1860-1863 | — 16 | | 77 | |
| 1864-1870 | 57 | +146 | 257 | +245 |
| 1871-1874 | 130 | | 322 | |
| 1875-1876 | 1 | —202 | 25 | —316 |
| 1877-1880 | — 72 | | 6 | |

[a]Madden, "British Investment . . . ," Table 10, p. 46.

Second, and perhaps more meaningful, is the evidence that although the average share going to America is only 20 to 25 per cent, the marginal share in terms of ratios of annual changes is much larger. Madden lists estimates of total British capital exports and exports to the United States, reproduced in Table 35, for selected periods from 1860 to 1880. The ratio of the increase in exports of capital to the United States to total increase of British capital exports from a trough period to a peak period (1860-1863 to 1871-1874) is 60 per cent. The ratio from peak to trough (1871-1874 to 1877-1880) is 64 per cent. However, in Chapter VI we also examine some recent estimates by Harvey H. Segal and Matthew

Simon. Their research suggests that the relative importance of the United States in explaining British long swings in net capital exports declines sharply after 1880, while their figures for 1860-1880 are approximately the same as Madden's.[66]

We began the tests by using estimates of the "need" for funds: as far as "pull" is concerned, we assumed that profit rates did not interfere with the appropriateness of using net investment in the railroad industry as a measure of external (to the industry) demand for funds over the long swing. On the English side we assumed that Cairncross' series of British home investment was an adequate measure of investment opportunities in the United Kingdom. We did not, however, use Poor's estimates of net railway mileage added since there is available a better estimate of investment activity in the rails from 1870 to 1914. Ulmer has recently derived an estimate of net capital expenditure in steam railroads that certainly should be a better index of external demand for funds.[67] Since we are primarily concerned with the explanation of the long swing in net capital imports rather than with larger secular movements, the trend was removed from all three series. The three series were also smoothed by a five-year moving average to eliminate minor short-run fluctuations.

The first test was a simple univariate one using only Ulmer's series (trendless and smoothed) as an explanatory variable and covering the span 1871-1914. The results are significant. The best fit occurs when net capital imports ($\dot{K}$) lag Ulmer's net expenditure in the railroads ($I_{US}$) by one year ($\bar{R}^2 = 0.624$) where the coefficient is positive and significant:

$$(1871\text{-}1914) \qquad \dot{K}^t = 6.7487 + 1.0189\ I^{t-1}{}_{US}, \quad \bar{R}^2 = 0.624.$$
$$(0.1271)$$

When, however, we add the Cairncross series of British home investment ($I_{GB}$), an extraordinary thing happens. Not only does

---

66. "British Foreign Capital Issues, 1865-1894," *Journal of Economic History*, XXI (December, 1961), 566-581.

67. Ulmer, *Capital in Transportation*, Table C-1, Col. 8, pp. 256-257. Incidentally, the movements of the Ulmer series are quite different from Poor's, indicating the inadequacy of the Poor series as a measure of investment activity.

the fit improve only slightly, but also the coefficient of $I_{US}$ (Ulmer) becomes insignificant.

$$(1871\text{-}1914) \quad \dot{K}^t = 914.45 - 0.0303I^t_{US} - 8.8473I^t_{BG}, \overline{R}^2 = 0.654.$$
$$(0.2000) \qquad (0.1556)$$

It would seem that Ulmer's series does not add much to the explanatory power of the Cairncross series. Over the long swing, and statistically, it seems that the rate of British home investment (see Table B-24) is inversely related to the rate of net capital inflow and that conditions in the American railroad industry are somewhat unimportant. This holds true, incidentally, under all reasonable lead-lag conditions.

In another experiment, the same bivariate regression was performed, but this time we excluded most of the fourth long swing, covering the period 1891-1914. Here the results are much more reasonable. The best fit is produced when neither the American nor the British series leads net capital imports. In this case

$$(1891\text{-}1914) \; \dot{K}^t = 699.2 + 0.4047 \; I^t_{US} - 6.6934 \; I^t_{GB}, \quad \overline{R}^2 = 0.891.$$
$$(0.1628) \qquad (1.3884)$$

This is much more encouraging. The long swing in the rate of net capital import into the United States is positively related with a similar swing in railroad development and inversely with the rate of British domestic investment. During the 1890's and until World War I, at least, the Ulmer and Cairncross series explain the net flow of foreign capital into the United States quite well. It should be mentioned at this point that from 1897 to 1915 Goldsmith breaks his direct estimate of net foreign investment into two parts: net changes in ascertainable foreign investment in the United States and net change in ascertainable United States investment abroad. The long swing in aggregate net capital movements seems to be primarily due to the movements in "net change in ascertainable foreign investments in the United States" which reflects the long swing much more clearly than "net changes in ascertainable United States investment abroad." The same relationship exists, incidentally, after 1919 and during the era in which the United States becomes a net exporter of capital.

Perhaps one reason why the fit is not better (but at the same time surprising that it is not worse) is the importance of short-term capital flow during the mid-1890's.[68] Clearly, our choice of the Ulmer and Cairncross series as explanatory variables of net capital movements was prompted by our knowledge of *long-term* foreign investment, while short-term capital flight may have acted so as to exaggerate aggregate net capital movements during the mid-1890's (although it does not seem to interfere with lead-lag relations). The argument has been suggested that the lag of net capital movements behind our "long-term" explanatory variables could have been produced by the movements of short-term capital. Even if foreigners did increase net purchases of long-term securities synchronous with upturns in our explanatory variables, the argument goes, this inflow of long-term capital might be temporarily offset by an opposite short-term capital flow—a plausible supposition if the net deficit on current account would be low or even a surplus at the lower turning point of the long wave.

Although it is possible that short-term capital movements obscure the meaning of our regressions here and in those that follow for the period 1879-1897, they do not seem to interfere with the similarity in timing and shape between long-term capital imports and total capital imports when such data are available. The similarity in shape can be seen in Chart 20 and Table 36. As far as timing is concerned, in two cases there are differences. In Graham's estimates long-term capital inflow peaks in 1873 in the annual data whereas *total* capital imports peak in 1872; but both peak in 1871 when the series are smoothed by a five-year moving average. In Goldsmith's estimates long-term capital outflow troughs in 1901, but *total* capital outflow troughs in 1900. In both these cases, long-term capital movements appear to lag behind total capital movements due to short-term capital flows. Thus, for the periods 1860-1878 and 1897-1915, short-term capital flows hardly explain the observed lag of total capital imports behind those variables which were chosen to explain long-term capital flows. Nevertheless, it should be made clear that, although

---

68. For a description of one phase of this period of short-term capital movements see Matthew Simon, "The Hot Money Movement and the Private Exchange Pool Proposal of 1896," *Journal of Economic History*, XIX (March, 1959), 31-50.

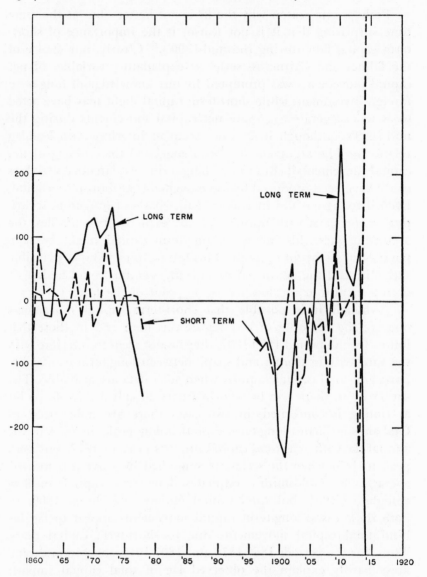

**Chart 20** United States Long- and Short-Term Capital Movements, 1860-1878 and 1897-1914 (in Millions of Dollars)

*Source:* 1860-1878, Graham; 1897-1914, Goldsmith

**Table 36** Long-Term and Short-Term Capital Imports into the United States, 1860-1878 and 1897-1915[a]

| Year | (1)<br>Long-Term<br>Capital<br>Estimates<br>[Outflow (+)] | (2)<br>Short-Term<br>Capital<br>Estimates[b] | (3)<br>Total Net<br>Capital<br>Estimates<br>[(1) + (2)] |
|---|---|---|---|
| 1860 | — 15 | 49 | 34 |
| 1861 | — 10 | — 90 | —100 |
| 1862 | 25 | — 12 | 13 |
| 1863 | 25 | — 17 | 8 |
| 1864 | — 80 | — 6 | — 86 |
| 1865 | — 75 | 31 | — 44 |
| 1866 | — 70 | 13 | — 57 |
| 1867 | — 74 | — 41 | —115 |
| 1868 | — 76 | 27 | — 49 |
| 1869 | —122 | — 43 | —165 |
| 1870 | —130 | 43 | — 87 |
| 1871 | —100 | 14 | — 86 |
| 1872 | —112 | — 95 | —207 P |
| 1873 | —145 P | — 22 | —167 |
| 1874 | — 51 | 23 | — 28 |
| 1875 | — 20 | — 6 | — 26 |
| 1876 | 50 | — 7 | 43 |
| 1877 | 100 | — 6 | 94 |
| 1878 | 150 T | 44 | 194 (T) |
| 1897 | 10 | 80 | 90 |
| 1898 | 48 | 66 | 114 |
| 1899 | 88 | 112 | 200 |
| 1900 | 218 | 103 | 321 T |
| 1901 | 245 T | 28 | 273 |
| 1902 | 135 | — 53 | 82 |
| 1903 | 21 | 133 | 154 |
| 1904 | 10 | 117 | 127 |
| 1905 | 83 | 11 | 94 |
| 1906 | — 68 | 46 | — 22 |
| 1907 | — 71 | 36 | — 35 |
| 1908 | 46 | 145 | 191 |
| 1909 | — 59 | — 84 | —143 |
| 1910 | —255 P | 26 | —229 P |
| 1911 | — 48 | 8 | — 40 |
| 1912 | — 23 | — 13 | — 36 |
| 1913 | — 87 | 229 | 142 |
| 1914 | 522 | —536 | — 14 |
| 1915 | 1579 (T) | —480 | 1099 (T) |

[a]1860-1878: Frank D. Graham, "International Trade Under Depreciated Paper —the United States, 1862-1879," *Quarterly Journal of Economics*, XXXVI (February, 1922), 222-273. 1897-1915: Goldsmith, *Study of Saving*, Vol. I, Tables K-1, K-2, K-3, pp. 1078-1085.

[b]Includes errors and omissions but not gold.

we purport to explain long-term capital flows, it is the *sum* of long- and short-term capital which we use as a dependent variable.

Another possible interference with the correlation between net capital flows and the Ulmer-Cairncross indices would be the exogenous government bond issue of the Treasury in an effort to stem the tide of gold in the mid-1890's. In 1895 more than $62 million worth of 4 per cent bonds were issued by the American government to protect the gold supply of the United States.[69]

The test again was repeated for a shorter span, 1895-1914, to eliminate completely the effects of the long swing of the 1880's and early 1890's. The results are more or less the same, however, with the best fit appearing when neither investment series is leading.

$$(1895\text{-}1914) \quad \dot{K}^t = 887.5 - 8.3654 \ I^t_{GB} + 0.3758 \ I^t_{US}, \ \bar{R}^2 = 0.914.$$
$$(1.3980) \qquad (0.1490)$$

The explanation for our poor results over the period 1871-1914 does not lie with the years between 1891 and the war, but rather with the decade of the 1880's. In a very general way, both net capital imports and the Ulmer series rise from the late 1870's to peaks in the 1880's and fall again to troughs in the late 1890's. But apart from the over-all similarity, the patterns of the long swings of these two series are strikingly different. Ulmer's series has a double peak, the first in the early eighties exceeding the second in the late portion of that decade, which is entirely absent in the net capital import series. Net capital flows rise quickly (although it remains a net outflow until 1880), but do not attain high levels of import in the early 1880's, do not reflect the severe depression of the mid-decade—a depression not unique to the rails alone—and do attain a higher level in the late 1880's. Our first task is to attempt an explanation for the dissimilarity of these two movements (net capital movements and the Ulmer series) over the long swing, which is not adequately explained by the addition of British conditions.

Since the number of observations is so small from 1871 to 1879, no formal analysis was attempted. However, it does seem that the Ulmer series leads net capital imports by two or three

---

69. Lewis, *America's Stake*, pp. 66-67.

years on the upturn from the late 1870's for reasons that are not applicable to later years.

Unfortunately we cannot, it seems, appeal to an argument that suggests the dissimilarity between net expenditure in American rails and net capital imports is due to the competing demands of other developing nations for British funds. For example, Latin American investment—especially the Argentine railroads—was quite popular in the late 1880's and early 1890's.[70] Competing demands for British, and perhaps European, capital do not seem to be a possible explanation since net British capital exports and net American capital imports have very similar patterns over the long swing, although American demands for British capital decline, from the 1870's to 1880's, as an explanation of total British capital exports over the long swing. Both series rise sharply from the late 1870's to 1882-1883, remain more or less constant until 1885, rise to a secular peak in 1888, and then fall until the late 1890's. The only difference in the time shape of the British capital export and American capital import estimates that might reflect competing demands for British funds is minor: from 1895 to 1900 net American capital imports fall very sharply to the trough while British net capital exports reveal only a mild reduction to their trough. It seems likely that we must rule out competing demands for British funds as an explanation for poor results covering the decade of the 1880's.[71]

Another possible explanation may have its source in Madden's research. His investigation supported the suspicion that the British investor was not a "risk lover" but a "risk averter." After 1870 English capital was predominantly in the rails of the developed and urbanized regions of the East, which left the task of Western expansion to the American, Dutch, and German investor. Is it possible that Eastern and Western railroad expansion were dissimilar enough to explain the poor correlation between

---

70. H. S. Ferns, *Britain and Argentina in the Nineteenth Century* (Oxford: Clarendon Press, 1960), especially Chapter XIII, pp. 397-435.

71. It must be emphasized that British investors were certainly interested in other geographic investments than the United States over this period. The point being stressed above is that the direction and rate of movements over the long swing are strikingly similar between the British and American series. It certainly seems obvious, however, that there is some positive correlation between U.S. demands for British capital and demands of other countries using it.

net capital movements and total net expenditure in the rails during the 1880's? There are numerous reasons for believing so.

A good argument can be presented that the severe recession in railroad expansion in the mid-1880's was caused, in great part, by the sharp decline in wheat production and exports and the secular fall of wheat prices (perhaps mainly due to the entrance of new major wheat suppliers: Russia and Argentina). In the annual estimates, wheat exports fall very sharply from a peak in 1880. In the quarterly data cited by Fels, the fall from the peak occurs in the fourth quarter of 1881.[72] Wheat prices also begin a steady fall from 1880 (or perhaps even 1878), reflecting the entrance of the new suppliers.[73] If it is true that the depression in the rails in the mid-1880's was a Western phenomenon tied to the conditions in the grain market, then it is quite possible that Eastern railway development was less affected than the United States as a whole.

A second argument is also suggested by Fels:

The character of railroad building in 1886 and 1887 differed from that in earlier cycles. Previous spurts of construction involved a good deal of activity by new and often shaky companies engaged in starting or completing their main lines. In the early 1880's this kind of work had largely been finished. The construction of 1886-87 was done by comparatively strong companies building feeder or complementary lines.[74]

Could it be that the nonspeculative investment atmosphere of the later part of the decades was more appealing to the essentially conservative nature of the British investor?

Unfortunately, the answer to most of these queries is in the negative. Poor's railroad mileage added breakdown into regions does not exhibit any dissimilarity between Eastern and Western movements, so that possible explanation suggested by Madden's research does not help us. This also holds true when we examine the movements of Eastern and Western first differences in Poor's

---

72. Rendigs Fels, *American Business Cycles, 1865-1897* (Chapel Hill: The University of North Carolina Press, 1959), p. 124.

73. U. S. Department of Commerce, *Exports of Farm Products from the United States, 1851-1908*, Bureau of Statistics, Bulletin No. 75 (Washington, D. C.: U. S. Government Printing Office, 1910) Table 3, p. 16.

74. Fels, *American Business Cycles*, pp. 138-139.

estimates of total capital account of the railroads in these regions. This does not necessarily rule out the possibility that different profit rates over the long swing in the Eastern railroads may interfere with the use of net expenditure figures as an estimate of external demand or external "need" for funds. It may be that, since the nature of railroad construction in the late 1880's was less speculative, British investors were more willing to purchase American assets. We shall return to this point later.

An obvious criticism of the use of investment series in explaining movements in net capital imports is that foreign investors are not attracted by the railroad industry's *demand* for funds, as reflected in Ulmer's net expenditure series or Poor's railway mileage added or total railroad bond issues, but rather by the estimated returns derived on the existing stock of assets issued by the rails in the past and present. The two conceptions may be quite the same in earlier periods when the existing stock of assets is very small and the flow is large, as in the period 1840-1860, for example. But they may move in different ways when the railroads are mature and the stock of assets large.

The best continuous series reflecting the attractiveness of American railroad issues that has a comparable British series is of stock prices. Since we know that railroad bond issues play a more dominant role in foreign portfolios than stocks (from 1870 to 1914), why choose a stock or share price series? The reason is simple enough. The British series of share prices is available as far back as the 1840's.

The movements in American railroad stock prices (see Table B-17) and British share prices (see Table B-25) give much better results. Again using smoothed and trendless data and covering the period 1873-1911, highly significant results occur when the American series leads by three years and the British by two:

$$(1873\text{-}1911) \ \dot{K}^t = 112.42 + 420.71P^{t-3}{}_{US} - 552.39P^{t-2}{}_{GB},$$
$$\bar{R}^2 = 0.83. \qquad\qquad (64.41) \qquad\qquad (72.52)$$

This result is not as good as that achieved for the period 1844-1860 (where $\bar{R}^2 = 0.91$, $P_{US}$ leading by one year, $P_{GB}$ leading by two years), and certainly one reason seems to be that we still have not adequately explained the 1880's. That explanation follows.

As evidence in almost all of our tests, foreign investors tend to lag considerably behind domestic investors in their willingness to increase their purchase of securities issued by the rails over the first half of the long swing in transportation development. They lag to a much lesser extent, if at all, in decreasing their purchases on the downswing. Thus, we might find that British investors were even slower to respond to the early boom in the railroads in the decade of the 1880's, since the Eastern rails, in which they had their main interests, lagged behind Western transportation development. This lag, incidentally, is not prevalent in later periods. The early boom itself is very sharp and abrupt with stock prices rising from 1877-1878 to a peak in 1881. Ulmer's series rises only very gradually at low levels until 1879-1880 and then jumps sharply to a peak in 1881-1882. After these abrupt peaks in all the railroad indices, there is an immediate and sharp depression that troughs in 1885. It seems reasonable to suppose that before foreigners began their lagging movement into railroad stocks and bonds, the peak was past and a recession prevalent in the industry. This would explain the low levels of net capital import in the early 1880's.

Why was there not a serious reduction in the rate of net capital imports in the mid-1880's or, for that matter, a net outflow of capital? Again the movements in railway bond issues, Ulmer's net expenditure of the railways, and Poor's railway mileage added exaggerate the seriousness of the depression in the railways, at least with respect to the attractiveness of their security issues in the eyes of foreigners. Not only was the fall in stock prices less severe, but also the low level in 1885 was still rather high compared to the late 1870's. Output and profits were much less severely affected by the depression:

Although the railroads appeared to be at the bottom of the trouble, their own business in physical terms was better than ever. . . . Although railroad profits in the aggregate probably held up pretty well, in many particular instances they were disappointing. Profit prospects declined more than actual profits . . .[75]

As indicated by Table 37, things were not that bad, and foreign investors must have felt it so. These facts, coupled with

---

75. Fels, *American Business Cycles*, p. 130.

the extensive fall in British share prices from 1882 to 1885, may explain why the rate of net capital inflow does not seriously reflect the fall in the railroad stock price or net expenditure indices.

When share prices recovered in the latter half of the 1880's, foreign investors, their frustration released after missing the first and more speculative boom, apparently were quite willing to purchase American securities. The time was certainly propitious

**Table 37** Indices of American Railroad Activity, 1877-1890

| Year | Freight Revenue[a] (000 missing) | Revenue Tons Carried[b] (000 missing) | Net Earnings[c] (000 missing) | Ton Miles Carried[d] (000 missing) |
|------|------|------|------|------|
| 1877 | $347,705 | | $170,977 | |
| 1878 | 365,466 | | 187,575 | |
| 1879 | 386,676 | | 216,545 | |
| 1880 | 467,749 | | 255,558 | |
| 1881 | 551,968 | | 272,407 | |
| 1882 | 485,778 | 360,490 | 280,317 | 39,302 |
| 1883 | 539,510 | 400,453 | 298,367 | 44,065 |
| 1884 | 502,870 | 399,075 | 270,891 | 44,725 |
| 1885 | 509,691 | 437,040 | 269,494 | 49,152 |
| 1886 | 550,359 | 482,245 | 300,604 | 52,802 |
| 1887 | 636,666 | 552,075 | 334,989 | 61,561 |
| 1888 | 639,201 | 590,857 | 301,631 | 65,423 |
| 1889 | 665,962 | 619,166 | 322,123 | 68,677 |
| 1890 | 734,822 | 691,344 | 346,921 | 79,193 |

[a]U. S. Bureau of the Census, *Historical Statistics of the United States: Colonial Times to 1957* (Washington, D.C.: U.S. Government Printing Office, 1960), Q 27, p. 428.
[b]*Ibid.*, Q 28, p. 428.
[c]*Ibid.*, Q 40, p. 428.
[d]*Ibid.*, Q 29, p. 428.

because British share prices hit a trough in the latter part of the 1880's.

There are two final comments that should be made at this point. The first is to underline the apparent importance of supply conditions in supporting and partially controlling the long swing in net capital imports into the United States. Although the interdependence of the British and American balance of payments will be discussed in Chapter VI at greater length, some points may be stressed here. Clearly, the severity of amplitude of these long swings in net capital inflow associated with the rate of transportation development in the United States is in part due to the inverse nature of British domestic investment opportunity. This needs no further amplification. But supply conditions apparently also have some important control over turning points, especially on the upswing of these long swings. That from 1873 to 1911 American capital imports lagged British capital exports at troughs suggests America was fortunate in not having to wait for conditions to be proper at the source of their capital imports. On the contrary, in 1880 Great Britain had been increasing its rate of capital export for three years and in 1900 for two. The same seems to be true of the 1840's but not of the 1830's.

The second point is to emphasize the difficulty of establishing a simple explanation of net capital movements over a period of forty-five years. That the results should be so good simply by appealing to British and American stock prices is rather astonishing. We may find that our more extensive, albeit tentative, explanation of the 1880's is not supportable at all, but rather that it is short-term capital movements attached (inversely?) to the state of the grain trade that explain the early 1880's. This latter hypothesis, however, does not seem very likely.

# V.

# BALANCE-OF-PAYMENTS
# DISEQUILIBRIUM
# AND THE LONG SWING

*An Introduction to American Nineteenth-Century Experience
with Balance-of-Payments Disequilibrium*

Due to the consistent response of commodity trade to variations in American growth, we have shown that with every long swing in United States history the components of the balance of payments have responded in a systematic fashion. Every Kuznets cycle upswing can be characterized as one of increasing trade-balance deficit (or deteriorating surplus) and of increasing capital inflow (or decreasing capital outflow). There is no exception to this generalization over the period 1820-1913. Similarly, we have seen that every Kuznets cycle downswing is typified by an improvement in the trade balance and by a reduction in the rate of capital inflow (or an increasing rate of capital outflow). This evidence in itself reflects astonishing historical consistency.

Given the fact that net capital flows partially offset the widely fluctuating trade balance and imparted some stability to the balance of payments, what was the net effect of the American long swing on our payments position? Did fluctuations in net capital movements consistently exceed fluctuations in the trade balance and thus in the current account, or vice versa? Expressed in more modern terminology, are Kuznets cycle upswings normally periods of gold outflow and dollar surplus? Or are upswings typically times of dollar scarcity, gold inflow, and balance-of-payments surplus? We shall find that generally in American history, under normal conditions, rapid growth has tended to generate payments surpluses, and sluggish growth payments deficits.

Examined either by themselves or relative to foreign price levels, domestic price movements do not have any consistent effect upon the *timing* of imports and thus upon the trade balance, over the long swing. This seems to be the only possible conclusion in light of the evidence presented in Chapter III. This does not imply that domestic price movements have not had substantial effect upon the trade balance in the past, for surely the *amplitude* of import-export movements is in part due to the fluctuation in the general price level (positively related to real-income movements). But there is little evidence of a regular relation between the timing of aggregate imports and domestic price levels over the long swing. The corollary is that movements in aggregate import values and thus in the trade balance are dominated mainly by the income variable or, perhaps, by movements in the components of income as well. Given this evidence, what we wish to explore in this chapter is not the specie-flow price mechanism for maintaining balance-of-payments equilibrium *directly* through price movements but rather whether gold flows reveal long swings at all (and thus if the net payments position responds consistently to the domestic long swing) and whether they can be related in some way to the movements in real income as a primary or secondary causative factor of long secular swings in American economic development.

Although an examination of the dynamics of the balance of payments in the context of growth and in a gold-standard environment must by definition include specie flows, there is another reason for investigating their nature and importance. Some contemporary economists, concerned with an examination and attempted explanation of the American long swing, have discarded the "real" cycle in favor of a monetary explanation. The long swing in the rate of growth of income, output, and productivity may indeed be apparent. But, they would argue, it is most likely to be autonomous and episodic and primarily due to the vagaries in the rates of change of the money supply. The principal proponent of the latter thesis has been Milton Friedman. In this chapter, however, no attempt is made to evaluate the Friedman hypothesis. On the contrary, we would like to explore the possibilities of explaining these long swings in the expansion of the money supply by dynamic adjustments in the balance of payments. Did the rate of gold flow over the United States borders play a major causative role in fluctuations of the money supply during American development, or did internal production of gold and variations in the money-gold ratio overshadow the importance of the gold flow?

The above is a simple statement of the problem. Considerably more difficult is the choice of an adequate model with which to search out the answers. This chapter on the research is far more problematic in two very important and related aspects. It seems particularly important to discard the usual classical specie-flow model, which is more applicable for short-run analysis, in favor of a model that is constructed in an environment of dynamic secular growth. For instance, fortified with the knowledge that price movements seem to have little consistent relation to the *timing* of trade-balance and import movements,[1] we are tempted to treat gold flows mechanistically as residuals, as an external market-clearing device quite independent of other balance-of-payments movements.

If specie flows were treated in that manner, our argument might proceed quite simply. Suppose we were to retain all the classical assumptions of the Hume model, yet attach some very important appendages: (1) there is a domestic long swing in real output (for the moment *unexplained*), fifteen to twenty years in duration, that seems to dominate trade-balance move-

---

1. That is, gold flows and resulting price movements may help complete the real transfer already initiated by income movements. On the other hand, it is suggested below that the occurrence of gold flows does not necessarily imply that the real transfer has not yet been completed since these flows themselves may satisfy demands in a domestically growing economy.

ments, and (2) net long-term capital movements are extremely important and not relegated, along with labor migration, to the minor role in which most classical economists have put them. If net capital flows (K) consistently exhibit greater or less amplitude in fluctuations over the long swing relative to the trade balance (TB), a twenty-year cycle in gold flows must certainly result. In the case of excessive fluctuation in K relative to TB, a peak inflow of K (and a trough in TB where import surplus is at a maximum) will coincide with the maximum rate of specie *inflow;* at all points over the domestic long swing, increments in the rate of inflow or outflow of K will exceed increments in the trade-balance deficit or surplus. Where fluctuations in the TB exceed those of K, a maximum *outflow* of specie is attained at the peak of K (trough in TB) and when domestic expansion is also at its peak. Under a gold-standard system, we have three possible movements in the net flow of gold over the United States borders. Either the TB consistently exceeds K in its amplitude over the long swing, K exceeds the TB consistently, or their amplitudes are approximately equal over the long swing in domestic expansion. In the first case, the rate of gold inflow will be inversely related to domestic activity; in the second, positively related; in the third, gold flows will reveal no long swing whatsoever. Thus, if we are to find support for the thesis that external gold flows have a strong influence upon the money supply—and already fortified with the knowledge that the rate of growth of the money supply is positively related to business activity with a lead[2]—then the amplitude of K must surely exceed that of the TB over those long swings in American economic development which are characterized by a negligible internal production of gold.[3]

But it is realistic or adequate to treat specie flows as mechanistic residuals? Can we consider it simply fortuitous that net

2. Milton Friedman and Anna J. Schwartz, "The Stock of Money in the United States, 1875-1955" (New York: National Bureau of Economic Research, 1958; mimeographed).

3. This conclusion follows under the assumption of coincident timing of the trade balance and capital movements. In fact, net capital movements lead the trade balance on the average, but hardly enough to interfere with the general supposition derived from the simple model above.

capital movements *did* exceed trade-balance fluctuations over the long swing in American development so that the money supply generally kept pace with real growth and apparently did not seriously cause short-run deficiencies in aggregate demand? Is it adequate to treat net capital movements as creating an independent pool of resources over the long swing out of which increasing import demands may be satisfied while *still* allowing the money supply to expand via net specie import? It seems more reasonable and correct to treat the problem in a general equilibrium framework. Clearly, if we consider only three markets—bonds, money, and goods—the upswing of a Kuznets cycle in output growth will generate an excess demand for goods that will be reflected in an increasing trade-balance deficit and an excess demand for money concomitant with the growth of real income. Both an excess demand for goods and for real-money balances may be offset by an excess supply of securities—a net inflow of foreign capital. Considered in this way (including a demand for money positively related in income-output in the model itself), a long swing in the rate of gold inflow, which tends to peak during boom, seems the less surprising hypothesis since there must have been a long swing in excess demands for real-money balances concomitant with variations in real-income growth.

The suggestion here is that in previous chapters we have exaggerated the independence of the movements in net capital flows and the trade balance. It is not quite enough to recognize the important relation between the export market and the rate of capital imports, especially prior to 1860. Nor is it enough to recognize that short-term capital and gold may be easily substituted for each other according to excess demands for money (i.e., for gold) left unsatisfied by domestic production. It seems absolutely necessary to recognize that if, for instance, excess demands for real-money balances are not satisfied by internal production and external flows of gold, interest rates and prices must move in a direction consistent with the correction of that imbalance by their effect upon the rate of import of capital and goods. It is still possible, of course, that capital movements may not respond to clear excess supply on the securities market and allow a complete satisfaction of excess demands for money. However, it seems that gold flows were *more* than sufficient to satisfy the demand for increases in real balances, since general price movements are positively related to real-income movements (the 1880's could be considered an exception to this rule).

In summary, the main point seems to be that gold flows cannot be treated simply as residuals, but must be considered as a very important part of the process of internal development, functionally related to excess demands in the domestic system. It is not quite correct to maintain, therefore, that gold flows fortuitously satisfied varying excess demands for money over the long swing due to excessive foreign capital imports (which resolved an excess supply of domestic securities), but excess demands for money over the long swing may have played an important part in causing those flows.

### Long Swings in Gold Flows: 1820-1913

The first question is this: do long swings in gold flows in fact exist in United States history? Before attempting an examination of net specie flows from 1820 to 1913, it might be advisable to review the criticism directed toward the accuracy of gold-flow data. In Appendix A, we review Morgenstern's attack upon the adequacy of "official" gold-flow data, a conclusion derived from an intercountry comparison of what should have been comparable data on source and direction of gold flows. He found little agreement among the "comparable" sources in his test and thus threw chilly criticism indeed upon the use of these data as *annual* estimates. But this should not necessarily discourage our use of gold-flow data for studying long secular swings, especially in view of the evidence we have found in support of their reasonable accuracy, at least with respect to our needs. In support of the gold-flow data, we have found striking coincidence between the *movements* in British figures for gold shipments between Great Britain and the United States and the American data for total gold flows. This coincidence between the data from two independent sources holds for periods of three to five years as an average but, of course, is much less clear in the annual estimates. Although the inadequacy (or likely in-

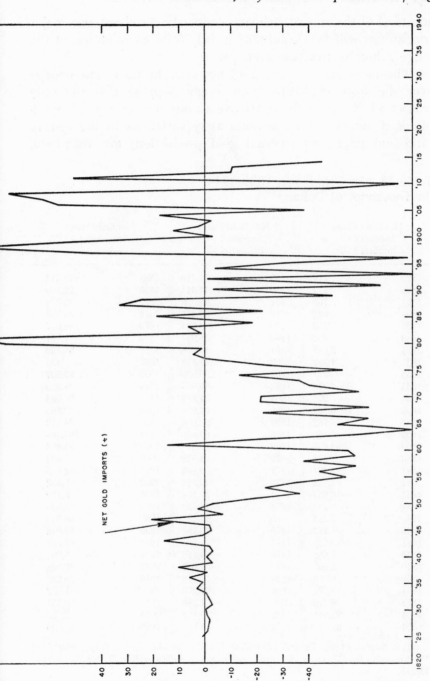

**Chart 21** Net Gold Flows over United States Borders, 1825-1914 (in Millions of Dollars; Positive Figures Are Imports)

*Source:* Table 38

accuracy) of the annual estimates cannot be dismissed, our major conclusions will derive support mainly from examination of the longer, three to five year averages.

The movements in net gold flows are by no means regular over the span 1825-1913. One might suppose that the only periods which satisfy the restrictive assumptions of a simple gold-standard model (which assumes away variations in the reserve ratio and important internal gold production) are 1825-1849,

**Table 38** Net Gold Flows, 1825-1914[a]
(In Thousands of Dollars)

| Net Gold Flows Exports (+) Imports (—) | | Net Gold Flows Exports (+) Imports (—) | | Net Gold Flows Exports (+) Imports (—) | |
|---|---|---|---|---|---|
| 1825 | — 213 | 1855 | 54,016 | 1885 | — 18,214 |
| 1826 | 377 | 1856 | 44,011 | 1886 | 22,209 |
| 1827 | 762 | 1857 | 58,578 | 1887 | — 33,210 |
| 1828 | 827 | 1858 | 38,437 | 1888 | — 25,558 |
| 1829 | 756 | 1859 | 58,983 | 1889 | 49,667 |
| 1830 | 602 | 1860 | 55,937 | 1890 | 4,331 |
| 1831 | 2,048 | 1861 | —14,868 | 1891 | 68,130 |
| 1832 | 1,332 | 1862 | 21,533 | 1892 | 496 |
| 1833 | 278 | 1863 | 56,632 | 1893 | 87,507 |
| 1834 | — 3,076 | 1864 | 89,485 | 1894 | 4,529 |
| 1835 | — 970 | 1865 | 51,883 | 1895 | 30,083 |
| 1836 | — 6,585 | 1866 | 63,001 | 1896 | 78,885 |
| 1837 | 782 | 1867 | 22,002 | 1897 | — 44,653 |
| 1838 | —10,462 | 1868 | 63,659 | 1898 | —104,986 |
| 1839 | 3,636 | 1869 | 21,871 | 1899 | — 51,433 |
| 1840 | 618 | 1870 | 21,579 | 1900 | 3,694 |
| 1841 | 2,321 | 1871 | 59,803 | 1901 | — 12,866 |
| 1842 | 1,548 | 1872 | 40,831 | 1902 | — 3,452 |
| 1843 | —16,658 | 1873 | 36,174 | 1903 | 2,109 |
| 1844 | — 247 | 1874 | 14,539 | 1904 | — 17,595 |
| 1845 | 2,234 | 1875 | 53,284 | 1905 | 38,945 |
| 1846 | 1,143 | 1876 | 23,184 | 1906 | — 57,648 |
| 1847 | —20,537 | 1877 | 344 | 1907 | — 63,111 |
| 1848 | 7,662 | 1878 | — 4,126 | 1908 | — 75,904 |
| 1849 | — 2,097 | 1879 | — 1,037 | 1909 | 47,528 |
| 1850 | 2,784 | 1880 | —77,119 | 1910 | 75,223 |
| 1851 | 19,261 | 1881 | —97,466 | 1911 | — 51,097 |
| 1852 | 36,416 | 1882 | — 1,789 | 1912 | 8,391 |
| 1853 | 23,016 | 1883 | — 6,133 | 1913 | 8,569 |
| 1854 | 37,438 | 1884 | 18,251 | 1914 | 45,500 |

[a]U. S. Bureau of the Census, *Historical Statistics of the United States, 1789-1945* (Washington, D. C.: U. S. Government Printing Office, 1960), Table M-47, pp. 243-245.

prior to the great era of American gold discovery, and 1879-1913, after the resumption of a specie standard and before World War I and the beginnings of the destruction of the gold-standard system. But for the moment we are only concerned with the movement of gold itself.

A description of the net movements of gold over United States borders seems best divided into three historical periods: 1825-1842,[4] 1843-1878, and 1879-1913 (see Table 38). As with the other elements of the balance of payments, the evidence of the long swing seems more apparent in the nineteenth century, and we will begin there. In general, the first period, 1825-1842, reveals a "long swing" in net gold flows with a maximum outflow in 1831, a maximum inflow in 1838, and a maximum outflow again in 1839 that continues at the same approximate rate until 1842 (see Chart 21). It does not seem clear that this long cyclic movement in net gold flows *is* dominated by the relative intensity of the swings in net capital movements (see Chart 11). Although import values behave violently during this early long swing in American development (indeed, more violently than at any time prior to 1929), export movements are also coincident with income movements and reveal wide amplitude over the secular swing such that they reduce the amplitude of trade-balance fluctuations. This, coupled with the first large influx of foreign capital in American history, a great deal of which was short-term and extremely responsive and accommodating to conditions in the balance of payments, produces movements in net capital flows in excess of trade-balance fluctuations. Here we find another interesting aspect of this first long swing. Whereas in later periods (post-1879) it is more the *relative* mildness of import movements that facilitates the dominance of capital movements over the balance of payments, here it is exports offsetting violent movements in imports to create relative stability in the trade balance.

---

4. Prior to 1825, gold and silver are aggregated in official accounts. As a result, this series must begin with that year. Prior to 1864, domestic exports of silver are included with gold but this inclusion is "probably small" (U. S. Department of Commerce, *Foreign Commerce and Navigation, 1914* [Washington, D. C.: U. S. Government Printing Office, 1915], p. 43). The data are given for fiscal years ending September 30, 1790-1842; June 30, 1843-1915; and calendar years thereafter (Chart 21).

As we have already suggested, it may have been the very climate of export markets which determined income-output growth and thus important movements.[5]

In the annual data, then, we do have a long secular movement in net gold flows generally similar to, but shorter than, swings in the other balance-of-payments components and the domestic series. The peak in gold inflow in the late thirties does indeed seem to occur in the vicinity of peaks in domestic activity, and the same seems to be true of the trough of the early 1840's. In this first long swing, dollar scarcity, gold inflow, and balance-of-payments surplus do seem consistent with rapid growth, while serious balance-of-payments deficits generally seem characteristic of the Kuznets cycle downswing.

We might tentatively suppose that a large inflow of gold might have furthered the boom of the 1830's and that the sharp curtailment and eventual outflow seriously activated the great depression of the 1840's. Net gold flows do respond in the 1830's and early 1840's as if they were satisfying variations in excess demands for real-money balances. The second question still remains: does the money supply respond consistently (expost) to the external flow of gold throughout the long cycle? At first glance, these general movements seem to be at least similar, but this is discussed further below.

For the next thirty-five or forty years the apparent compliance with the original thesis exhibited from 1825 to 1842 disappears (see Chart 21). Internal gold production usurps the importance of external supply in satisfying excess demand. Net gold flows during the years 1843-1848 are extremely erratic and volatile, and no general movement can be discerned until 1849. This begins, of course, the era of American gold discoveries. From 1850 to 1879 there is a large sustained rate of net gold outflow in every year except 1861. Although there are two long swings in gold flows during these years, the secular movements in net gold flows behave *inversely* to domestic activity. This is certainly consistent with the notion that this period of gold discovery was one of excess money supply. The first long swing in

---

5. See Chapter II and Chapter IV.

net gold flows rises from the low level of net inflow in the late 1840's, and the rate of outflow increases sharply to 1855. After that time, there is a clear retardation in the rate of increase in outflow. The "long swing" terminates with a brief inflow in 1861.

This secular movement in net gold flows clearly reflects a different set of conditions. Whereas prior to 1850 and after 1875 the rate of change in net capital imports exceeds that of the deficit in the trade balance and current account, from 1850 to 1861 the opposite is the case. Fluctuations in the trade balance exceed those of capital movements, and the long swing in gold flows has a maximum outflow at the peak in domestic activity rather than a maximum *inflow* as seen at the peak in 1838. The third long swing behaves in the same way with a maximum outflow in 1864 and a long secular fall to a maximum inflow in 1881.

This period from 1849 to 1861 is an unusual one in United States history, with respect to the balance of payments, and deserves special attention. All other gold-standard periods prior to World War I exhibit both an excessive amplitude in net capital movements relative to the fluctuation in the trade balance (and current account) and a concomitant long swing in net gold inflows *directly* correlated with real-income movements. This "long swing," 1849-1861, produces net gold flows *inversely* related to real-income movements. But as we shall see, net gold outflows still are positively related to (negative) excess demands for real-money balances. To repeat, the explanation for excessive movements in the trade balance relative to net capital movements lies in the low levels of net capital inflow (and, thus, rather small changes in the rate of inflow) relative to trade-balance fluctuation and not in unusually high levels in the trade-balance deficit. Other than this there seems to be nothing distinctly unusual about balance-of-payments movements during that period.

There are two points which must be made clear at this time. First, we are not discarding this period from examination only because it does not satisfy our simple assumption that there should be no substantial internal production of gold. Second, the relative dominance of trade-balance fluctuations is *not* due to any unusual fluctuation in the amplitude of the trade balance alone (relative to other long-swing experience) but is due to the un-usually low levels of net capital inflows relative to our expecta-tions. This second point is important. The internal supply of gold does not appear to force itself outside of the domestic system via the usual gold-standard process. Trade-balance move-ments are not excessive enough to suggest that the internal sup-ply of gold forced itself onto the world market via the effect of domestic prices upon import demand and export supply, which were in excess of expected income effects.

The relatively low levels of capital movements can be ex-plained by any number of possible causes, but we will not at-tempt to examine them exhaustively here. We might suggest, however, that this period of the late 1840's and the 1850's was a time of railroad boom not only in the United States but also in the rest of the world. There was competition for British long-term credit. It is also true that British investors were still hesitant about investing in American securities after their heavy losses of the early forties from the state repudiations and defaults. It may also be that the Crimean War seriously interrupted the flow of capital, especially short term, to the United States. Be-tween 1853 and 1855, long before the panic of 1857 and the slackening in railroad construction, the net inflow of capital abruptly fell by more than half. The Crimean War itself ac-counts, in part at least, for the tremendous increase in gold out-flow from 1853 to 1855.

Two previously suggested explanations remain. First, since there is surely no excess demand in the domestic money market but rather excess supply due to the Western gold discoveries, we may find that the movements of long-term interest rates are extremely mild during the 1850's compared to the long swings of the 1830-1840's, 1860-1870's, 1880's, and the first decade and one-half of the twentieth century. Second, with gold increasingly in excess supply, it is quite likely that gold substituted directly for short-term foreign capital. With empirical verification, these two suppositions alone would give sufficient support for our general equilibrium model.

The gold discoveries in the West were a tremendous and

fortuitous boon to American growth. In the period 1849-1861 there was not the normal need for a larger rise in capital imports than in the trade balance or current account (inverted). A large domestic gold supply paid for a balance-of-payments deficit engendered by rapid growth. The need for adding external gold to the domestic stock did not exist. With the Western gold discoveries an increasing excess supply of real-money balances was created, while both long- and short-term securities must have found their excess supply greatly reduced (at the same time it is surprising that an increased excess demand on the goods market is not reflected in trade-balance movements, although it is reflected in import movements alone).

At the outset of our study of the United States balance of payments, it seemed most fruitful not to treat capital movements simply as accommodating short-term movements that tend to satisfy excess demand or supply in the merchandise trade balance, but rather predominately as movements of a long-term sort that are not dictated directly by conditions in the balance of payments.[6] On the contrary, it seemed more correct to treat net capital flows as occurring independent of import demand (in excess of export supply) and as an external stimulus to accelerated growth. This still seems to be the most helpful approach, but we must also allow for gold flows, their effect upon the domestic money supply and, in turn, their effect upon the divergence between the actual and the natural rates of interest. If there is no pool of long-term external credits and if imports are a requisite for export expansion at a later time, there can be serious interference with maximum growth performance: either too much of the internal resource stock is devoted to import substitution (imports which are at a comparative disadvantage *at this point* in the development process), monetary disequilibrium occurs, or necessary import demands are not satisfied. But in our simplified model of the gold-standard system, we assumed that the stock of gold cannot be augmented internally. If it can,

---

6. We also thought, and still think, that direct investments, the loans from which were paid in kind, played a very small part in United States balance of payments: that is, for example, an exchange of American railroad securities for simultaneous import of railway material.

as in the years 1849-1861, we have at least partially removed one of our constraints: monetary disequilibrium is averted.[7]

The period 1861-1879 requires a different explanation. An examination of the relative movements in net capital inflow and the trade balance no longer has relevance as an explanation of the dynamics of net gold flows, either as a measure of balance-of-payments disequilibrium or a measure of excess demands for real-money balances. The United States left the gold standard early in 1862 and suspended convertibility of Union currency into specie. Based on a paper standard, a freely fluctuating exchange rate was maintained throughout the years 1862-1878. Gold flows no longer represent potential monetary disequilibrium during this period, nor are they approximate measures of balance-of-payments disequilibrium. (It may be true that the *desire* to readopt the gold standard at prewar parity in the 1870's had a substantial effect upon that decade of development.) For the seventeen years 1862-1878 gold can be treated as just another export commodity susceptible to fluctuations in foreign demand, vagaries in price expectations, and export supply. The exchange rate must adjust any resulting disequilibrium in the balance of payments.

From the termination of the War for the Union to resumption in January 1879, there is a secular fall in the rate of outflow of gold reflecting the gradual exhaustion of the gold fields in the West. Nevertheless, the rate of gold outflow seems to be positively related to the "real" long swing. It accelerated in the booms and slowed down in the slumps. From 1865 to 1873 the downward trend in outflow slows down, whereas after 1873 (except for 1875) there is a sharp reduction in the rate of outflow until 1877 (see Chart 21).

With the end of that great era of gold discovery and with resumption early in 1879, the movements in net gold flows again exhibit a long swing similar in time shape to that found in the 1830's and 1840's (see Chart 21). If we begin with the resumption year 1879, we find net gold flows rise to a maximum

---

7. Disequilibrium in this sense implies a potential interruption in pace of development of the long swing due to an unsatisfied excess demand for money and insufficient aggregate demand.

inflow in 1881, fall to a large outflow in the mid-1880's, rise to a large inflow again in the late 1880's, and finally fall to a period of great gold outflow in the 1890's. As with the long swing of the 1830's and 1840's, we again find a positive correlation between general income movements and gold inflow. That is, with "normal" conditions again satisfied, it appears that balance-of-payments surplus becomes characteristic of the upswing and deficit characteristic of the downswing of the Kuznets cycle.[8]

This long secular swing in gold flows has the same double-peaked nature that is common to many other domestic and foreign trade series: there is a peak in the early and late 1880's with a sharp dip in the middle of that decade. Over the long swing in the balance of payments, net capital movements generally have more violent amplitude than the merchandise trade balance and the current account. The evidence of long swings in the rate of gold flows certainly suggests that they may play some role in aggravating similar fluctuations in internal development. Although we have yet to examine movements in the money supply, it does seem plausible that high growth rates achieved early in the secular swing could be explained in part by the stimulus of large specie inflows and that the severity of the depressed mid-1890's could be explained in part by monetary stringency and the tremendous outflow of gold. The causation may run the other way *as well:* in the early and late 1880's excess demand for money concomitant with rapid output growth should have been partially satisfied by large gold inflows; in the mid-1880's and the 1890's unimpressive growth and severe depression should have facilitated an outward flow of gold.

After 1899 the evidence of long secular swings in net gold flows is less obvious although here again, during a "normal" period of American development, the upswing of a Kuznets cycle appears to generate balance-of-payments surplus and vice versa on the downswing. The last three years of the nineties temporarily interrupt the long cyclic movement in gold flows. From

---

8. The period 1879-1900 was extensively examined in Jeffrey G. Williamson, "Real Growth, Monetary Disturbances and the Transfer Process: The United States, 1879-1900," *Southern Economic Journal,* XXIX (January, 1963), 167-180. In that article the results of the author's research, in terms of the real transfer problem, were applied to an intensive examination of this one period in American history.

1897 to 1899 there is a very sharp inflow of gold which interrupts a more gradual increase in inflow from the 1890's to 1908 (see Chart 21). Thus we find an increasing rate of inflow to 1898, followed by a decreasing rate of inflow reaching an outflow in both 1900 and 1905. Apart from this uncooperative interlude, the secular pattern of gold inflow and domestic activity are fairly similar. In the annual data Riggleman's building index peaks in 1909 and troughs during the war, while the rate of net gold inflow increases to 1908 and then falls to a maximum outflow in 1910, which is sustained until 1914.

The sharp increase in net gold inflow over the three years 1897-1899 is due to the unusual increase in the export surplus within the merchandise trade balance. After 1899 the long swing in the trade balance is exceptionally mild—an adjective which applies to both the export and import time series over this period—and thus the fluctuations in net capital movements generally exceed those of the trade balance. From 1900 to 1908 there is a gradual drift toward an increasing rate of gold inflow concomitant with this last historical boom in net capital imports. But from 1908 to 1910 the increasing rate of gold outflow is not accompanied by a reduction in the rate of capital inflow, since net capital movements do not peak until 1910, but is attributable to a worsening in the trade balance. After 1910, however, the sustained outflow of gold is paralleled by a diminution in the net inflow of capital and eventually by a net outflow. Although the evidence is a little less clear-cut, it does appear that gold movements from the mid-1890's to World War I behave in a fashion roughly consistent with the postulated time shape of excess demand for money concomitant with real output growth.

To summarize, we have seen that during the five long swings from 1820 to 1913 and during periods of "normalcy," there appears to be a consistent relation between the net payments position and the domestic long swing. When the United States was committed to a specie standard and without significant internal sources of gold, increasing imports (or decreasing exports) of capital and gold occurred together. On the Kuznets cycle upswing, America enjoyed an increasing balance-of-payments surplus, and on the downswing, increasing payments deficits, gold outflow, and dollar surplus were the rule.

*Gold Flows and Long Swings in the Money Supply: 1879-1913*

Do gold flows help explain movements in the domestic money supply?[9] The period 1825-1842 reveals rates of gold inflow positively related to domestic activity. The same is true for the period 1879-1896 and, to a lesser extent, 1897-1913. The two swings embraced by the dates 1843 and 1878 do not reveal such patterns. We have explained the inverse nature of the first (1843-1861) by the discovery and exploitation of Western gold deposits and have discarded the second since it was a period in which the United States favored a paper standard (1862-1878). It remains to be determined whether the flow of gold did indeed have an influence upon the domestic money supply at any point during those years (1825-1842 and 1879-1913) when an important internal gold supply was lacking.

This does not mean that long swings in the money supply and gold flows should be in evidence throughout the years 1825-1842 and 1879-1913. The evidence is very thin, as far as we can see, regarding a long swing in the money supply during the fifteen years prior to World War I. The same is true of gold flows (see Chart 22). But should we anticipate finding a rather precise relation between the changes in the money stock and the external movement of gold? Given no internal source of gold and that the United States maintains an approximately constant ratio between the gold stock and the money stock the relation is less a functional one and more a definitional one. One might suppose that there was really no instant in United States history when the ratio between the gold stock and the money stock remained constant. The important point is whether the flow of gold over United States borders offsets variations in the ratio

---

9. Although no evidence has been found to the contrary, it would be quite a different matter to show that variations in the *excess demand* for money (and goods, as well as an excess supply of securities) cause the long swing in gold flows and to determine the nature of these behavioral relations. The problem of the remainder of this chapter is much simpler: do long swings in gold flows play a major role in determining the *supply* of money?

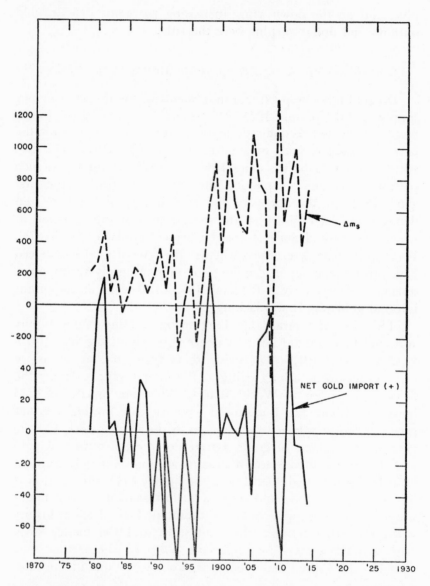

**Chart 22** Changes in the Money Supply and Net Import of Gold, 1879-1914 (in Millions of Dollars)

*Source:* Table 39

**Table 39** Net Gold Flows and Changes in the Money Supply, 1879-1914

| Year | Net Gold Flow[a]<br>Outflow (+)<br>Inflow (—)<br>(thousands<br>of dollars) | Net Change<br>in<br>Money Supply[b]<br>(millions<br>of dollars) |
|------|------|------|
| 1879 | —  1,037 | 220 |
| 1880 | — 77,119 | 267 |
| 1881 | — 97,466 | 457 |
| 1882 | —  1,789 | 95 |
| 1883 | —  6,133 | 217 |
| 1884 | 18,251 | —  47 |
| 1885 | — 18,214 | 73 |
| 1886 | 22,209 | 246 |
| 1887 | — 33,210 | 196 |
| 1888 | — 25,558 | 83 |
| 1889 | 49,667 | 181 |
| 1890 | 4,331 | 365 |
| 1891 | 68,130 | 111 |
| 1892 | 496 | 451 |
| 1893 | 87,507 | — 282 |
| 1894 | 4,529 | 36 |
| 1895 | 30,083 | 253 |
| 1896 | 78,885 | — 211 |
| 1897 | — 44,653 | 216 |
| 1898 | —104,986 | 655 |
| 1899 | — 51,433 | 897 |
| 1900 | 3,694 | 344 |
| 1901 | — 12,866 | 958 |
| 1902 | —  3,452 | 673 |
| 1903 | 2,109 | 513 |
| 1904 | — 17,595 | 462 |
| 1905 | 38,945 | 1,088 |
| 1906 | — 57,648 | 792 |
| 1907 | — 63,111 | 710 |
| 1908 | — 75,904 | — 454 |
| 1909 | 47,528 | 1,301 |
| 1910 | 75,223 | 505 |
| 1911 | — 51,097 | 815 |
| 1912 | 8,391 | 1,005 |
| 1913 | 8,569 | 378 |
| 1914 | 45,500 | 730 |

aDerived from Table 38.
bDerived from Table B-15.

as well as in domestic supplies and at least partially dominates the money supply.

Most of this section will be devoted to the period beginning with resumption (1879) and ending with the Federal Reserve Bank System and World War I (1913-1914). The money supply figures, taken directly from the Friedman-Schwartz tables, include currency outside banks and total demand and total time deposits at commercial banks. The money stock data and, therefore, changes in the money stock are given for the year ending August from 1875 to 1881 and for the year ending June from 1882 to 1915. Since our gold-flow data are also for the fiscal year ending June 30, we do not have the problem of comparability and "manufactured" lags which were prevalent in our analysis in Chapter III (see Table 39).

From 1879 to 1881 there is an upswing in both series (an increase in the money supply and an increasing rate of gold inflow: see Chart 22), and there is positive conformity with no lag between the two estimates. This conformity is true of *both* the annual data and three-year movements as a whole. Not only do gold flows over United States borders and increments to the money stock move in the same direction, but also their relative amplitudes seem to be strikingly similar. The next four years, 1881-1884, are also ones of conformity, as the two series again exhibit similar relative amplitudes. Both series then fall to an intermediate trough, with a reduction in the money supply in 1884 coinciding with an outflow of gold in that same year. From 1885 and until 1892 gold flows do not seem to dominate changes in the money supply over the period as a whole, although *annual* movements of the two series coincide. The rate of increase in the money supply attains a secular peak in 1892 almost as great as that of 1881, while net gold flows fall secularly from a peak in 1887 as the rate of outflow increases. But again from 1892 to 1896 the two series conform not only in the annual data but also by reaching a secular trough in 1893 and remaining at low levels; 1893 and 1896 are years of depletion in the money stock and they are also years of severe outflow of gold.

Over the eighteen years, 1879-1896, the money supply and

the net flow of gold exhibit long swings very closely related. Comparing annual movements, there are only four years in which the two series do not move in the same direction: 1886, 1887, 1889, and 1895. The correlation is only a little less strong over the long swing as a whole. Both series rise to a secular peak in 1881, fall to an intermediate trough in 1884, and rise again in the late 1880's. The only period of disagreement seems to be on the downturn. Gold flows fall from an intermediate peak inflow in 1877 to a severe rate of outflow in 1893. The money stock, however, continues to expand (although at a decreasing rate) until 1892 before it succumbs to the movements in the rate of gold outflow. Thus, even though annual movements in the rate and direction of net gold flow seem to dominate the money supply from 1879 to 1896, this is not true of "secular" movement from 1888 to 1892. The explanation of this conflict, at first glance, would seem to lie primarily in the ratio between the money and domestic gold stock; this ratio rises abruptly from 1888 to 1893 and seems to offset the secular fall in net gold flows (see Chart 22).

The upswing from the severe trough of the mid-1890's is extremely abrupt and large in both series. Gold flows rise from a large rate of outflow in 1896 to a tremendous inflow in 1898 and, to a lesser extent, 1899. The money supply also has a sharp rise from the trough of 1896 to a peak in 1899. In the following five years, 1900-1904, conformity is again the rule in annual movements but less so over a longer time span. The minor peak in the money supply in 1901 is, relatively, much larger than that of the gold inflow. After 1904, however, any suggestion of agreement between the rate of net gold flow and changes in the money supply disappears. The yearly estimates 1909-1914 do not have any similarity in movement. The most obvious case of flagrant violation of the hypothesis, however, is the period 1905-1910. The gold-flow series rises to a large peak net inflow in 1908 and falls to a large net outflow in 1910, while the money supply *falls* to a trough in 1908 and rises to a peak in 1909. Over the period 1900-1913 eight years reveal net gold flows and changes in the money stock moving in opposite directions. And there are no periods of from three to five years when these two series move in a similar way.[10]

The explanation for this apparent unimportance of net gold flows in influencing the rate of expansion or contraction of the money supply over the long swing does not lie with the internal production of gold. Alaskan discoveries notwithstanding, the movements in the ratio of the money stock to the domestic gold stock is the major explanation for the lack of correlation between the two series. Especially after 1904, the "reserve" ratio fluctuates abruptly from year to year, but it also rises secularly from 1900 to 1913.[11]

Both these series have long, mild secular movements rising from low levels at the turn of the century to peaks at the end of the first decade and then falling to the war. Over the decade and one-half prior to 1913 and when smoothed by a five-year moving average, both series have a double peak. The first peak is in the last years of the nineteenth century and the second at the end of the first decade of the twentieth century. This can hardly be accepted as very strong evidence in support of the thesis, however, since there is major disagreement in both the annual estimates and over periods of three to five years from 1904 to 1914.

To be absolutely sure that it was not a third variable but gold flows themselves which caused the apparent striking similarity between changes in the money supply and net gold movements, we observed movements in the domestic stock of monetary gold (see Table B-15). These estimates include coin and bullion in the Treasury vaults and coin in circulation and in national banks.[12] From 1874 to 1900 there can be no doubt that the external movements of gold dictate the level and amplitude of changes in the gold stock (see Chart 23). The domestic production of gold does

---

10. Edward Shaw has pointed out that the poor correlation between the net flow of gold and changes in the money stock from 1904 to 1913-1914 has been somewhat exaggerated. Although the secular relation becomes less clear, there is a definite pattern of relationship over the short cycle: a large inflow of gold coincides with monetary expansion in the initial year of the short cycles beginning 1905, 1909, and 1912.

11. The relation between the net flow of gold and changes in the American monetary gold stock is discussed below.

12. Both the net gold flow and domestic gold-stock figures are for fiscal years ending June 30.

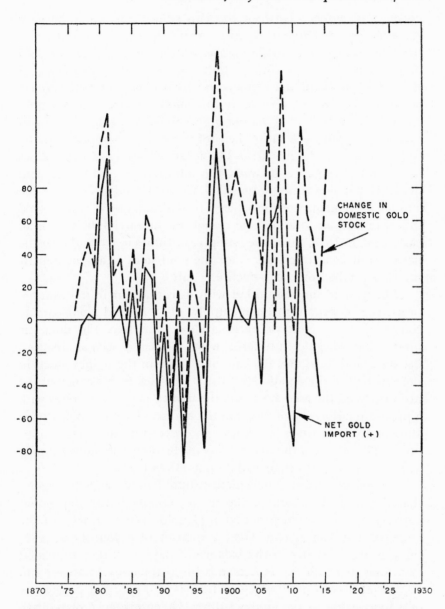

**Chart 23** Net Change in Domestic Gold Stock and Net Gold Flows, 1876-1915 (in Millions of Dollars)

*Source:* Tables 38 and A-15

create a divergence between the two series, but that difference remains approximately constant over this quarter of a century so that the annual and secular movements in the rate of net gold movements dictate the time path of changes in the monetary gold stock. Clearly then, any explanation for the apparent divergence between the rate of change in the money stock and net gold movements over United States borders must lie in fluctuations in the money–gold stock ratio (i.e., 1888-1892). This applies equally well to the period 1905-1913. The internal supply of gold causes significant divergence between the additions to gold stock and net external flow only from 1900 to 1905, and even here the annual movements are the same. Thus, although the rate of gold inflow falls to an intermediate trough in the early 1900's from an early peak in 1898, the money supply continues to expand over the period, but at a *lesser rate* since the gold stock is augmented by internal production (at a declining rate).

The general impression left with us is that our initial assumptions (unimportant internal supply of gold and approximate constancy in the "reserve" ratio) are too restrictive. The domestic production of gold interferes with a precise secular relation between gold flows and the rate of change in the money stock in the first half of the decade 1900-1910. The lack of constancy in the ratio between the gold stock and the money supply interferes with a precise relation in *both* the annual and secular movements from 1904 to 1914. At times the flow of gold over international borders does seem to dictate the movements in the domestic money supply (1879-1904) and at others it does not (1905-1914).

On the one hand this evidence should be enough to suggest that the rate of growth of the money supply is not dependent entirely upon internal production of gold or the vagaries of the domestic banking system. Over a quarter of a century at least, there is a long swing in the balance of payments (not unrelated to a long swing in excess demands for real-money balances) and in the net flow of gold which in turn is an important progenitor of a long swing in the money supply. Given evidence of positive correlation between gold flows and the rate of change in the money stock, we must draw the causation this way. There is no lag, and if it were the money supply (expost) which caused the movement in gold via prices and the trade balance (or via the interest rate and capital flows), one would surely exist. On the other hand, conditions in the balance of payments over the long swing do not consistently control variations in the money supply over the postresumption period 1879-1914.

One more tentative conclusion might be established at this point. We have some evidence, it seems, which would seriously muddle an hypothesis that it is the rate of change in the money supply which *precipitates* the long swing in the rate of economic development. Gold flows cause the movements in the money supply over most of the period from 1879 to 1904. But the rate of net gold flow over United States borders, we think, is predominately caused by income movements and excess demands for real-money balances.[13] How can secular movements in the money stock be *caused* by movements in the external flow of gold synchronous with other balance-of-payments fluctuations and, at the same time, *cause long swings in the balance of payments via income movements?*

*Gold Flows and Long Swings in the Money Supply: 1834-1863*

Abramovitz has compiled an estimate of the total money supply "in the hands of the public" for 1834-1863 (see Table B-16). Whether this is a meaningful series to use may be questionable, but it is the best estimate available. It is also true that our gold-flow estimates are likely to be less accurate for this period. Finally, the money supply is estimated as of the first of each year while the gold-flow data are estimated as of the middle of each year. The flow of gold may have, therefore, an artificial lead of one-half year.

The results are hardly conclusive (see Chart 24). With a "manufactured" lead of approximately one year, the flow of gold conforms with increments to the money supply only over the

---

13. The flow of gold *was* facilitated by excessive fluctuations in net capital movements. These variations in excess demands for real money balances could have been satisfied by price deflation or by income reduction via insufficiencies in aggregate demand. Fortunately, foreign capital helped clear the securities market and allowed the inflow of gold to take place. It therefore helped eliminate several monetary difficulties which could have interfered with maximum growth performance on the upswing of the long wave.

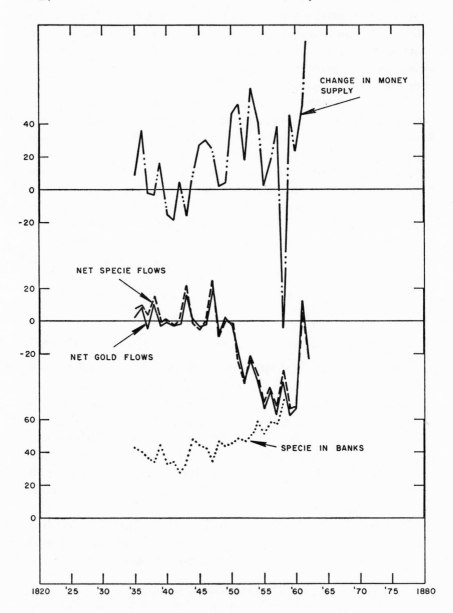

**Chart 24** Net Gold Flows, Net Changes in Money Supply, and Specie in Banks, 1835-1862 (in Millions of Dollars)

*Source:* Tables 38, A-1, and A-16

period 1837-1843 (a period when the Specie Circular was effective?). After the peak in 1838 the rate of gold inflow declines to a protracted trough of gold outflow covering the years 1839-1842 before rising again in 1843. The movement is the same in the money supply series with a one-year lag. The money supply reaches a secular trough and contraction 1840-1843. It appears that approximately half of the years from 1834 to 1849 reveal positive evidence. We cannot even appeal to the less elegant argument that the flow of gold controls the major turning points in the money supply series since the secular peak in expansion of the money supply in the hands of the public occurs in 1836 while the peak inflow of gold occurs in 1838. The Specie Circular explains the fall in the money supply after 1836. The increasing inflow of gold up to 1838 may be partially explained by the same condition and the hoarding that followed. After the late 1840's, of course, both the flow of gold and the money supply are controlled by the gold discoveries of the American West.[14]

In contrast to this negative evidence, from 1835 to 1850 there is an excellent correlation between specie in commercial banks (see Table B-16) and the net flow of gold (see Chart 24). This suggests that either the "money supply in the hands of the public" is an incomplete estimate of the money supply proper, certainly not a very promising hope especially during the period of the 1830's and 1840's, or, much more likely, the ratio between the gold stock and the money supply is not constant. In this con-

---

14. George Macesich argues quite differently in a recent article. Although he concedes that the correlation between gold imports and the money supply is poor, he considers this an inapplicable comparison. Short-term capital held in foreign banks by Americans is also a part of the reserve base upon which the money supply can expand. He is of the opinion that the money supply is therefore primarily determined externally since it is highly possible that the fluctuation in the ratio of gold to money is only apparent. If we could sum gold and net short-term capital holdings, the correlation would be much more impressive. This may explain an absolute difference between changes in the money supply and gold stock but it is hard to believe that over a period of four years (1834-1838) one year finds short-term capital movements interfering with the relation between the money and gold stocks while not in another. Nor can we see why this would explain impressive differences in secular peaks over the long swing between the two series. For the present, the argument must remain unresolved (George Macesich, "Sources of Monetary Disturbances in the United States, 1834-1845," *Journal of Economic History*, XX [September, 1960], 407-434; see also Jeffrey G. Williamson, "International Trade and United States Economic Development: 1827-1843," *Journal of Economic History*, XXI [September, 1961], 372-383).

nection, there is a great deal of evidence in early American banking history which suggests that there were few banks operating under a fixed reserve ratio. The fluctuation in the "reserve" ratio may also reflect the struggle between Biddle's Second Bank and Jackson's "hard currency" proponents.

### Summary

Given a nation which is on the gold standard or a bimetallic standard dominated by gold, there is reason to suppose that the rate of change in the money stock over the domestic long swing will be controlled partially by conditions in the balance of payments and the flow of specie. If the net flow of gold is significant enough to offset any contrary movements in the ratio between the gold and money stock and if it also overshadows domestic production, then it becomes an important determinant indeed. But the flow of gold over the long swing is *not* in the form of an equilibrating mechanism in the balance of payments. Apparently the assumptions necessary to make this an equilibrating mechanism over a long swing of fifteen to twenty years are not fulfilled in United States experience. Not only do long swings in the balance of payments and in specie flow persist, but also the general price level does not seem to play the major role in conditioning the trade balance over the long swing. It seems more logical, therefore, to treat the flow of gold as a movement attempting to remove *internal* disequilibrium (excess demands for real-money balances concomitant with variations in real-income growth over the long swing) than as a simple short-run mechanism for adjusting external imbalances.

Not only do long swings in net gold flows exist (1825-1842, 1849-1861, and two swings between 1879 and 1913), but also in all but one case, 1849-1861, they move in *sympathy* with business activity. Maximum inflow generally conforms with peaks in domestic activity. If anything, the specie-price mechanism is disequilibrating in the short-run sense since it responds in a fashion which may tend to magnify the long swing rather than dampen it. In a growth model which includes a money demand function, these gold flows are *equilibrating*. The positive correlation between rates of economic development and rates of gold inflow seems to be due to the more violent amplitudes of net capital movements relative to the trade balance over the long swing. Thus, not only do net capital movements allow maximum growth performance to continue over long periods of time, but they add further impetus to domestic growth by supplying in increasing amounts a widening base for liquidity expansion on the Kuznets cycle upswing. And to repeat, this cannot be considered purely a fortuitous circumstance. On the contrary, the balance-of-payments components form a part very closely related to the whole of the general equilibrium growth matrix. The flow of gold seems to respond in a functional way to excess demands for money over the long swing in real income: it is fortuitous in the sense that net capital flows are excessive enough to oversatisfy excess demands for real-money balances while, if net capital inflows had not been forthcoming in increasing amounts, severe interference with maximum growth performance might have occurred prior to the secular peak.

The period 1842-1861 is the only exception during the nineteenth century to the less restrictive hypothesis that gold inflow is positively related to income movements over the long swing. It is not, however, an exception to a model which states that net gold flows are conditioned by excess demand in the money market. During this time span, for various and complex reasons, net capital movements were not sufficient to finance the usual expanding trade deficit. But this was also a period of unusual domestic gold production, which allowed continued development without enormous needs for foreign capital. The export of gold financed that deficit, and yet domestic gold production was still large enough to allow the domestic system sufficient liquidity. An excess supply of money released gold from the domestic system.

But if there are long swings in the rate of net gold flows that are positively related to (exante) excess demand for real-money balances, do they have a consistent relation with the rate of growth of the money supply (expost)? We have found that in some periods the internal production of gold reduces the importance of external gold flows (1849-1861). In other periods fluctuation in the reserve ratio dispels such a relationship (1825-1842, 1904-1914), while in 1862-1878 America gives up the gold-standard system entirely. When both assumptions have been satisfied—minor fluctuations in the reserve ratio and unimportant domestic gold production—net gold flows become a powerful and consistent determinant of rate of change in the money stock (1879-1904). For a quarter of a century at least, long swings in net gold flows explain the same secular movement in the money stock.[15]

This evidence certainly has important implications for theories which regard the growth of the money supply as entirely episodic, exogenous, and a function of the vagaries of the banking system. It also throws a very dark shadow on the hypothesis that these long swings in economic growth, in United States history, are primarily induced by monetary conditions. For a quarter of a century at least, 1879-1904, it does not seem possible that secular movements in the money stock can be *caused* by gold flows synchronous with movements in the balance of payments and, at the same time, *cause* long swings in the balance of payments via income movement.[16]

---

15. Even in periods when the *secular* movements of the two series are not alike, *annual* movements do coincide. Thus, this does *not* eliminate the possibility that gold flows explain the apparent turning points of domestic activity even when the over-all secular movement of domestic activity is unlike that of the changes in the money stock.

16. Unless, of course, we consider rates of change in the money stock as the important independent variable rather than absolute levels of the money stock relative to real income. In this case, the two statements in the above paragraph may not be inconsistent but only unsuitable partners. Moses Abramovitz has pointed out that the problem of whether the money supply contributed to the demise of the boom of the 1880's cannot be resolved simply in terms of acceleration or retardation in the growth of the money supply. The rate of expansion of the money supply may become a difficulty not when it suffers retardation but when that rate falls below some critical level (depending on the complex growth of liquidity demands). One must agree that although the money supply was expanding rapidly from 1885 to 1892, we cannot decide whether it was fast enough just by examining a chart of the money supply itself. See Williamson, "Real Growth . . . 1879-1900," pp. 178-179.

# VI.

## COMPARISON AND INTERACTIONS WITH THE BRITISH BALANCE OF PAYMENTS, 1820-1913

### The Problem

There are two excellent justifications for including a brief examination of nineteenth-century British balance of payments (see Table B-19) with a more extensive investigation of domestic long swings and their effects upon the American balance of payments. Since there is preliminary evidence of a long swing in many British domestic series *after* 1870, especially in home investment,[1] it seems fruitful to study British experience in order to throw further light upon the question of Kuznets cycles in internal development and their effect upon the international flow of goods, capital, and specie.

Realistically, we should anticipate different secular movements in the balance of payments of an important capital exporter from

---

1. Cairncross, Matthews, Lewis and O'Leary, and Thomas, among others, have shown the most interest in the evidence of long swings, or Kuznets cycles, in British home and foreign investment.

those of a chronic capital importer, even when faced with the evidence of internal long swings in both the lending and receiving nations. But as with the relation between American internal development and her capital imports, British capital exports should exhibit an inverse relation with the pace of internal development or with domestic outlets for domestic savings. That is, when the pace of British internal development was low, English investors should have shifted increasingly to more lucrative investments abroad, just as when American business experienced retardation there was a net reduction in capital imports or even a serious net export of capital.

Dissimilarities may arise for at least two major reasons. First, because of its resource endowment and small size, foreign trade played and does play a much greater role in the British system than in the American. Thus, although British and American experience may *both* reflect an inverse relation between domestic and foreign investment over the Kuznets cycle, net foreign investment assumed a much more important role as a determinant in British aggregate demand than in American. Cairncross estimated that between 1875 and 1914 a little more than 40 per cent of British capital investment was in net capital exports, while in 1913 the share was as large as 50 per cent.[2] This averages about *three or four times* the American estimates (presented in Chapter IV): in the post-1860 period the highest share of net capital imports in total capital accumulation was 27 per cent, while the average share from 1870 to 1900, *during periods of positive inflow alone,* lies between only 10-15 per cent (see Table 33).[3]

---

2. A. K. Cairncross, *Home and Foreign Investment, 1870-1913* (Cambridge: Cambridge University Press, 1953), pp. 2, 4.

3. Of course, *changes* in net foreign investment would be more pertinent than absolute levels in determining the relative importance of capital movements as a stabilizing component of aggregate demand. However, United States fluctuations in the import of capital are not so much more violent than British variations in the export of capital. For that matter, it is also true that net capital flows are not precise measures of net foreign investment.

Cairncross' estimates are consistent with some recent comparisons of the importance of external trade (exports plus imports of goods) as a share of total income. Deutsch and Eckstein estimate that from 1860 to 1920 British external trade was 50-60 per cent of national income. The same share in the United States was 15-20 per cent during the period 1819-1839 and 10-15 per cent from 1859 to 1909. Thus again British trade played a role about four to five times that of the United States in their respective economies (K. W. Deutsch and A. Eckstein, "National Industriali-

Apart from relative internal conditions, we should anticipate much less violent fluctuations in aggregate output and income over the long swing in home investment, due to the offsetting effects of changes in net capital exports on aggregate demand. British import demand, therefore, should reveal mild fluctuations, since imports are generally written as some function of national output. In this respect, however, Cairncross, Lewis and O'Leary, and Matthews put the argument in much stronger terms than either Thomas or we would. The former imply that evidence of a long swing in British national output, and in all expenditures related to it, would be lacking. It seems more cautious, but more nearly correct, to suggest that a dampening of the domestic long swing occurred and that severe depressions and excessive booms in aggregate demand at the troughs and peaks of long swings in the rate of development were more likely to be avoided. Although severe fluctuations in aggregate demand may have been cushioned over the long swing, this does not imply a constant growth path of capacity output or that fluctuations in domestic investment were completely offset.

The second major difference between British and American balance-of-payments movements over the Kuznets cycle would lie in export movements. As a capital exporter, especially under the assumption of mild import fluctuations, the rate of expansion of the export industry ought to be very closely related to the out-flow of foreign capital. Whereas American experience revealed import movements dominating the trade balance to facilitate the real transfer, we should expect that British trade-balance fluctuations were dominated, and the real transfer facilitated, by exports. And finally, since export movements should be inversely related to long swings in British home investment, the trade balance should have reached peak deficits at high levels of British home investment and at low levels of net capital exports—movements, though caused in a different manner, precisely like those found in United States experience.

Besides using this excursion into British balance-of-payments history in a comparative manner, there is a second and perhaps

zation and the Declining Share of the International Economic Sector, 1890-1959," *World Politics,* XIII [January, 1961], 267-299).

more pertinent justification for the research which follows in this chapter. We have attempted with some success to include conditions in Great Britain as an explanatory factor of American net capital imports, but did American Kuznets cycles also have *direct* effects upon British economic conditions via balance-of-payments movements?[4] That is, did fluctuations in United States import demand have profound and direct effects upon total British exports, was the American market too small, did other developing nations take up the slack, or were all the factors in effect? The problem can be reworded more elegantly to ask whether or not the United States simultaneously created its own increasing supply of foreign capital on Kuznets cycle upswings by dominating fluctuations in the rate of expansion of British export markets and thereby creating a concomitant trade-balance surplus in Great Britain; if not, the interrelationship becomes much more subtle.

The second possible direct influence is through prices of traded goods. We may find that any evidence of a mild long swing in British import demands is eliminated by raw material and foodstuff price movements. If grain and cotton prices dominate British import price movements, American export prices in cotton and, to a lesser extent, grain may have had a profound influence upon British imports *in current prices,* at least prior to 1860-1870. Before the 1860's American export prices were positively related to domestic activity, while over the nineteenth century as a whole British and American internal development moved inversely. It is likely that British import demand moved inversely with American export prices, and thus it seems reasonable to expect that American export prices had a smoothing influence on British imports in current prices.[5]

We have seen in earlier chapters that supply conditions of investment funds in Great Britain played an important role in determining the amplitude of American net capital imports over

---

4. *Indirect* effects are those which the migration of labor had upon income and prices in both nations.

5. Chapter III showed that United States imports and import prices exhibit a reasonably significant positive correlation over the long swing. This *may* be explained in the same manner since in this case American import demand and British export prices move in sympathy. Given our assumptions above, it is more likely that British imports and import prices move inversely.

the Kuznets cycle. The final direct effect of United States balance of payments upon British balance of payments might include an examination of the importance of American security markets in influencing British capital exports. It is not necessary that America's share of British capital export was large, only that its fluctuations in demand for British capital were excessive enough to dictate long swings in British capital exports.

It should be frankly admitted at the outset that the research and analysis which follows is much less extensive than our examination of American balance of payments. This chapter actually raises more questions than it answers, especially with regard to the framework of the Atlantic economy envisioned by Brinley Thomas or the broader interactions in nineteenth-century development of capital-scarce, agricultural, raw-material-producing nations and capital-rich, manufactures-producing nations. The major question of the evidence of long swings in Australian, Argentine, Canadian, and other nations' development and international interactions over the course of nineteenth-century expansion must be deferred until a later time.

*British Imports: 1820-1913*

Our expectations concerning import movements are supported by the data.[6] Even after removing the trend, British imports in current prices reveal no evidence whatsoever of long swings (see Table B-20). What the trend removal *does* exhibit are longer movements associated with "Kondratieff" swings in import prices. In the trendless series, British imports in current prices fall steadily for about twenty years from the mid-twenties to the mid-forties, rise consistently over a longer period of thirty years until the mid-1870's, fall to a secular trough in the mid-1890's, and then expand until World War I. Not surprisingly, this con-

---

6. All the British balance-of-payments estimates are taken from Albert H. Imlah's most recent publication, *Economic Elements in the Pax Britannica* (Cambridge, Mass.: Harvard University Press, 1958). Imlah utilizes the same techniques employed by North and Simon in estimating nineteenth-century net capital flows. (See Appendix A.) However, it should be noted that Imlah's transportation account, which is an important part of his balance of payments, has been the subject of criticism. See particularly the article by Douglass C. North and Alan Heston, "The Estimation of Shipping Earnings in Historical Studies of the Balance of Payments," *Canadian Journal of Economics and Political Science*, XXVI (May, 1960), 265-276.

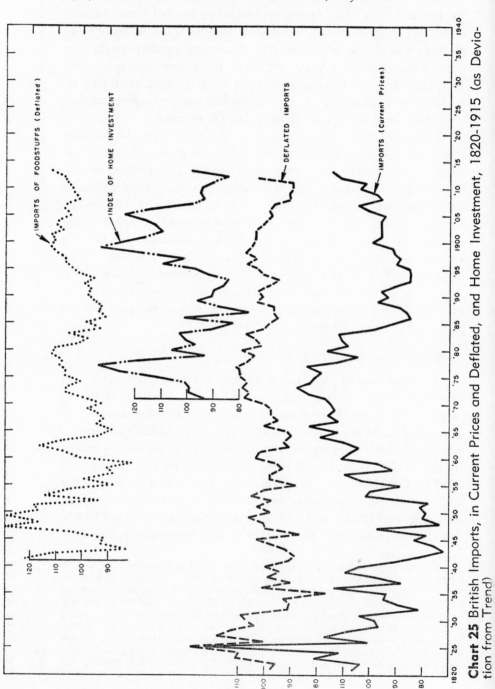

**Chart 25** British Imports, in Current Prices and Deflated, and Home Investment, 1820-1915 (as Deviation from Trend)

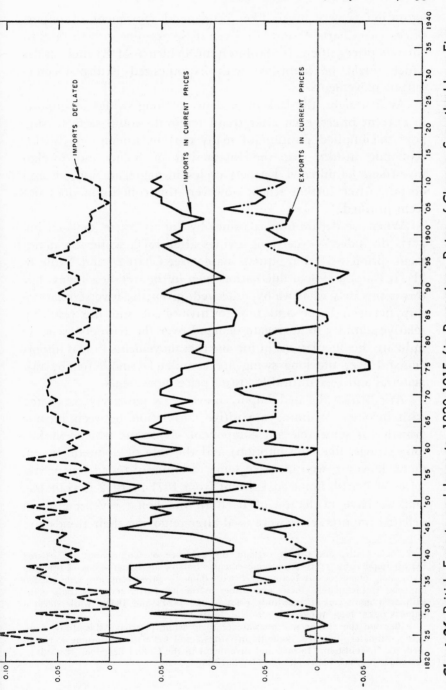

**Chart 26** British Exports and Imports, 1820-1915 (in Percentage Rates of Change, Smoothed by a Five-Year Moving Average)

*Source:* Tables A-19 and A-21

figuration is very much like the general movement of import prices (see Charts 25 and 26). Even if we examine growth rates in current prices, there is absolutely no evidence of Kuznets cycles which might be identified with hypothesized British income-output movements.

At first sight, the lack of evidence of long swings in imports in current prices, even after trend removal, would seem to support the implied position of many current students of British economic history that the interaction of home and foreign investment eliminated Kuznets cycles in aggregate income and output. After further study, however, this conclusion does not seem justified.

When we deflate import values by import prices, deflated imports do indeed reveal long swings after 1860, while the movements prior to 1860 are questionable (see Chart 25 and Table B-21). It is not a violent fluctuation even in the trendless index, but this is precisely what we hypothesized, given the inverse relationship between home and foreign investment and the resulting relative stability in aggregate demand over the Kuznets cycle. So mild are the fluctuations in income that movements in real import demand over the long swing are completely smothered by raw material and agricultural foodstuff price movements.[7]

Are British deflated import movements positively correlated with income? Assuming a positive correlation between income growth (or some relevant component of income which exhibits long swings, like consumption) and the rate of domestic investment, however, we can make some meaningful tests.[8] Cairncross' series of British home investment from 1871 to 1913 is available, and we have made use of it. Both the home investment and deflated imports series were used after removing their trends and

---

7. Incidentally, one cannot explain the evidence of long swings in deflated British imports by terms-of-trade movements. Imlah's net barter terms of trade do reveal long swings positively correlated with domestic investment and with deflated imports. Unfortunately, these long swings in the net barter terms of trade occur with even more violent amplitude prior to the 1850's and 1860's, while deflated imports reveal long swings only *after* the 1850's.

8. Because the author was unaware of them while preparing this study, Feinstein's estimates of British domestic investment and net national income were not used (C. H. Feinstein, "Income and Investment in the United Kingdom, 1856-1914," *Economic Journal*, LXXI [June, 1961], 367-385).

smoothing. A simple univariate regression exhibits a positive cor-relation between the two series where the explanatory power of domestic investment ($I_{UK}$) over deflated imports ($M_D$) is surprisingly high:

$$(1871\text{-}1913) \qquad M_D = 73.47 + 0.2597 I_{UK}, \qquad R^2 = 0.837,$$
$$(0.0190)$$

and as we might have expected, the coefficient of $I_{UK}$ is low, 0.26, reflecting the relative mildness of income movements compared with domestic investment.

The conclusion then is that not only were there long swings in deflated imports, but also they were positively related to "income" movements. Nevertheless, they seemed to have been mild enough to be eliminated by active and inversely correlated import price movements. When deflated imports were at high levels in the late 1840's and early 1850's, import prices reached a secular trough. When deflated imports troughed in the mid-1860's, prices achieved fantastic heights. Finally, when deflated imports peaked in the late 1890's, prices again fell to a secular trough. Although general world price movements were little different from British import price movements, the violence in amplitude of those prices surely must be explained in part by supply conditions in the American cotton and grain markets prior to 1870-1880 (see especially Chapter II). Thus, it is the variation in agricultural and raw material prices from the general world price trend which removes the evidence of long swings in British import demand. For approximately two decades, the late 1860's and the 1870's, American wheat exports play a fairly important role in dictating the state of the grain market, while prior to 1860 the cotton market is almost entirely dominated by American exports. And both these commodities make up by far the largest share of British imports.[9]

One more observation might be made before passing on to the more violent swings in export movements. Deflated imports reveal Kuznets cycles after the late 1850's and until 1913, but the

---

9. With regard to cotton imports and import prices, see Imlah, *Economic Elements,* pp. 103-104.

evidence of long swings *before* the American Civil War is thin indeed. There is a long swing in deflated food imports, to be sure, but this may be explained by a major British policy change into free trade. This may also explain the mild secular "swing" in deflated imports over the 1830's and 1840's. No explanation can be offered for the severe fall in deflated imports in the early and mid-1830's.

This lack of long swings in British history prior to the 1850's is also true, we shall see, of net capital exports, which had configurations more like seven- to ten-year than twenty-year cycles, and of merchandise exports, which did not reveal long swings until the late 1840's and early 1850's. Was the same thing true of British income movements?

Since net capital exports were certainly no more severe in their amplitude and were less important as a share in total investment prior to the 1860's,[10] any explanation of observed stability in income-output movements should be attributable to the pattern of British home investment itself. In this respect, Thomas disagrees with Lewis and O'Leary since he believes that there is no evidence of British building cycles from 1830 to 1850.[11] Cooney, in a recent article, puts the argument in even stronger terms: "The first main point to be made here is that there does not seem to be enough evidence to establish the existence of a (roughly) twenty year building cycle in British history before 1870."[12] Cairncross and Weber also support the view that, prior to 1850 at least, there is evidence of indigenous seven- to ten-year cycles but none of building cycles.[13] Based mainly on Shannon's brick index,[14] Cairncross and Weber date major peaks in 1819, 1825, 1836, and 1847 and major troughs in 1821, 1832, and 1842.

---

10. R. C. O. Matthews, *The Business Cycle* (Chicago: University of Chicago Press, 1959), p. 222.

11. Brinley Thomas, *Migration and Economic Growth* (Cambridge: Cambridge University Press, 1954), p. 175.

12. E. W. Cooney, "Long Waves in Building in the British Economy of the Nineteenth Century," *Economic History Review*, Second Series, XIII (December, 1960), 258.

13. A. K. Cairncross and B. Weber, "Fluctuations in Building in Great Britain, 1785-1849," *Economic History Review*, Second Series, IX (December, 1956), 283-297.

14. H. A. Shannon, "Bricks—a Trade Index," *Economica*, N.S. I (1934), 300-318.

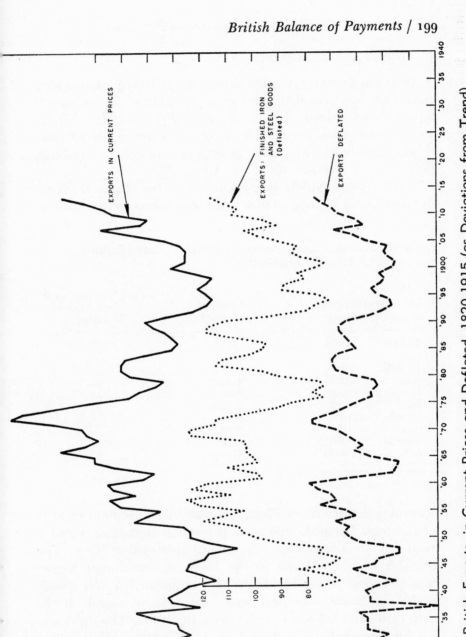

EXPORTS IN CURRENT PRICES

EXPORTS: FINISHED IRON
AND STEEL GOODS
(Deflated)

EXPORTS DEFLATED

**Chart 27** British Exports, in Current Prices and Deflated, 1820-1915 (as Deviations from Trend)

*Source:* Tables A-22, A-23, and Thomas, Table 103, p. 293

## British Exports: 1820-1913

Over the Kuznets cycle, the movements in British exports were much more apparent than those in imports. Generally, the rate of expansion in British exports was inversely related to deflated imports (and thus, presumably, to income) and exhibited more violent amplitude. This is true in both rates of change (see Chart 26) and in the trendless series (see Chart 27).

Nevertheless, exports in current prices (see Table B-22) are also dominated by long secular price movements so that without

**Table 40** Dating of Long Swings in British Deflated Exports and Imports[a] (Trend Removed)

| Deflated Exports (trendless) | | Deflated Imports (trendless) | | Lead (+) or Lag (—) of Imports over Exports Inverted |
|---|---|---|---|---|
| Trough | 1848 | | | |
| Peak | 1860 | | | |
| Trough | 1864 | | | |
| Peak | 1871 | Trough | 1864 | +7 |
| Trough | 1878 | Peak | 1877 | +1 |
| Peak | 1882 | Trough | — | — |
| Trough | (1885) | Peak | — | — |
| Peak | (1889) | Trough | 1886 | —4 (+3) |
| Trough | 1901 | Peak | 1898 | +3 |
| Peak | 1913T | Trough | 1910 | +3 |

[a]Where T means last year in series.

examining deflated exports first, it is somewhat difficult to identify long swings. Deflated exports as percentage deviations about a trend exhibit almost four long swings (see Table B-23). The first rose from low levels in the 1840's to increasingly higher rates of export in the late 1850's and terminated with a trough in the mid-1860's. The next long swing rose to a peak in the early 1870's and fell to a trough late in the 1870's. The third rose to a double peak in the early and late 1880's, with an intermediate trough between, and then fell to a trough at the turn of the century. Exports then expanded continually up to 1913 and the war. These long swings are less evident in the trendless current price series, but even there they are quite clear in rates of change (see Chart 26).

The dating for deflated exports and imports with their trends removed is given in Table 40. After 1870 the inverse correlation between export and import movements is quite striking, with imports generally leading by from one to three years.[15] Prior to 1870, however, the inverse relationship almost disappears, while before 1850, of course, there is not enough evidence of a long swing in imports to date them. The inverse relationship between

**Table 41** Comparison of Long-Swing Dating of United States Deflated Imports and British Deflated Exports[a] (Trend Removed)

|  | (1)<br>U.S. Deflated Imports (trendless and annual) | (2)<br>British Deflated Exports (trendless and annual) | Lead (+) or Lag(—)<br>of (1) over (2) |
|---|---|---|---|
| Trough | 1821 |  |  |
| Peak | 1836 |  |  |
| Trough | 1843 | 1848 | +5 |
| Peak | 1854 | 1860 | +6 |
| Trough | 1862 | 1864 | +2 |
| Peak | 1872 | 1871 | —1 |
| Trough | 1878 | 1878 | 0 |
| Peak | 1883 | 1882 | —1 |
| Trough | (1885) | (1885) | 0 |
| Peak | (1888) | (1889) | +1 |
| Trough | 1898 | 1901 | +3 |
| Peak | 1913T | 1913T | 0 |

[a]Where T means last year in series.

imports and exports seems to have become more consistent and precise as the century progressed. Can we go one step further and suggest that the same would also hold true of net capital exports and the rate of home investment?

Deflated British exports moved inversely to deflated British

---

15. Since imports lead exports in almost all cases, one might expect to find income or domestic investment movements also leading exports. This would seem to throw weight behind the argument that Juglar cycles in British experience after 1870 are only superficial cycles caused by the incomplete compensation between capital exports and domestic investment over a larger swing of twenty years. See especially Matthews, *The Business Cycle,* p. 223.

imports, at least over most of the latter half of the nineteenth-century, but they also moved *directly* with United States import fluctuations. This is true for the period after the late 1840's and until 1913, but there is no long swing in deflated British exports from 1820 to 1850. (There *was* a long swing in the rates of growth of exports in current prices over the nineteenth century as a whole, including 1820-1850. This is discussed extensively below.) Table 41 compares the dating of deflated British exports and deflated American imports. Although there is obvious similarity in movement and timing throughout—but not in amplitude—the lead-lag relationship is much better in the latter half of the nineteenth-century. Indeed, the timing of the British and American

**Table 42** Comparison Between British Exports to the United States and Total British Exports, by Decades, 1850-1913

| Years | British Exports to U.S. ÷ Total British Exports | Net Change in British Exports to U.S. ÷ Net Changes in Total British Exports |
|-------|:---:|:---:|
| 1850-1859 | 0.19 | 0.14 |
| 1860-1869 | 0.13 | 0.17 |
| 1870-1879 | 0.14 | 0.39 |
| 1880-1889 | 0.18 | 0.38 |
| 1890-1899 | 0.19 | 0.45 |
| 1900-1909 | 0.16 | 0.19 |
| 1910-1913 | 0.16 | 0.20 |

series is so close after 1860, especially in a comparison of annual data, as to suggest that American import demand played an important role in determining the rate of expansion of total British exports.

Fortunately we can apply a better test than this to determine the importance of the American market in conditioning the state of the British export industry. We can compare increments in total British exports to foreign countries and British exports to the United States—data which are available in the British *Parliamentary Papers*. Were Kuznets cycles in the rate of expansion of British exports in current prices caused by violent fluctuations in

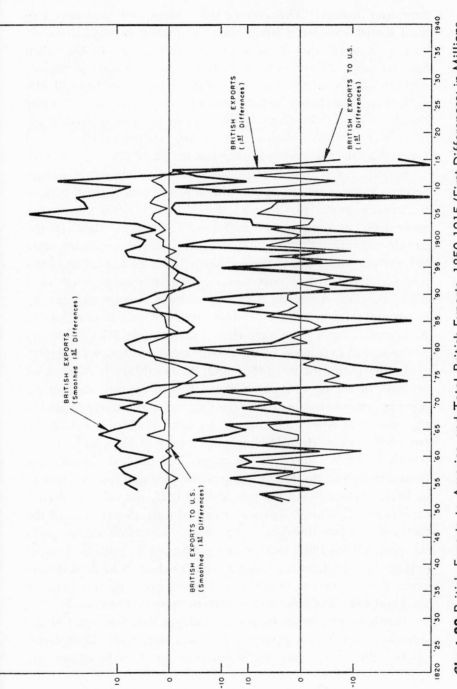

**Chart 28** British Exports to America and Total British Exports, 1850-1915 (First Differences; in Millions of Pounds Sterling)

*Source:* British Parliamentary Papers

American demand? The average share of exports to America in total British exports is significant: the highest average share occurred between the decades of the 1880's and 1890's when approximately 20 per cent of British exports to foreign nations went to the United States. The marginal share, the ratio of first differences, was much larger, reaching its highest share in the decade of the 1890's when 45 per cent of changes in British exports were attributable to changes in exports to the United States. The decade averages are given in Table 42.

Perhaps even more impressive is the striking similarity between the movements of first differences in total British exports to America shown in Chart 28. From 1850 to 1900 these series move together both in the smoothed and annual data. In the decade and one-half after 1900, the series exhibit much less similarity when American markets apparently ceased to play as vital a role for the British export industry over the long swing (and when the last American frontier, Canada, began to play an important role). It should be clear, however, that fluctuations in American demand must have been a major cause for long swings in the rate of expansion of the British export industry 1850-1900.

In the period of the 1830's and 1840's, although there is no evidence of a long swing in deflated British exports, current exports in rates of change do reveal a long swing positively related to movements in American imports. In rates of change, British exports fell to a trough in 1824, reached a peak in 1834, and fell to a trough in 1839. United States imports, in rates of change, rose from a trough in the 1820's to a peak in 1833 and fell to a trough in 1842. Averaged over the period 1833-1842, the value of British exports to the United States constituted only 15 per cent of the total value of British exports. The *proportional* fluctuations, as in the period 1860-1900, were much greater. The average ratio of changes in exports to the United States to changes in total British exports was as high as 58 per cent. There is only one year between 1833 and 1842 when the series move in opposite directions.

Matthews concluded from this evidence that "the state of the American market was therefore the most important single factor in bringing prosperity or depression to British export industries."[16] There are two problems, however, which surround such a strong conclusion concerning the effect of American import demand on English industry during the 1830's and 1840's. First, American imports in current prices *and* deflated exhibited long swings. Why were British exports affected only in current prices? This was not true of the later years. Second, the fluctuation in British exports in current prices was extremely mild, even in rates of change, and certainly nothing like those which appeared after the 1860's. It is thus difficult to believe that American import demands seriously imposed long-swing fluctuations on the British export industry at this stage of the nineteenth century, and certainly there is no evidence that the British economy as a whole was enmeshed in the long-swing mechanism. It seems more likely that the direct effects of the American long swing on British development began during the period 1848-1864, when evidence of Kuznets cycles in British exports became clear (although the British domestic economy at this stage was not yet undergoing long swings).

There is another interesting aspect of this comparison. Prior to and after 1870, when both series are expanding rapidly, increases in British exports exceed increases in exports to the United States. This is to be expected over a long period where secular expansion of the export industry is not dependent upon United States demand alone. It is also true that changing American factor proportions must have tended to cause a proportional shift out of British exports over a period of time. But at troughs of long swings, things are quite different. Prior to 1870 and in periods of depression in the American market, total British exports decrease at a lesser rate than American imports from Great Britain. After 1870, however, changes in total British exports have more violent movements during *both* booms and prolonged depressions over the Kuznets cycle. This suggests to us that prior to 1870 only the United States was undergoing long swings in demand for British products whereas after 1870 other developing nations with demands for British manufactures must also have been undergoing long swings that were similar in timing to American movements.

---

16. R. C. O. Matthews, *A Study in Trade Cycle History: 1833-1842* (Cambridge: Cambridge University Press, 1954), pp. 43-44.

This conclusion seems consistent with earlier movements as well, since Matthews' figures show negative first differences in British exports to the United States during American depressions from 1833 to 1842. We shall return to this point below in our discussion of British capital exports.

### British Balance of Trade: 1820-1913

Thus far we have seen only dissimilarities between America and Britain in the flow of goods over the long swing. Nevertheless, it does seem that long swings in United States development had an immediate effect upon British conditions through British export movements and, to a much lesser extent, via British import prices.

The similarities begin with balance-of-trade movements. Just as with American trade-balance movements, the British trade-balance deficit grew progressively worse during periods of domestic boom over the Kuznets cycle, while it became less unfavorable during periods of domestic depression and massive capital export. But after 1860 American trade-balance fluctuations inversely related to domestic expansion over periods of from fifteen to twenty years were almost entirely due to violent income, and thus import, movements. British trade-balance fluctuations were certainly less violent, but their significant amplitude was due entirely to fluctuations in the rate of export expansion since imports in current prices reveal no long swing. Thus an improvement in the British trade balance during depressions in domestic investment is not normally to be explained by a reduction in import values (although real import demand decreases) but rather by an expansion of export values.

Long swings in the British balance of trade really did not begin until 1860. However, if we choose a somewhat arbitrary date of 1847, we find the trade balance exhibits a mild secular improvement from the large deficit of this year up to 1859. The trade balance became sharply unfavorable from 1850 to the mid-1860's but remained constant and finally improved gradually up to 1872. From 1872 to the late 1870's the trade balance was progressively unfavorable but then reversed and became progressively more favorable until 1886. From 1886 until 1902 the trade

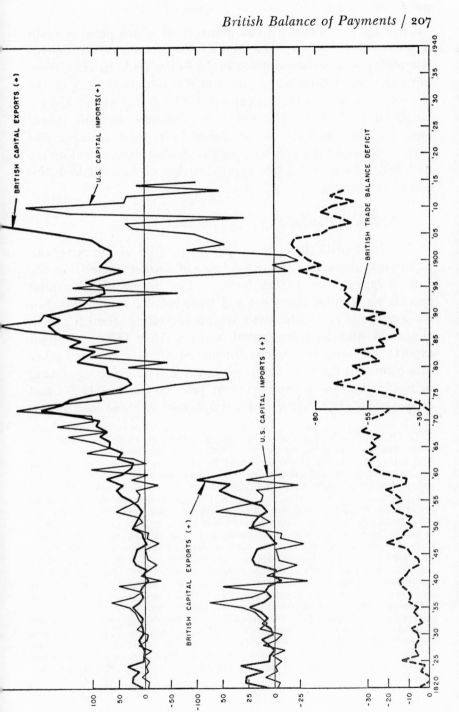

**Chart 29** British Trade Balance and Net Capital Exports (in Five Hundred Thousands of Pounds Sterling); United States Net Capital Imports (in Millions of Dollars), 1820-1915

*Source:* Tables A-1 and A-19

balance again deteriorated cumulatively, at which point it again improved until about 1911 (see Chart 29). Severe movements resembling long swings did not begin in the trade balance, then, until the late 1850's, which are also the initiating years of the more violent long swings in exports.[17] The dating of deflated exports, the trade balance, deflated imports, and domestic investment is shown in Table 43. It should be noted that imports in current prices do not exhibit long swings, but deflated values are included only as a further approximation of hypothesized "income" movements.

### British Net Capital Exports: 1820-1913

In the British balance of payments, just as in American experience, the most obvious evidence of Kuznets cycles is in the flow of capital over British borders. The timing of net capital exports was similar to export and trade-balance movements, but the amplitude of capital flows was more violent—though not as violent as American net capital imports. After 1870 net capital exports and home investment did indeed complement each other in a consistent fashion. Nevertheless, there is no evidence of long swings in the rate of capital export prior to the late 1850's and early 1860's. After that time the amplitudes of those long swings

---

17. Although rates of growth of imports in current prices do not reveal long swings over the nineteenth century as a whole and deflated imports do not reveal long swings prior to the 1850's, the period 1828-1841 *does* exhibit a movement in import values (in rates of change) similar to export movements. Indeed, this is the *only* period when import values indicate evidence of something akin to the long-swing mechanism. Apparently, although real-income movements do not seem to reveal a long swing 1820-1840 and thus similarly for deflated imports, price fluctuations (primarily American cotton prices) are severe enough to cause a movement in import values similar to, and exceeding in rate of change, export movements. Thus, in spite of the long swing in rates of change of exports in current values from 1824 to 1839, the trade balance does not reflect it in such a way as to extend the evidence of long swings in the trade balance (positively related to export movements) back before the 1850's. Compared to the other nineteenth century movements this is indeed a very unusual period in English history. One cannot help but be further impressed with the dissimilarity between British secular movements prior to the 1850's and afterwards. Apparently, the long swing, which was already so evident in United States development, either had not yet foisted itself upon English development or whatever endogenous conditions were necessary to generate the long swing were not yet in evidence. Surely the popularized mechanism of the interaction of the Atlantic economy was not the same prior to 1850 as after that year.

in capital flows unquestionably become more severe. Prior to the late 1850's net capital exports from Great Britain played a much smaller role in British development and in total investment. It is also true that prior to the late 1850's any fluctuations in net capital exports seem to have been primarily to the seven- to ten-year variety, peaking in 1835, 1844, 1850, and 1859 while troughing in 1840, 1847, and 1853. At least from 1830 to 1845 net capital exports moved consistently with building indices.[18] Nor is this

**Table 43** Long-Swing Dating for the British Trade Balance, Deflated Exports, Deflated Imports, and Home Investment[a]

| | Inverted British Trade Balance Deficit (annual data) | Deflated Exports (trendless) | | Home Investment[b] (trendless) | Deflated Imports (trendless) |
|---|---|---|---|---|---|
| Trough | 1847 (?) | 1848 | | | |
| Peak | 1859 | 1860 | | | |
| Trough | 1868 | 1864 | | | |
| Peak | 1872 | 1871 | Trough | 1871 | 1864 |
| Trough | 1877 | 1878 | Peak | 1877 | 1877 |
| Peak | — | 1882 | Trough | — | — |
| Trough | — | (1885) | Peak | — | — |
| Peak | 1886 | (1889) | Trough | 1887 | 1886 |
| Trough | 1902 | 1901 | Peak | 1899 | 1898 |
| Peak | 1911 | 1913 T | Trough | 1912 | 1910 |

[a]Where T means last year in series.
[b]Taken from Thomas, *Migration*, Table 100, p. 290.

positive relation inconsistent with experience after 1870, when domestic and foreign investment moved inversely over the long swing, for in that period as well domestic and foreign investment move positively over *short* cycles.[19]

From a peak outflow of capital in 1859, net capital exports fell to a trough in 1862. The first complete swing rose from that trough to an extremely high level of capital outflow in 1872 and then fell to a severe trough in 1877. This long swing rose rather gradually to the end of the decade of the 1860's before the massive outflow peaking in 1872. The second secular swing rose from a

18. Cairncross and Weber, "Fluctuations in Building . . . ," p. 285.
19. Cairncross, *Home and Foreign Investment.*

trough in 1877 to a peak in 1890 and then fell into the prolonged depression of the 1890's, the poorest year being 1898. From the decade of the 1890's, capital exports continued to increase until 1913, especially sharply from 1905 to the war (see Chart 29).

The general pattern and timing of these long swings in the net export of capital conform very well to our expectations (see Table 44). The net export of British capital is positively correlated with the trade-balance deficit, home investment, and

**Table 44** Long-Swing Dating of Net British Capital Exports Compared with Other Balance-of-Payments Components and Home Investment[a]

| | Net Export of British Capital | Deflated Exports (trendless) | | Trade Balance (deficit) | Home Investment Deflated | Deflated Imports (trendless) |
|---|---|---|---|---|---|---|
| Trough | — | 1848 | Peak | 1847 (?) | | |
| Peak | 1859 | 1860 | Trough | 1859 | | |
| Trough | 1862 | 1864 | Peak | 1868 | | |
| Peak | 1872 | 1871 | Trough | 1872 | 1871 | 1864 |
| Trough | 1877 | 1878 | Peak | 1877 | 1877 | 1877 |
| Peak | — | 1882 | Trough | — | — | — |
| Trough | — | (1885) | Peak | — | — | — |
| Peak | 1890 | (1889) | Trough | 1886 | 1887 | 1886 |
| Trough | 1898 | 1901 | Peak | 1902 | 1899 | 1898 |
| Peak | 1913T | 1913T | Trough | 1911 | 1912 | 1910 |

[a]Where T means last year in series.

deflated imports. On the average, net capital exports lead deflated exports by about two years (the lead would possibly be longer if export movements were expressed in annual data). We find home investment (inverted) leading net capital exports by one or two years, similar to the lead of deflated imports over deflated exports. Thus, foreign and domestic investment do not quite mesh over the long swing. It may be quite true that this lag of British savers moving out of domestic and into foreign investment explains the apparent evidence of a Juglar cycle.

Although the evidence seems to support the hypothesis that American import demands played an extremely important role in determining the level and movements of British exports, at least after 1850, it is more difficult to make the same statement for capital flows. Surely the timing and general pattern of British exports and American imports of capital were extremely similar. Nevertheless, it is difficult to say much more than this for the nineteenth century as a whole due to the limited quantitative information available. After the late 1850's it is clear that American capital imports move as if they dominated British capital exports due to the similarity of timing and pattern over the long swing. But could this be the result of long swings in other countries as well?

A comparison between the contributions of American demands for imports of British goods and capital to fluctuations in total British exports of goods and capital is extremely interesting. Recall from Table 42 that net change in commodity exports to America as a share in total changes in British commodity exports reached its peak level of importance during the decade 1890-1899. The importance of American demands apparently increases up to that decade and declines thereafter. The secular pattern in the relative importance of American demands for British investment, however, is somewhat different.

Two pieces of evidence show that, at some stages in the nineteenth century, United States demands for British capital were clearly the major determinant of the long-swing pattern in British capital exports. One source of evidence which positively points to the importance of American demands for capital lies in Madden's research.[20] Table 35 shows that 60-65 per cent of the fluctuations in British capital exports from 1860 to 1880 were due to fluctuations in American demands for capital over the long swing! If this were true of all the long swings in the nineteenth century, we would conservatively conclude that American demands did indeed directly determine the extent and timing of British capital export fluctuations over the long swing.

More recent research by Simon and Segal, however, tells a more complete story (which at the same time confirms Madden's results). Using their data constructed from quantitative information on British new capital issues, we find that the rela-

---

20. John J. Madden, "British Investment in the United States, 1860-1880," Conference on Research in Income and Wealth (New York: National Bureau of Economic Research, 1957; mimeographed), Table 10, p. 46.

tive importance of North American new issues to total issues is the following: over the upswing 1867-1874 changes in the rate of North American issues explain 72.3 per cent of total changes in issues while on the subsequent downswing 1874-1877 the figure is 68.7 per cent.[21] These ratios are very similar to the Madden estimates and do indeed confirm the notion that American demands for British capital dictated total variations in British capital exports.[22] But the interesting aspect of the Segal-Simon data is that it reveals a sharp decline in the relative importance of American demands for British capital in the following decades. The ratio of net changes in American issues to net changes in total issues is 27.4 per cent on the long upswing 1877-1889 and 25.9 per cent on the subsequent downswing 1889-1893! The evidence thus far suggests, therefore, that up to the 1850's violent fluctuations in American demands for British capital had little effect upon variations in total British capital exports. After 1860, however, and until 1880 variations in American demands over the long swing produced similar long swings in total British capital exports. From 1880 to 1900 the relative importance of American long swings falls to rather low levels and can no longer be considered the definite cause of British variations in capital exports. As far as the period 1896-1913 is concerned, there seems to be little doubt that variations in Canadian demands for British capital become the geographic cause for long swings in British capital exports.[23]

What is the implication of all this evidence? It would seem that it takes a combination of *three* things to cause a long swing in net capital movements in the case of this capital exporter. Long swings in the demand for capital in the United States were not enough to cause similar British movements (i.e., pre-1850's) either because the United States was too small as a source of demand or, *and more likely,* one of the other two necessary

---

21. Derived from Harvey H. Segal and Matthew Simon, "British Foreign Capital Issues, 1865-1894," *Journal of Economic History*, Vol. XXI (December, 1961), Appendix Table, p. 579.

22. North America includes, of course, both Canada and the United States. This accounts for the somewhat higher Segal-Simon figure relative to the Madden results.

23. See, for instance, John A. Stovel, *Canada in the World Economy* (Cambridge, Mass.: Harvard University Press, 1959).

ingredients was missing. If income growth was approximately constant in the rest of the world outside of the United States, it should have been relatively simple for British investors to shift between American securities and those of other countries according to the vitality of American development and the return on capital, as was apparently the case prior to the 1850's. Thus, a long swing in American development and demands for foreign capital need not be reflected in total British capital exports. Nor,

**Table 45** Comparison of Long Secular Movements in American Net Capital Imports with Canadian, Australian, and Argentine Movements, 1850-1915[a]

|  | U.S. Capital Imports (net) | Canadian Capital Imports (net)[b] | Australian Capital Imports (net)[c] | Argentine Capital Imports (net)[d] |
|---|---|---|---|---|
| Peak | **1853** | | | |
| Trough | 1858 | | | |
| Peak | 1872 | 1873 | | |
| Trough | 1878 | 1879 | | 1880T |
| Peak | 1888 | 1890 | 1886 | 1888 |
| Trough | 1900 | 1897 | 1906 | 1900T |
| Peak | 1910 | 1912 | 1913T | |

[a]Where T means first or last year in series.

[b]Penelope Hartland, "Canadian Balance of Payments since 1868," *Trends in the American Economy in the Nineteenth Century* ("Studies in Income and Wealth," Vol. XXIV [Princeton, N. J.: University Press, 1960]), pp. 717-755.

[c]Roland Wilson, *Capital Imports and the Terms of Trade* (Melbourne: Melbourne University Press, 1931).

[d]John H. Williams, *Argentina International Trade Under Inconvertible Paper Money, 1880-1900* (Cambridge, Mass.: Harvard University Press, 1920).

for that matter, did long swings in British exports of goods (1848-1864) have an immediate impact upon the pattern of growth of the British economy.

One of the missing ingredients may be the lack of similar and inverse movements in the pace of development of the lending country. If Great Britain was undergoing a long swing as well, surely one would also expect to find a long swing in the rate of British capital export. The problem, then, is why there is so little evidence of long swings in British internal development prior to the 1850's. Can we suggest that American long swings in some indirect way triggered movements in Great Britain? This seems a more likely hypothesis than to attribute the creation of a domestic long-swing mechanism in Great Britain to something purely endogenous to the British system. For why do British and American movements exhibit this curious and suspicious inverse relation, and why do British long swings come relatively late in the century after the United States had been undergoing them for some time?[24]

The hypercyclical fluctuations which appeared in British building in that period [1850's and 1860's] owed their timing and amplitude largely to the impact on British industry, by way of migration and foreign investment, of the succession of long waves which had marked the development of the American economy since the 1830's.[25]

The second ingredient which seems to be in evidence after 1870 and not before, and which may help explain the appearance of Kuznets cycles in British capital exports after 1860, is the possible new occurrence of long swings in the pace of growth in more newly developing raw-material and foodstuff-producing nations. Not only did Canada exhibit what were obviously long swings in their consumption of foreign capital after 1870 (and mainly British: 68.8 per cent during the period 1900-1913[26]), but also their movements were inversely related to British internal development (see Table 45). This hardly should be surprising since Canada reasonably can be considered simply as another frontier in the American Western settlement.[27] But South America, and especially Argentina, also appears to have undergone the long-swing mechanism post Civil War. This is less true of the other "empty" countries.

24. H. J. Habakkuk reveals some skepticism concerning the interrelated Atlantic economy hypothesis. "There are reasons of domestic origin why the relation between British building fluctuations and the trade cycle should have changed and, in particular, why a long wave of building activity should have appeared" ("Fluctuations in House-Building in Britain and the United States in the Nineteenth Century," Journal of Economic History, XXII [June, 1962], p. 205).

25. Cooney, "Long Waves in Building . . . ," p. 267.

26. Stovel, Canada, p. 119.

27. Indeed, that frontier, like the American, was supplied by Eastern United States capital; 24.7 per cent of Canadian capital imports during 1900-1913 came from Americans (Stovel, Canada, p. 119).

...the long swings that we have observed are largely ascribable to the fluctuations in the North American and South American series, which comprise 50 per cent of the capital called during the thirty-year period [1865-1894] and much larger shares during the expansion phases of the long swings.... there is little trace of the two-swing pattern in the Australian, Asian and African series.[28]

For that matter, fluctuations in net capital imports into Canada and Argentina may have been the effect, not the cause, of fluctuations in British capital exports.

Thus, after 1880 when the relative importance of the United States in contributing to variation in British capital exports had declined, America may have already initiated the necessary conditions elsewhere to make the long swing interaction self-sustaining. The United States may have helped create long-swing patterns in Great Britain to produce the "push," and she may have also initiated long-swing "pull" patterns inversely related to those of Great Britain via, among other routes, the effects of American development upon raw material and foodstuff prices.

This chapter did not intend to examine exhaustively the possible direct interactions between British and American balance of payments. Nor was it intended to determine and test the causes of British balance-of-payments fluctuations over the long swing. What has been attempted here is to leave open the door so ably set ajar by Brinley Thomas in his examination of the interactions in the development of the Atlantic economy. The general impression in this preliminary analysis is that if there is indeed a systematic relationship between British and American development in the nature of a Kuznets cycle, that mechanism did not have its source in Great Britain but rather in the United States. If that statement is supported by future research, then it is only a small step to imagine how the powerful inverse rela-

---

28. Segal and Simon, "British Foreign Capital . . . ," p. 570. Given the information presented above, it becomes difficult to find much agreement with Saul's conclusion that "Britain was able to isolate herself to some extent, and other countries to a larger extent, from the effects of slumps in certain parts of the world by changing the direction of her capital exports" (S. B. Saul, *Studies in British Overseas Trade 1870-1914* [Liverpool: Liverpool University Press, 1960], p. 112). For information regarding the Argentine experience, see, for instance, A. G. Ford, "Flexible Exchange Rates and Argentina, 1885-1900," *Oxford Economic Papers*, N.S. X (October, 1958), 316-338, and *The Gold Standard, 1880-1914: Britain and Argentina* (New York: Oxford University Press, 1962).

tion in Anglo-American development spilled over into other more newly developing nations with factor endowments similar to those of the United States.

It seems clear that a large part of the Anglo-American interaction can be explained by the direct effects upon the British export industry of fluctuating United States demands for imports. Nevertheless, this is not meant to depreciate the importance of labor migration as an explanation for the inverse pattern of growth between these two countries. Long swings in American demands for imports can be traced back at least to 1820, but migration of labor from Europe to America did not really attain impressive heights until the 1840's and 1850's. Long swings in British development do not seem to be in evidence before that time, but do very soon afterwards. However, we now have an alternative hypothesis: from 1848 to 1864 British exports (current and deflated) showed definite long swings, but net capital exports and home investment did not. Could these fluctuations in British exports reflect an initiation of the transfer of American long swings into British development via demands for British exports? It seems more likely, however, that the interaction was a result of both the demand for goods and for migrants. Variations in American import demands strengthened the inverse movement, which became clear after the first really important flow of factors, notably labor, across the Atlantic.

# VII.

## EPILOGUE:
## A MODERN RESUMPTION
## OF ALTERNATION
## BETWEEN DOLLAR
## SCARCITY AND SURPLUS?

### Introduction

Throughout this study we have attempted to present a description and analysis of the secular pattern in the nineteenth-century American balance of payments. Prior to World War I, the long swing had a reasonably consistent and impressive impact on the components of the balance of payments. Furthermore, as presented in Chapter V, the domestic long swing in United States growth produced rather singular effects on the net position in the balance of payments. Under "normal" nineteenth-century conditions (when this country was committed to a gold standard and without significant internal sources of gold), decades of rapid domestic growth *and* accompanying inflationary pressures were ones characterized by tendencies toward increasing balance-of-payments surplus. Because of the excessive variations in the rate of net capital movements, rapid growth and accompanying relative price inflation generated (under "normal" conditions) dollar *shortage,* while periods of secular stagnation and sluggish growth tended to generate dollar *surplus* and severe gold drains.

The public reaction to these periods of severe dollar crisis strikes a familiar contemporary chord. In the middle of the 1890's, as in the late 1950's, another great debate on our balance of payments began. This was the era in which Bryan made his eloquent reference to the "cross of gold," and the Private Exchange Pool Proposal was outlined to deal with the hot money movement.[1] Most of that decade following the rapid growth of the 1880's was characterized (like the late 1950's and early 1960's) by relative stagnation, high unemployment, and excess capacity. As Abramovitz dates it, it included the trough of a long swing. It was also, to repeat, a period of serious deficit and gold outflow.

It is our feeling that American post–World War II experience with surplus and deficit *may* be much less unique than most economists imply. We should be the first to admit, however, that the most available portion of our history, the two interwar decades, does not appear to be very helpful in offering historical precedent for an understanding of contemporary dollar problems. One has to glance further back in history, into the pre-1913 era which the rest of this book examines, to find significant similarities between past and present.

The theme of this chapter, then, is that current problems with our balance of payments can be more intelligently understood when compared with past American experience with the long swing. The suggestion that conditions in our balance of payments since about 1950 and over periods longer than the business cycle have been very closely related to the general pace of American postwar development is certainly not original to this book. Nevertheless, there has not been, to our satisfaction, a serious attempt to review our recent balance-of-payments history

---

1. Matthew Simon, "The Hot Money Movement and the Private Exchange Pool Proposal of 1896," *Journal of Economic History,* XIX (March, 1959), 31-50.

in the light of our knowledge of variations in United States growth during the ten or fifteen years since the war.

## A Review of Nineteenth-Century Experience

What were the underlying component movements in the balance of payments which tended to produce alternations between dollar surplus and deficit? Over the nineteenth and early twentieth centuries, long swings in merchandise imports are apparent in the data. These long-run variations reveal, not surprisingly, high positive correlations with the levels of income, output, and investment, but with a small lag. Leaving aside exports for the moment, we find the long swing in import demands created similar patterns in the trade balance and current account. During periods of rapid growth on the upswing of a Kuznets cycle in internal development, the trade balance became progressively worse, reflecting a tendency toward increasing excess demands in the domestic market. Generally the trade balance and current account lagged considerably behind domestic *growth rates;* peak deficits in the trade balance did not occur on the average until five years after retardation had set in. These periods of progressive deterioration in the trade balance alternated with periods of progressive improvement, lagging by about four years, when our growth was sluggish and seriously involved with periods of severe recessions, unimpressive recovery, and factor employment. The trade balance improved, as the simplest trade models predict, merely because income and prices were relatively low or growing at a low rate.

What about the role of exports in our nineteenth-century balance of payments? Mintz has shown us that exports always have had a very complex relationship with our business cycle.[2] This has been true of the long swing also. As we have seen, in no portion of our pre-1913 history has the pattern of aggregate exports interfered with the dominance of aggregate imports in producing a long swing in our trade balance such as to make increasing trade-balance deficits typical of periods of rapid growth

---

2. Ilse Mintz, *American Exports During Business Cycles, 1879-1958,* Occasional Paper No. 76, (New York: National Bureau of Economic Research, 1961).

and surplus typical of slow growth. During some stages of our development (approximately 1820-1860), exports moved in a positive relation with our growth over the long swing. During other periods (approximately 1860-1880), exports moved independently of the domestic long swing. But during the four decades of export stability prior to the 1920's, the relationship was, if anything, inverse, with periods of laggard growth being ones of rapid export expansion. In spite of their inconsistent pattern prior to World War I, however, any uncooperative movement in aggregate exports over the long swing was swamped by the pattern of imports.

If an increasingly large trade-balance surplus was coincident with domestic retardation and eventually temporary stagnation, how do we explain the normal tendency towards dollar surplus and gold drain during these same periods? The answer, of course, is that alternations in the trade balance were actually overfinanced by similar but more striking fluctuations in net capital imports. Ragnar Nurkse and others have pointed out that the nineteenth century did not know of a chronic sterling shortage due to the British willingness to export capital in increasing amounts.[3] But as we have already seen, this condition did not eliminate the tendency towards recurring dollar surplus and sterling shortage in the United States. Extensive periods of rapid development were accompanied by increasing relative rates of return on American securities. Thus, increasing trade-balance deficits were accompanied (not always synchronously) by sharply rising net capital imports (or sharply declining net capital exports). Furthermore, the fluctuations in net capital imports were only negligibly offset by changes in the flow of payments on that accumulating debt. In this way, potential balance-of-payments deficits generated by periods of rapid growth were transformed into actual payments surpluses by an excessive outflow of securities that were earning increasingly higher relative returns.

So much for a brief review of past payments experience. The question immediately arises as to the relevance of our pre-

---

3. Ragnar Nurkse, "International Investment Today in the Light of 19th Century Experience," *Economic Journal*, XLIV (December, 1954), 744-758.

1913 experience to contemporary problems. Do these distinctive long swings persist in the recent two decades, and are they of the same nature and magnitude as those of our nineteenth-century history? Perhaps it would be wise to discard immediately such emotive terms as long swings and Kuznets cycles and talk less pretentiously in terms of variations in growth rates however explained. Surely significant long-run variations in growth rates have occurred in the postwar era, but they certainly have been milder than those of the past. But there are other more serious questions. Has the period since 1950 been one of "normalcy" similar to the placid atmosphere of the nineteenth-century trade? Can we appeal to the all-pervasive term "normalcy" to explain the messy balance-of-payments history of the interwar period? Are imports of a composition today that make them respond differently to contemporary domestic conditions? Is the trade balance now tied to capital movements? This is just a sample of the questions which come to mind, but the issue is clearly whether there is enough similarity between past and present environments to expect similar patterns in our contemporary balance of payments.

## *Postwar Development in United States Balance of Payments*[4]

Perhaps it would be wise at the outset to make clear just what part of our postwar experience we shall attempt to explain. First, this chapter does not consider the effects of the short-run business cycle on the balance of payments. We are concerned with much longer-run conditions in our payments position. But at the same time, this brief excursion into our recent balance-of-payments history does not consider the possibility of this country's involvement in a fundamental secular disequilibrium. Between the years 1946 and 1961 the United States lost something in the neighborhood of $2.7 billion worth of gold; from 1950 to 1961 the figure is close to $7.2 billion. The size of the secular deficit is even more impressive, of course, when it is measured in terms

---

4. The data for this section are taken from the following sources: 1945-1955, from U. S. Department of Commerce, *Balance of Payments, Statistical Supplement* (Washington, D. C.: U. S. Government Printing Office, 1958); 1956-1961, from recent issues of the *Survey of Current Business.*

of gold flow and increase in liquid dollar holdings abroad. What we are primarily concerned with here is the sharp long-term fluctuations that have occurred around that deficit level since the late 1940's and especially since 1950.

Very generally, and to give by necessity a brief descriptive review, the United States balance moved decisively into an increasingly serious deficit only in 1958. Using the rate of change in gold and liquid dollar asset position as a frame of reference, beginning with 1950 the United States deficit declined steadily. This trend of improvement in our payments position, although it was not great and suffered interruption, persisted until the mid-1950's. In the autumn of 1956 and the greater part of 1957, the United States actually found itself enjoying a surplus. At this point there is a sharp line of demarcation: toward the end of 1957 we moved back into a deficit position which became worse and has remained at alarming levels until the present. If we regard the period from 1956 to 1958 as an extraordinary combination of circumstances perhaps it may be more accurate to say that long-term pressures to increase the size of the United States deficit were apparent as early as 1956. The abrupt transition from surplus in 1957 to tremendous deficit in 1958 would seem to support this view.

Thus far the description of the movements in our payments position has covered the period beginning 1950. Is this an arbitrary delinenation? Suppose we set our task to include an explanation of the changes in our payments position since 1946 or 1947? Initially, our conclusions would seem to be somewhat different: the payments position moves secularly—despite the interruptions of 1950 and 1957—from a surplus position in the late 1940's to a deficit in the late 1950's and early 1960's. It is our opinion that the pattern from 1945 to 1950 is explained by the *exogenous* effects of reconstruction and the overwhelming importance of government transactions in the balance of payments. (For the same reasons, we disregard the World War II years as well.) The more *systematic* and endogenous pressures, which this chapter attempts to identify, existed during this period in the private account but were overshadowed by the movements in the public account. It is only with the beginning of the 1950's that *systematic* effects make themselves felt. Thus the discussion of the effects of American growth on the net payments position begins with 1950, while investigation of the payments components may cover the earlier period.

To idealize and generalize the patterns, then, the period of rapid United States growth from 1950 to the mid-1950's was a period of improvement in the United States balance of payments (although it was *not* one of consistent surplus). Serious balance-of-payments problems only begin to arise in the late 1950's, with the inauguration of an extended period of sluggish development in the American economy. This relationship seems to be interrupted only temporarily by the unusual international circumstances of late 1956 and of 1957.

Thus far we have only the loose correlation between the net payments position and American growth performance. The trade balance, however, also seems to have a pattern similar to those of the pre-1913 era. During a period of impressive American growth, the trade balance shrank from a high level in 1947 to a very small surplus in 1953. Now surely a good part of the severe deterioration in our export surplus during the late 1940's was due to the abrupt contraction of American assistance in postwar reconstruction. (One may contest more strongly that the deterioration in our export surplus reflects the devaluation of 1949.) Nonetheless, the trade balance continued to shrink until 1953 and remained at low levels up to 1955. With 1956 it began to show significant improvement. If we again disregard the unusual nature of 1957 and 1958 (inflationary boom, material shortages abroad, and the Suez crisis in 1957, bad harvest in Europe in 1956, and a reversal of these conditions in 1958) as well as 1959 (the steel strike and the invasion of the "compacts"), then the trend has been towards significant improvement in our trade balance during the seven years 1956-1962. This again is consistent with American history and with our elementary notions of the effect of domestically generated income movements (of the Harrod-Domar rather than Abramovitz-Solow type[5]) on the

---

5. As asserted below, rapid growth tended to generate dollar shortage or payments surpluses due to the enormous response of capital movements to that growth. Rapid growth did not generate surplus via the trade balance and thus not by, as

trade balance. Rapid growth and significant price inflation were coincident with a reduction in the trade-balance surplus and relative stagnation with an improvement in our trade-balance position.

But is it as simple as that? Are the *causes* of the trade-balance fluctuations in the postwar period common to those of the pre-1913 era? It is at this stage of the comparative analysis that significant differences arise. As we have seen historically, exports have never seriously contributed to the pattern of long swings in the trade balance and current account. The relationship between Kuznets cycles in income and price movements were only negligibly affected by exogenous shocks and by the complex effects of systematic productivity changes on import substitutes and exports. Is it primarily the dominating pattern of imports which produces this configuration in the contemporary trade-balance surplus?

Although the nature of the current domestic long swing has been much milder than those of the past, it still seems clear that aggregate imports have not revealed very striking fluctuations over recent patterns in our growth (see Chart 30). It is true that aggregate imports (trendless) rise from low immediate postwar levels to a significant peak in 1951 and then fall consistently into the sixties. But surely a large portion of the boom culminating in 1951 is due to the inflation of primary product prices during the Korean conflict (and the 1949 devaluation?). If the import series was adjusted for the excessive movements related to the Korean War, then the pattern of aggregate imports would be even milder. Indeed, when aggregate imports are deflated by the Department of Commerce import price index, then very little of the long swing in imports remains even in the trendless data. Does this suggest that imports reveal a relationship with postwar American growth performance inconsistent with

---

Kindleberger calls it, Abramovitz-Solow growth of the technological sort (C. P. Kindleberger, "Foreign Trade and Growth: Lessons from British Experience since 1913," *Lloyds Bank Review* [July, 1962]). Much of our present long-run dollar problem (if it exists) may be due to low Abramovitz-Solow growth over and above the long-swing pattern. Nevertheless, it is argued here that the decade variations in our postwar payments position, apart from its longer-run level, is due primarily to the relationship between capital flows and economic growth.

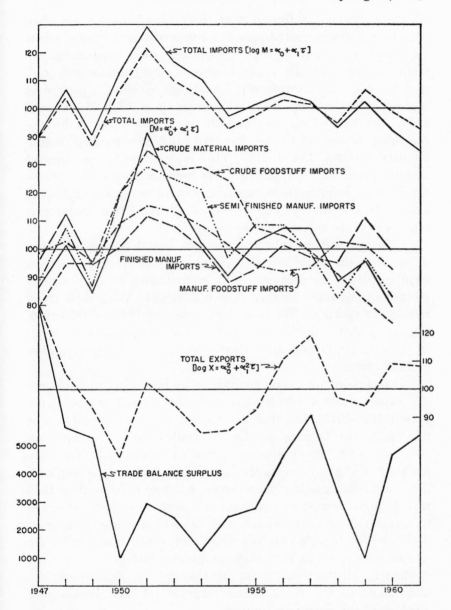

**Chart 30** United States Trade Balance and Its Components, 1947-1961 (in Millions of Dollars)

*Source: Survey of Current Business*

the past? Perhaps so, but an interesting complication arises when imports are disaggregated into five commodity groupings. Chart 30 reveals that four of these groupings reflect long-swing patterns. Crude materials, crude foodstuffs, semimanufactures and, to a lesser extent, manufactured foodstuffs all show a pattern of increasing imports up to 1951, remaining at high levels until 1953, and then falling continuously up to 1960 (except for the short-run boom in crude materials and semifinished manufactures around 1955-1957). The nonconformist is finished manufactures, which apparently has been an important enough bundle to minimize the long-swing pattern in aggregate import values. In the pre-1913 era, we will recall, these five components tended to move together rather consistently.

Although import values (trendless) reveal a positive correlation with the trade-balance surplus, aggregate export patterns seem to play a far greater role in contributing to the long-run pattern in the trade balance than historically. With their trend removed, exports decline from high levels in 1947 to 1953-1955. Following that low, they increase to, and remain at, high levels in the late 1950's and early 1960's (except for the interruption of 1958-1959).

At this point we should summarize by indicating that it is not the export pattern which lacks historical precedents (e.g., the period 1880-1915), but that the apparent importance of export movements in helping produce a trade-balance configuration consistent with history appears at first to be unusual. Throughout most of the nineteenth century, import fluctuations dominate the trade balance and current account, while exports after 1860 reveal fairly consistent stability. However, we have observed in Chapter III that the violence of those long swings in imports declines progressively over the nineteenth century so that by the two decades prior to 1915 they reveal long swings only in rates of change. Furthermore, it appears that exports *do* dominate the movements in the trade balance during the first decade and one-half of the twentieth century.

As far as the export pattern is concerned, we might be able to fit that experience, expost, into American postwar growth experience. First, it is quite possible indeed that domestic price inflation has had a significant effect upon the pattern of exports during the postwar period. These price movements have not been entirely independent of the rate of United States growth. Second, the export pattern may simply reflect our "capacity" to export, that periods of excess capacity and sluggish growth in domestic demand may be ones in which foreign demand can compete successfully for United States products. It should be clear from Chapter II that the pattern of United States exports during three of four decades prior to World War I can in good measure be explained by the combination of these two factors. Third, the pattern of exports may simply reflect American willingness to export private and public capital abroad. The prime historical example of such a balance-of-payments mechanism is nineteenth-century Great Britain. To grossly overgeneralize, America facilitated the real transfer over the long swing by variations in import demands; England facilitated the real transfer by variations in aggregate exports.[6]

Given that the trade balance deteriorates during periods of rapid growth and improves during periods of poor growth performance, how do we explain the opposite pattern in our net payments position? In our view, the answer to this question clearly lies in the private capital account. Net capital exports fell sharply and with few interruptions from extremely high levels in 1947 to 1953-1955 (see Chart 31). From the mid-1950's to 1961 net capital exports increased sharply and fairly consistently except for the interruption in 1959 (again with a lag behind retardation in domestic growth). But public capital movements, although they may explain a large part of our export patterns especially in the late forties and early fifties, do *not* explain the pattern of total United States capital exports. Net private capital

---

6. This may seem to suggest that it would be more fruitful to examine British nineteenth-century experience for historical answers to current American experience with dollar scarcity and surplus. However, in spite of the fact that the United States is now a net exporter of capital and in that respect similar to a nineteenth-century Great Britain, the British nineteenth- and the American twentieth-century economies have a more significant difference. Because of the inverse relation between British home and foreign investment, and because of the size of the latter, long-swing fluctuations in British income and output are hardly discernible in the nineteenth century. This, of course, is not the case for nineteenth- or twentieth-century America (see Chapter VI).

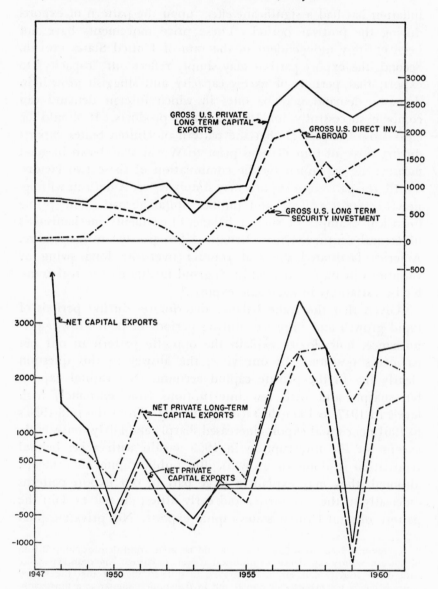

**Chart 31** United States Capital Movements, 1947-1961 (in Millions of Dollars)

*Source: Survey of Current Business*

exports fell from a high in 1946 to a net *import* position in 1953. They rose abruptly after 1955 and remained at those high levels until 1961 (again, with the exception of 1959). Except for the years 1946 and 1947, it is private capital which dominates the pattern in net capital account. Years of rapid growth in the United States economy are ones which apparently produce successively smaller rates of net capital export; periods of sluggish growth and apparent relatively low returns on capital are ones of increasing capital export. So significant are those fluctuations that they overshadow the trade-balance pattern and tend to produce dollar surplus during years of generally unimpressive growth.

Furthermore, this long-run pattern in our net private capital account is not explained simply by short-term capital movements. The net long-term private capital position shows stability or even a slight but steady decline in the rate of export up to 1955. After that point it reveals the same pattern as the net capital position, but 1959 is still a year of significant long-term capital export. One is tempted to firmly conclude, therefore, that the long-run pattern in our net payments position during the 1950's and 1960's can be explained by relative profit opportunities and returns on securities which, though difficult to quantify, should have significant positive correlation with domestic income-output movements. But we are still left with unanswered questions concerning the relative importance of short-term capital movements.[7]

The verbal model which we have described in this chapter predicts that the balance of payments will improve during periods of rapid domestic growth and deteriorate during sluggish periods of growth. Mintz has clearly shown that this model requires that the deterioration in the current account be less than the decrease in capital outflow (increase in capital inflow) in periods of rapid growth and vice versa for periods of slow growth. The evidence clearly supports this for both the "normal" pre-1913 periods and for the post–World War II period. But the question now arises as to whether it is short-term or long-term capital movements

---

7. The comments that follow below were stimulated by the excellent criticisms Ilse Mintz expressed at the December, 1962, meetings of the American Economic Association held in Pittsburgh.

which produce this result. Mintz has suggested that changes in the long-term capital account are not large enough by themselves to offset changes in the current account between the two periods 1950-1955 and 1956-1961. Thus, it would appear that it is only after including changes in the short-term capital export account that we get a balance-of-payments deficit coincident with slow growth and surplus with rapid growth.

In order that our model really explain American postwar experience with the balance of payments, short-term capital movements must also be explained by variations in domestic growth. Following Kindleberger's classification,[8] we would have to show that a very large portion of short-term capital movements during the 1950's and 1960's were of the income rather than autonomous, speculative, or equilibrating sort. Has the movement in short-term capital been dominated by variations in relative profit opportunities and thus closely tied to variations in domestic growth? Furth has asserted that the fairly small portion of short-term capital which represents speculation against the dollar is insignificant compared with the bulk of American capital that went abroad in the late 1950's simply because of the relative improvement in profit opportunities.[9]

The results of empirical studies that have attempted to explain short-term capital movements during the postwar era are conflicting. In an excellent study for the Joint Economic Committee, Philip Bell concluded that the 25 to 30 per cent of short-term capital (during 1960-1961) which was not tied directly to United States exports exhibited very little sensitivity to interest rate differentials.[10] The Federal Reserve Bank of New York, however, has stated that their research suggests just the opposite: that interest rate differentials are important.[11]

---

8. C. P. Kindleberger, *International Short-Term Capital Movements* (New York: 1937), pp. 7-13.

9. J. H. Furth, "U. S. Balance of Payments in the Recession," *Quarterly Journal of Economics*, LXXIII (May, 1959), 197-206.

10. [Philip W. Bell], U. S. Congress, "Private Capital Movements and the U. S. Balance of Payments Position," *Hearings Before the Joint Economic Committee of the Congress of the United States*, 87th Cong., 2nd Sess., 1962, Part 6, "Factors Affecting the United States Balance of Payments," pp. 395-481.

11. [Frederick H. Klopstock], U. S. Congress, *Hearings Before the Joint Economic Committee of the Congress of the United States*, 87th Cong., 2nd Sess., 1962, "State of the Economy and Policies for Full Employment," p. 488.

We do not intend to answer, in this chapter or in this book, the question as to whether variations in short-term capital flows during the post–World War II period are related to domestic growth variations or exogenous factors. But if short-term capital movements are not related to domestic growth variations in the same fashion that long-term capital flows appear to be, why does the response of aggregate net capital movements to domestic long swings seem to have such historical consistency? In the pre-1913 period we have no reliable estimate of the distribution of net capital movements between short and long term. Nevertheless, in each of our "normal" periods in American history the net capital account has responded in precisely the same fashion, with total changes in net capital account exceeding changes in the current account during each of these downswings of the Kuznets cycle. Are we to believe that in every case short-term capital movements followed the same pattern as long-term due to factors completely unrelated to the domestic long swing? Our intuitive feeling is that there is little question that short-term capital movements are intimately related (in a consistent fashion) to domestic variations in growth just as with other components in the balance of payments. The nature of the relationship, however, is not obvious and certainly needs further study.

Direct investment never played an important role in the American capital position prior to World War I. But the fact that it does today does not seem to obliterate the tendency for net private capital movements to be "sensitive" to long-run domestic conditions, as was the case in the nineteenth century. Both private long-term security investment and direct investment reveal this pattern. Certainly part of the extremely sharp movements in net capital exports from 1953-1955 to 1957 can be explained by the tremendous increase in direct investment in petroleum. Nevertheless, the striking increase in net capital exports persists even after discounting for the abrupt rise in direct petroleum investment during these years. As a matter of fact, long-term investment in securities exhibits a pattern even more suggestive of a close correlation with American growth. Beginning with 1950, net long-term investment in securities gradually declines to a net capital *import* position in 1953, then expands continuously to a high level of net capital export in the years 1958-1960.

Finally, some comment should be made on the role of long swings in other countries. It would be extremely fruitful to examine closely the nature of growth patterns abroad. How much of the movement in the American balance of payments is due to domestic growth variations and how much to European? Is the growth pattern of Western Europe consistent with United States balance-of-payments movement during the 1950's and 1960's? Has the inverse nature of the interaction between nineteenth-century British and American economies re-emerged, and how important is the inverse relation, or lack of it, in explaining alternations between dollar scarcity and surplus? These are indeed intriguing questions. But it should be remembered that the peculiar and consistent response of our balance of payments to the domestic long swing exists in both the early and late nineteenth century, while the inverse interaction between the Anglo-American economies does not become significant until after the Civil War.

### Conclusion

It seems that the pattern of our net capital account cannot be dismissed by an appeal to such explanations as the gradual process of returning to the "normalcy" of the 1920's and earlier. We find it difficult to attribute the sharp rise of net capital exports from the mid-1950's to the early 1960's as simply a lagged readjustment of the international community to a renewed period of relative international stability and relatively unimpeded trade. Nor can we find a great deal of sympathy for the view that the pattern of net long-term private investment is simply the reflection of such exogenous accidents as the creation of a common market in Europe. The pattern of American long-term investment abroad applies not only to European, but to Canadian and Latin American investment as well.

Although these comments on post–World War II experience have been directed in the spirit of offering suggestive hypotheses rather than substantive proof, the policy conclusions inherent in the model are striking and worthy, it seems, of at least cursory examination. The policy implications are both optimistic and unorthodox. A monetary and fiscal policy that recognizes a conflict between the achievement of full employment accompanied by rapid growth and achievement of balance-of-payments equilibrium, and chooses the latter goal, may only solve short-run balance-of-payments problems while perpetuating a long-run dollar problem. On the other hand, a domestic policy which is effective in achieving the goals of full employment and rapid growth may in the long run reduce the size of the American deficit. Whether or not our payments deficit would disappear is another question entirely, but it is conceivable that once again in the 1960's we will find the literature flooded with articles on causes and cures of the new dollar shortage.

# APPENDIX A

# THE NATURE

# OF THE DATA

## Net Capital Movements

Needless to say, in order for an analysis of secular movements in nineteenth-century American capital flows to be at all meaningful, we must be convinced of the reliability of the historical balance-of-payments data (see Table B-1).[1] It must be emphasized at the outset that it would be much too demanding to expect substantiation of the *annual* net capital movements estimates (hereafter called K). First, verification of annual estimates of K would be desirable but unnecessary, given the scope of this inquiry, for we are concerned with long secular swings in the United States balance of payments. Second, it is not the purpose of this book to re-do the tremendous amount of excellent paleontological work

---

1. Although there have been others, the most recent and presumably the most reliable estimates of nineteenth-century American balance of payments have been constructed by Douglass C. North in "The United States Balance of Payments, 1790-1860," *Trends in the American Economy in the Nineteenth Century* ("Studies in Income and Wealth," Vol. XXIV [Princeton, N. J.: Princeton University Press, 1960]), pp. 573-627 (this volume is hereafter cited as *Trends*), and by Matthew Simon in *Trends*, pp. 629-715. We have depended heavily on these estimates throughout the research. For the period 1901-1918 prior to the publication of official (but not necessarily accurate) statistics, we have used Raymond W. Goldsmith's estimates of capital movements which appear in his *A Study of Saving in the United States* (Princeton, N. J.: Princeton University Press, 1955).

that North and Simon have contributed to our historical knowledge. In addition, it is far from evident that any substantial improvement could be made upon these estimates for the nineteenth century. For these reasons, only a summary verification of the North-Simon K estimates, over fairly long time periods, is attempted here; that is, of the secular movements of K in direction and general amplitude and decade by decade.

We attempt to substantiate the North-Simon figures in four ways. First, using Goldsmith's direct and indirect estimates of net capital movements (1897-1919), we have found close conformity between the results of the two estimating techniques.[2] The method of indirect estimation used by North, Simon, and Imlah involves the estimation of all elements in the balance of payments except K; by appealing to the accounting identity in the external balance, we find K appears in the residual.

Independent of the residual or indirect estimates, Goldsmith also developed figures for net capital movements using the direct technique. Depending heavily on the work done by Dickens,[3] Goldsmith has compiled all "ascertainable foreign investments in the United States" and "ascertainable United States investments abroad," year by year, from 1897 to 1919. Since "ascertainable" capital movements estimated by the direct technique by no means exhaust total capital movements due to the paucity of capital flows data, the aggregate direct estimates do not coincide with the aggregate indirect estimates. The difference between these two series, exhibited on Chart A-2, becomes progressively smaller as we move farther into the twentieth century and obtain more adequate data. Nevertheless, Goldsmith's indirect estimates reveal remarkable conformity to the direct estimates in direction and amplitude over the period 1897-1919. This, it seems, is excellent evidence of the accuracy of the net capital movements estimates constructed by the residual, or indirect, method for that period alone. But it also speaks well for Simon's K estimates covering 1861-1900. There is no justification for believing that the accuracy

---

2. *Study of Savings*, Vol. I, Tables K-1 through K-7, pp. 1078-1093.
3. Paul D. Dickens, "The Transition Period in American International Financing: 1897-1914" (unpublished Ph.D. dissertation, George Washington University, 1933).

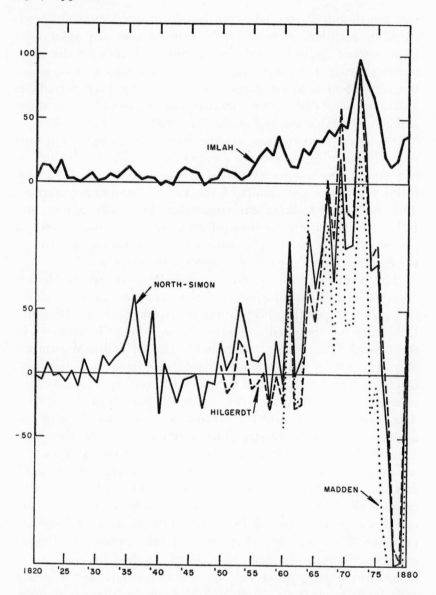

**Chart A-1** British Net Capital Exports (in Millions of Pounds Sterling); United States Net Capital Imports Estimates (in Millions of Dollars), 1820-1880

*Source:* See Text

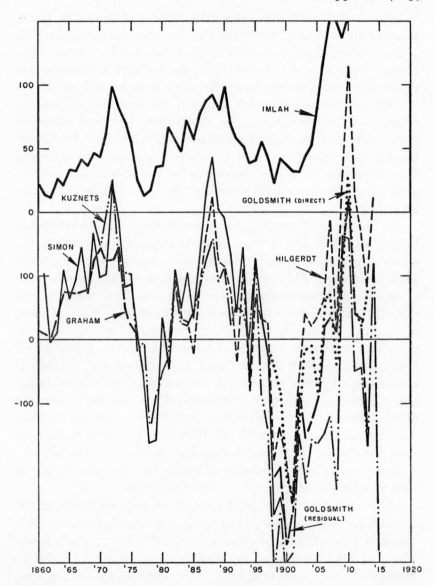

**Chart A-2** British Net Capital Exports (in Millions of Pounds Sterling); United States Net Capital Imports Estimates (in Millions of Dollars), 1860-1915

*Source:* See Text

of the unofficial estimates of service balance items or of specie data are substantially better for the last years of the nineteenth and first years of the twentieth century than for 1861-1896. Thus there is little reason to believe that the indirect K estimates are significantly more accurate for 1897-1919 than for 1861-1896.

But Goldsmith's research supports the accuracy of Simon's estimates in another way. The Goldsmith (Dickens) series of direct estimates overlaps the indirect estimates done by Simon. During these four years, 1897-1900, the two series for net capital movements—estimated independently by Goldsmith and Simon—move in sympathy in both direction and general amplitude (see Chart A-2).

In the second method of substantiating the North-Simon figures we have found that there is nothing inherent in the residual technique that introduces a bias. During the period 1919-1956 (as in the 1897-1919 estimates), we find that the two methods of estimation produce similar results. In the official data,[4] beginning 1919, the direct estimate method is used, and incompleteness or inaccuracy accounts for the large residual of errors and omissions[5] in the balance-of-payments account. However, if we include errors and omissions in the direct estimates of the net capital movements, the time path of this residual sum—net capital movements estimated indirectly—conforms almost precisely with the direct estimates of K (see Chart A-3). This piece of evidence does not, obviously, remove the 1820-1900 estimates of K from suspicion, for we would find it especially necessary to examine the accuracy of the service balance estimates for that period, but at least it adds further weight to our confidence.

This brings us to a third method of substantiation of the K estimates. All the independent, and nonofficial, estimates of K (most of which fall within the period 1860-1919) generally agree. The indirect estimates of net capital flows done by Goldsmith (1897-1919), Graham (1862-1876), Williams-Bullock-Tucker, Kuznets (1869-1919), North (1790-1860), Simon (1861-1900), Hilgerdt

---

4. U. S. Department of Commerce, *Balance of Payments, Statistical Supplement* (Washington, D. C.: U. S. Government Printing Office, 1958), pp. 10-13.

5. Most economists feel that errors and omissions are mainly attributable to unrecorded short-term capital movements.

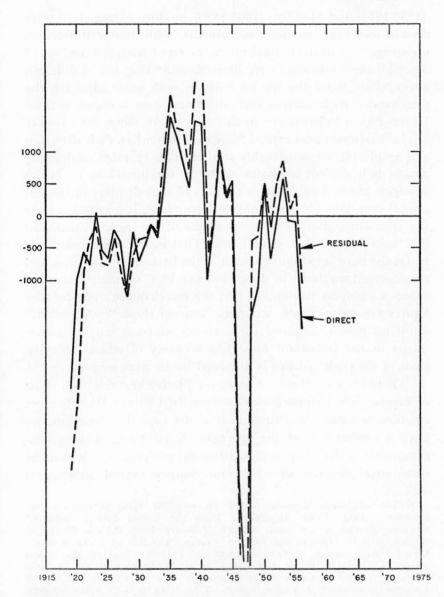

**Chart A-3** United States Net Capital Imports, Residual and Direct Estimates, 1919-1956 (in Millions of Dollars; Positive Figures Are Imports)

*Source:* See Text

(1850-1914) and Madden (1860-1880) produce extremely similar decade and even five-year movements, with minor differences occurring only in the annual estimates (see Charts A-1 and A-2).[6] Since all these estimates were derived by making use of different assumptions about the service balance, with some adjusting the merchandise trade balance and others not, these K estimates must be considered independent in this respect. Although the *absolute* levels of estimated net capital flows vary somewhat, their direction and amplitude are remarkably similar. This revealed conformity among independent estimates might be considered by us as the strongest piece of evidence in support of the adequacy of the net capital flow data. However, and unfortunately, it may reflect only the apparent stability or unimportance of the service balance in the United States current accounts. That is, the trade balance is by far the most important element in the balance of payments, and the observed similarity in these "independent" estimates may only reflect a common assumption that the merchandise trade balance figures are more or less accurate. None of these "independent" estimates have questioned the accuracy of trade balance movements in any important way. The accuracy of official compilations of the trade balance is discussed in the next section.

There are also, of course, some qualitative histories of the flow of capital over United States borders. In Chapter IV, when we examine the cause and directions of net capital movements, we have a further test of the aggregate K estimates. The general conclusion of that chapter relative to our problem here is that the qualitative histories of nineteenth-century capital movements

---

6. Goldsmith, *Study of Saving*, Vol. I, pp. 1079-1085. Frank D. Graham, "International Trade Under Depreciated Paper—the United States, 1862-1879," *Quarterly Journal of Economics*, XXXVI (February, 1922), 222-273. Charles L. Bullock, John H. Williams, and Rufus S. Tucker, "The Balance of Trade of the United States," *Review of Economic Statistics*, I (July, 1919), 213-268. Simon Kuznets, "Technical Tables Underlying Series in *Supplement to Summary Volume on Capital Formation and Its Financing*" (New York: National Bureau of Economic Research, 1957; mimeographed), Table T-13, p. T-25. Folke Hilgerdt, *Annual Figures for the Balance of Payments of the United States, 1850-1914*, United Nations Department of Economic Affairs, Research Memorandum No. 9, n.d. John J. Madden, "British Investment in the United States, 1860-1880," Conference on Research in Income and Wealth (New York: National Bureau of Economic Research, 1957; mimeographed), Table A-1, p. A-2. North *Trends*, Table 3, p. 581. Simon, *Trends*, Table 27, pp. 699-705.

fully support these quantitative estimates derived by the indirect technique. And, incidentally, both North and Simon attempt to evaluate the comparability of their estimates of the net accumulating balance of indebtedness suggested by contemporary nineteenth-century observors. Simon finds reasonable correspondence between his estimates and the direct estimates, in spite of their fragmentary and subjective character, published by nineteenth-century observors.[7] North feels that his figures check rather well with "reliable direct estimates of foreign debt in 1837 through 1839, 1843, 1853 and 1857."[8]

In sum the estimates between 1820 and 1846 check with the partial estimates and the complete direct estimates for the period. After 1847 the possible error resulting from undervaluation of imports and the size of certain hard-to-estimate invisible items is more serious. However, the direct estimates during the last decade corroborate the estimates of the net balance and the cumulative debt figures, suggesting that errors in the separate components are counterbalancing.[9]

There still remains another source of support of a weaker sort for these indirect estimates of net capital flows, and that arises in the estimates of British capital movements over British borders (see Table B-19). It is especially true throughout the nineteenth-century that by far the bulk of investments flowing into the United States had its source in Great Britain. In the later half of the nineteenth century, American securities played an important role in British portfolios. One might expect, then, to find a positive correlation between the directions and amplitudes of the rate of net capital outflow from Great Britain and the rate of inflow into the United States. This conformity should hold true at least over long periods of from twenty to thirty years and would involve an independent check of the estimates of United States net capital inflows. The similarity between the movements in Imlah's estimates of British capital exports and American net capital imports from 1860 to 1900 is shown in Charts A-1 and A-2.[10] Both the

---

7. *Trends*, pp. 698-707, esp. pp. 706-707.
8. *Trends*, p. 576.
9. *Ibid.* For a summary of the comparability between the direct and indirect estimates of American net indebtedness, see pp. 622-627.
10. Albert H. Imlah, "British Balance of Payments and Export of Capital, 1816-1913," *Economic History Review*, Second Series, V (1952-1953), 234-239. A more

Table A-1 Dating of Long Swings in Net Capital Movements over United States Borders, 1820-1919 (Annual Data)

| | North | Simon | Hilgerdt | Kuznets | Graham | Madden | Goldsmith | Imlah (British capital exports) | Range in Years: Latest Date—Earliest Date (excluding Imlah) |
|---|---|---|---|---|---|---|---|---|---|
| Trough | 1827 | | | | | | | | |
| Peak | 1836 | | | | | | | | |
| Trough | 1840 | | | | | | | | |
| Peak | 1853 | | 1853 | | | | | 1859 | 0 |
| Trough | 1858 | | 1858 | | | | | 1862 | 0 |
| Peak | | 1872 | 1872 | 1872 | 1873 | 1872 | | 1872 | 1 |
| Trough | | 1878 | 1879 | 1878 | | 1879 | | 1877 | 1 |
| Peak | | 1888 | 1888 | 1888 | | | | 1890 | 1 |
| Pcak | | 1900 | 1901 | 1900 | | | 1900 | 1898 | 0 |
| Trough | | | 1910 | 1909 | | | 1910 | | 1 |

British estimates and the American estimates were compiled by means of the indirect method of estimation, and the similarity of ante-bellum movements is most welcome evidence for the adequacy of the North-Simon estimates over long secular periods. The dating for all these independent estimates is given in Table A-1.

In summary, our feeling is that we cannot be very far in error by using the most recent estimates of net capital movements derived by North and Simon. (The Goldsmith estimates for 1897-1919 are not in question since adequate *direct* estimates are also available that support Goldsmith's indirect measurement.) We might, it is true, be less confident of these net capital flow estimates if we were concerned with shorter periods. Over the long swing, however, we have found general conformity in direction, timing, and amplitude between available indirect and direct estimates of net capital movements, and general conformity among *all* independent estimates published in recent years. But, admittedly, this is not conclusive evidence, since the trade balance dominates the foreign balance and each of these writers has more or less accepted the official estimates of the merchandise trade balance. Clearly, the only adequate means of checking the reliability of the net capital movement data would be to reconstruct the only balance-of-payments component which is not official: the service balance. This would take far too much time, however. The skeptical reader is encouraged to examine the thorough methods used by North and Simon to derive this balance.

## The Merchandise Trade Balance

Mercantilism has produced at least one wholesome result: it has led governments to keep relatively full and careful records of imports and exports. No other type of trade has so long or so adequate a statistical record. Of course the economist who is using these data for any purpose complains of their defects; by the nature of his calling he is an ungrateful creature who must begin an investigation by pointing out the limits of the data in scope and in reliability. We follow this time honored precedent; but we wish that the available

---

recent publication and revision of these earlier estimates appears in Imlah's *Economic Elements in the Pax Britannica* (Cambridge, Mass.: Harvard University Press, 1958), Table 4, pp. 70-75.

records of domestic production and exchange were equal to those of foreign trade.[11]

There are two reasons for establishing the reliability of merchandise trade figures (see Table B-1). First, since the merchandise trade balance is by far the most important item in the current account, its accuracy is essential if the balance-of-payments residual, net capital movements, is itself expected to be reliable. Second, we are also concerned with import and export movements by themselves, and therefore reliability is a welcome attribute. If the reader is interested in an extensive examination of the difficulties and possible inaccuracies of merchandise trade data, he should refer to North's and Simon's work, for we will only summarize their comments here.

The general implication in the literature of those economists who have shown interest in the American balance of payments during the nineteenth century is that the merchandise trade figures over this period are relatively accurate and certainly complete. We should feel even more optimistic toward these estimates since our concern is less with the annual estimates or even short cyclic movements than with decade movements. Nevertheless, the "official" trade-balance figures of the nineteenth century do present problems which North and Simon attack vigorously and feel they have adequately solved.

Simon's problem of compiling estimates of the merchandise trade balance (1861-1900) is, of course, somewhat less difficult than North's, which covers an earlier period (1790-1860), due to the superiority of techniques of recording official data in the later period. Simon has assumed the export data to be accurate and has thought it necessary to make only one adjustment. Prior to April 1, 1893, only exports transported on marine vessels were recorded in the official data on aggregate exports. Legislation in 1893 required all exporters to clear goods shipped by railroads and other land vehicles *as well as* by marine vessels. Under the conditions prior to 1893 and after the beginning of the post–Civil War railroad boom "discrepancies between 'reported' exports and

11. Wesley C. Mitchell as quoted in Ilse Mintz, *Trade Balance During Business Cycles*, Occasional Paper No. 67 (New York: National Bureau of Economic Research, 1959), p. 6.

'actual' exports became considerable. . . . The extension of the American railroad net to the Canadian and Mexican borders and the growth of their railroad systems increased the volume of overland trade and aggravated the situation."[12] These adjustments to include overland trade certainly add to the accuracy of the export figures.

The import data is much less adequate and much more difficult to adjust. Simon has applied two modifications to the import data. The first directly concerns the valuation of imports by customs authorities. The tariff act of March 3, 1883, included a clause which called for the dutiable value of imported goods to be computed at less than actual cost and cost to importer. The difference between the two costs was written explicitly:

The cost of transportation, shipment and trans-shipment, with all the expenses included, from the place of growth, production or manufacture whether by land or water, to the vessel in which shipment is made to the United States; the value of the usual and necessary sacks, crates, boxes or covering of any kind in which such merchandise is contained; commission at the usual rates, but in no case less than 2½ per centum, and brokerage, export duty, and all other actual or usual charges for putting up, preparing, and packing for transportation or shipment.[13]

The method of evaluation was eliminated with the act of June 10, 1890. Under the provision of this act, imports were estimated at the actual market value or wholesale price of the goods at the port of export.[14] In the official data from 1883 to 1890 imports are undervalued and Simon makes an adjustment for this inadequacy.

In spite of the more effective means of combating illegal undervaluation and smuggling of imported merchandise after the Civil War, the maintenance and abutment of a system of highly protective tariffs in the late nineteenth century did not eliminate illegal operations. Simon's adjustment, however, becomes progressively less from 1860 to 1900 due to the improvements in

12. Simon, *Trends,* p. 631.
13. U. S. Department of Commerce, *Commerce and Navigation of the United States, 1886* (Washington, D. C.: U. S. Government Printing Office, 1887), p. xi, as quoted in Simon, *Trends,* p. 639.
14. Simon, *Trends,* p. 642.

methods with which the Customs Administration attempted to stem smuggling and illegal undervaluation.[15]

North's problem of adjustment of the merchandise trade figures is somewhat more difficult since the official data is less adequate for the first half of the nineteenth century, although the trade figures certainly are as good or better than most domestic series. Thus we can place less confidence in the annual estimates despite the adequacy of the trade figures in describing secular movements over periods of five to ten years.

The quality of the trade data recorded after 1820 changes substantially. After 1820, by law, the total value of all imports was ascertained regardless of their duty status. The act of 1820 resulted in the compilation of complete foreign trade statistics for the first time. The problem of undervaluation of imports still existed, especially after the Walker Tariff of 1846, which put all duties on an ad valorem basis. The amount of undervaluation clearly increased and the possible error becomes, therefore, more significant.[16] The estimates of exports are complete after 1820 (except for overland exports, which were relatively unimportant from 1820 to 1860 due to an inadequate railroad network), and the only major difficulty would arise in valuation. Since there was no intent to evade the law (no pecuniary gain would be derived therefrom), under- or overvaluation can not be very important. As a matter of fact, slight undervaluation seems to have been most probable, but North considers it "unlikely to have been very significant."[17] The official export data is therefore used without adjustment since they seem to be fairly accurate.

Imports present a more serious problem. The value of all imports after 1820 were ascertained at the customhouse "regardless of whether they were subject to ad valorem or specific duties or were free goods."[18] The import statistics are therefore complete. Nevertheless, valuation may seriously interfere with the accuracy of import statistics.

While the import figures were comprehensive in coverage, their accuracy was a subject of extensive contemporary debate. The under-

---

15. *Ibid.*, p. 644.
16. North, *Trends*, p. 603.
17. *Ibid.*, p. 602.
18. *Ibid.*

valuation of ad valorem duty imports could be and frequently was profitable. The debate became more acrimonious after the Walker Tariff of 1846 was enacted. It placed all duties upon an ad valorem basis and reduced the penalties for undervaluation.[19]

North thus has allowed a larger upward valuation of imports for 1846-1860 than before 1846.

In summary the value of imports, 1820-32, is probably approximately correct. . . . Between 1832 and 1846 a small allowance should be made for undervaluation on ad valorem goods and between 1846 and 1860 a larger allowance must be made because of the abolition of specific duties and the shift to ad valorem duties.[20]

The general conclusion one is forced to reach when examining the official balance-of-payments data is that the merchandise trade figures are by far the most accurate. The adjustments made by North and Simon, however, are certainly important. The general feeling of contemporary economists toward the adequacy of the United States merchandise trade figures seems to be one of confidence, and the North-Simon adjustments must surely add to that feeling.

### Service Balance

This is by far the most difficult aspect of United States balance-of-payments accounts to discuss with regard to accuracy. Our major concern in examining long swings in the balance of payments is in terms of the flow of goods, capital, and specie, and we are therefore only indirectly interested in the estimated service balance. Although there are official estimates of merchandise trade and net specie movements beginning early in the nineteenth century (specie flows will be discussed below), there are none for trade in services, and the problem of deriving estimates of net capital movements arises mainly in the service balance. Thus, in order to derive indirect estimates of K, approximation and knowledgeable guesses as to size, sign, and variation of the service balance are necessary. The service balance includes, of course, the shipping balance, which only assumes relative importance prior to the

---

19. *Ibid.*, p. 603.
20. *Ibid.*, pp. 603-604.

1850's; the passenger balance, which assumes an important role with the great flow of migration after the 1840's and with the concomitant flow of immigrant funds and emigrant remittances; and the financial balance, which is a direct function of the flow of capital over United States borders. The main differences between the North-Simon estimates of net capital movements and the others discussed in the first section of this appendix should arise primarily in their assumptions about the service balance, for which no official data exists.

Let us state at the outset of this discussion that no attempt will be made to evaluate the *accuracy* of the North-Simon estimates of the service balance and the reasonableness of their assumptions. Since we are not concerned primarily with the estimates of the service balance but rather with the flow of goods, money, and capital, there is no compulsion to convince the reader of the accuracy of the service balance. With regard to the importance of the service balance in deriving indirect estimates of net capital movements, the first section of this appendix should be adequate. There is no plan, therefore, to review the methods and assumptions which North and Simon used to construct their estimates of the service balance. For that purpose the reader may once again refer directly to their work. However, we should devote some attention to a brief examination of the behavior of the service balance in fact and pose some questions about that balance.

We might first examine the importance of the service balance by determining the time shape of the current account, for it is from the current account (less specie flow) that the residual, net capital movements, is derived. Posed in another way, does the trade balance consistently dominate the current account, dictating its level, direction, and violence of movement? The answer to this question is most certainly in the affirmative. Chart A-4 shows this remarkably consistent relation during the period when official estimates are available. From 1919 to 1956 and in every year except 1946 and 1955, the movements in the current account are dominated by the trade balance. Although some periods reflect a larger service balance than others, 1922-1930 and 1950-1956, the time paths of these two series are precisely the same. Now there are three possible explanations of this behavior: either the service

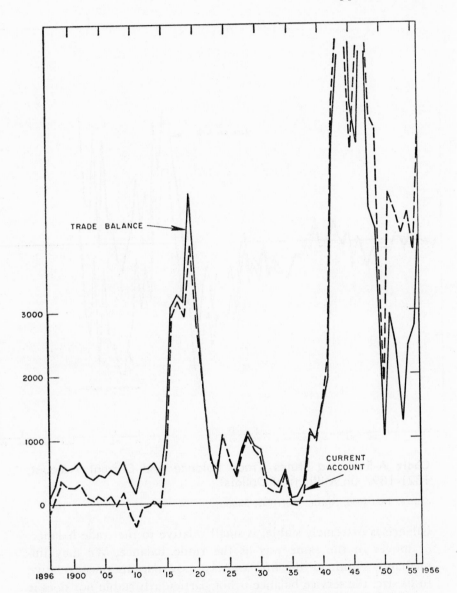

**Chart A-4** United States Trade Balance and Current Account, 1896-1956 (in Millions of Dollars)

*Source:* 1896-1900, Simon; 1901-1918, Goldsmith; 1919-1956, Balance of Payments (1958)

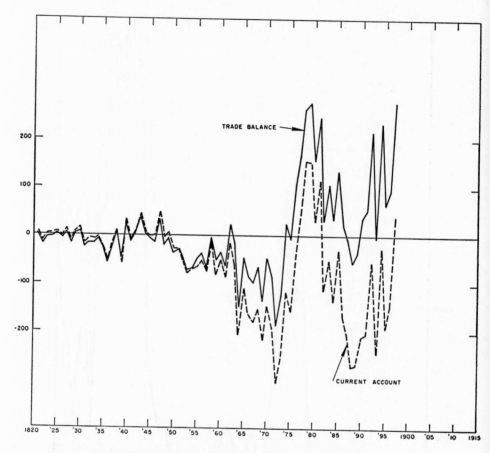

**Chart A-5** United States Trade Balance and Current Account, 1821-1897 (in Millions of Dollars)

*Source:* 1821-1860, North; 1861-1897, Simon

balance is extremely stable, is small relative to the trade balance, or moves in the same way as the trade balance. We may immediately eliminate the first and last explanations since, relative to its size, the service balance is not particularly stable nor does it move consistently over time in the same way that the trade balance does.

But this apparent unimportance of the service balance in shaping the time path of the current account is not just true of the post–World War I period. It is also true from 1820 to 1919 with only 1846, 1851, and 1879 as exceptions (see Chart A-5). Although from 1919 to 1956 it seems to be the relative smallness of the service balance which accounts for its unimportance, this is not the case over most of the nineteenth century. The service balance assumes extremely large proportions with the migration of capital and people sometime after 1850.

Incidentally, the apparent unimportance of the service balance in influencing the movements in the current account is not peculiar to United States experience. Imlah has also pointed to the same phenomena in the British balance of payments, where the service balance is extremely important and in excess of the trade balance. In both the American case from 1840 to 1919 and the British case over the nineteenth and twentieth centuries, the service balance is *not* small, but it still does not interfere with the general conformity between trade balance and current account movements.

To summarize, the American service balance prior to 1840 and after 1919 is small relative to the trade balance (and thus its relative movements are small) since these dates embrace the beginning and end of almost a century of major movements in capital and labor. It is not the stability of the service balance (pre-1840 and post-1919) which causes the conformity between the trade balance and the current account, but rather its smallness. It would take a very large, and unlikely, error to have understated the service balance so greatly on the *absolute* level as to create this apparent smallness. However, from 1840 to 1919 there is a great deal of similarity between British and American experience. During an extensive period of international factor movement, the service balance becomes a function of the flow of interest and dividends (and thus net capital inflow), emigrant remittances, and immigrant funds (and thus the inflow of people). Although both have very large service balances, a combination of *relative* stability *and* approximate synchronization with the trade balance over the long swing allows the trade balance to dictate movements in the current account.

### Net Gold Movements

We have examined in turn the flow of capital, trade in merchandise and, trade in services with regard to source of data and probable accuracy for our purpose of studying long swings in the balance of payments. Since we make important use of it in Chapter V, we must also attempt an evaluation of the accuracy of specie flow statistics (see Table B-1). Beginning in 1825, there are official compilations of the flow of silver and gold over United States borders, but before that time gold and silver are aggregated.[21] A second and minor difficulty exists in the official data prior to 1864 when domestic exports of silver were included with gold, but this inclusion "is probably small."[22] And finally during the years 1790-1842, the data is given for the fiscal year ending September 30; for 1843-1915, the fiscal year ending June 30; and for post-1915, calendar years. These problems are quite minor in the face of the recent sharp criticism that specie-flow data has received.

Morgenstern's findings are alarming indeed.[23] His research revealed no consistency whatsoever between country gold statistics. This comparison of total gold shipments among the United Kingdom, Germany, France, and the United States was for isolated years between 1900 and World War I. Thus German shipments of gold to France were very different from French receipts of gold from Germany; British imports of gold from the United States did not favorably compare with American shipments of gold to Great Britain and so on. This is a serious criticism of the usefulness of gold statistics indeed, but recalling Mintz's rebuttal that "[Morgenstern's] sharp criticism of trade statistics applies to data on trade between countries, not to total trade,"[24] a simple test of their accuracy was attempted. We tried to allow for Mintz's qualification by aggregating British, French, and German imports of American gold and comparing this sum for those isolated years with the aggregate of American exports to Great Britain, France, and Germany. Although the conformity of

21. U. S. Bureau of the Census, *Historical Statistics of the United States, 1789-1945*, M 47, pp. 243-245.

22. U. S. Department of Commerce, *Foreign Commerce and Navigation, 1914* (Washington, D. C.: U. S. Government Printing Office, 1915), p. 43.

23. Oskar Morgenstern, *The Validity of International Gold Movement Statistics*, Special Paper in International Economics No. 2 (Princeton, N. J.: Princeton University Press, 1955).

24. *Trade Balance During Business Cycles*, p. 6.

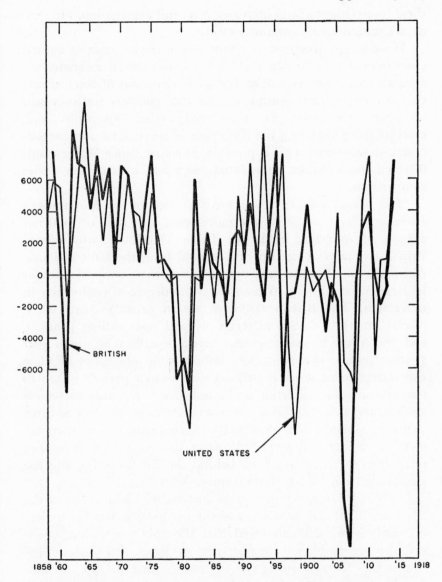

**Chart A-6** Net British Gold Imports from United States (in Thousands of Pounds Sterling); Net United States Gold Exports (in Ten Thousands of Dollars), 1858-1914 (Positive Figures Are British Imports and United States Exports)

*Sources:* British Data from Parliamentary Papers; United States Data from Table 38

these intertrade statistics increased after this aggregation, Morgenstern's criticism still remained valid.

If we accept Morgenstern's criticism of the accuracy of annual estimates (it may be that the United States official estimates are accurate and the others not so, but we have no way of determining the validity of such optimism), are the gold-flow statistics still adequate and useful for examining cyclic movements and, especially, for analyzing the time path of specie flow over periods of five to ten years? This is possible, of course, since Morgenstern directed his attention to isolated years and not to time series comparisons.

The period 1858-1914 was used as a test of the Morgenstern criticism. Chart A-6 shows the movements over time of total net *exports* of American gold (see Table 38) plotted with official British estimates of net imports of gold from the United States. Although the absolute difference between these two series might be large, what we wish to examine is the degree of conformity in movement. The British estimates are in calendar years while official American data is in terms of fiscal years ending June 30, and thus American estimates may have a superficial lag of one year at some points. However, the conformity in *movement* of these two independent series is striking over secular periods of ten to twenty years. The direction and amplitude is certainly extremely similar, and this also seems true over shorter movements of three to five years. Only from 1896 to 1907 is there any serious disagreement in timing and amplitude. Over this period the American series is as much as two years behind the British series, and the amplitude from 1905 to 1908 is quite different.

Although Morgenstern may be justified in his criticism of the adequacy of annual estimates and the use of such data for statistical analysis, we are convinced that the gold-flow estimates are certainly acceptable for our purposes. An interesting aspect of the comparison revealed in Chart A-6 may be that the poorest conformity between British and American annual estimates occurs from 1898 to World War I, and this may explain why Morgenstern's results were so negative. In any event, we have used the official American estimates of net specie flow without adjustment or much uneasiness throughout this study.

# APPENDIX B

## Tables

**Table B-1** United States Balance of Payments, 1820-1935 (in Millions of Dollars)[a]

| Year | Exports | Imports | Trade Balance Deficit(—)[b] | Net Specie Import(+)[b] | Net Capital Inflow (+) | Cumulative Balance |
|------|---------|---------|------------------------------|---------------------------|-------------------------|---------------------|
| 1820 | 69.7 | 74.5 | — 4.8 | | — .7 | 86.7 |
| 1821 | 54.6 | 54.5 | + .1 | — 2.4 | — 5.0 | 81.7 |
| 1822 | 61.4 | 79.9 | — 18.5 | — 7.4 | + 8.3 | 90.1 |
| 1823 | 68.3 | 72.5 | — 4.2 | — 1.3 | — 2.0 | 88.1 |
| 1824 | 69.0 | 72.2 | — 3.2 | + 1.4 | — 1.0 | 87.1 |
| 1825 | 90.7 | 90.2 | + .5 | — 2.6 | — 6.8 | 80.3 |
| 1826 | 72.9 | 78.1 | — 5.2 | + 2.2 | + 2.6 | 82.9 |
| 1827 | 74.3 | 71.3 | + 3.0 | + .1 | — 10.0 | 72.9 |
| 1828 | 64.0 | 81.1 | — 17.1 | + .8 | + 11.4 | 84.3 |
| 1829 | 67.4 | 67.1 | + .3 | + 2.5 | — 1.5 | 82.8 |
| 1830 | 71.7 | 62.7 | + 9.0 | + 6.0 | — 7.9 | 74.9 |
| 1831 | 72.3 | 95.9 | — 23.6 | — 1.7 | + 14.1 | 89.0 |
| 1832 | 81.5 | 97.0 | — 15.5 | + .3 | + 6.8 | 95.7 |
| 1833 | 87.5 | 103.1 | — 15.5 | + 4.5 | + 13.5 | 109.2 |
| 1834 | 102.3 | 110.8 | — 8.5 | + 15.8 | + 18.8 | 128.0 |
| 1835 | 115.2 | 139.5 | — 24.3 | + 6.7 | + 30.0 | 158.1 |
| 1836 | 124.3 | 180.1 | — 55.8 | + 9.1 | + 62.2 | 220.3 |
| 1837 | 111.4 | 133.1 | — 21.6 | + 4.5 | + 22.6 | 242.9 |
| 1838 | 105.0 | 97.9 | + 6.1 | + 14.2 | + 5.3 | 248.1 |
| 1839 | 112.3 | 159.6 | — 47.4 | — 3.2 | + 49.1 | 297.2 |
| 1840 | 123.7 | 100.2 | + 23.4 | + .5 | — 30.8 | 266.4 |
| 1841 | 111.8 | 125.4 | — 13.6 | — 5.0 | + 7.6 | 262.0 |
| 1842 | 99.9 | 98.0 | + 1.9 | — .7 | — 6.2 | 243.8 |
| 1843 | 82.8 | 43.3 | + 39.5 | + 20.8 | — 22.2 | 221.6 |
| 1844 | 105.7 | 104.7 | + 1.1 | — .4 | — 4.7 | 216.8 |
| 1845 | 106.0 | 115.4 | — 9.4 | — 4.5 | — 3.8 | 213.0 |
| 1846 | 109.6 | 122.6 | — 13.0 | — .1 | — .8 | 212.2 |
| 1847 | 156.7 | 127.3 | + 29.4 | + 22.2 | — 26.6 | 193.7 |
| 1848 | 138.2 | 154.6 | — 16.4 | — 9.5 | — 5.7 | 196.0 |
| 1849 | 140.4 | 146.9 | — 6.5 | + 1.2 | — 8.3 | 193.2 |
| 1850 | 144.4 | 180.5 | — 36.1 | — 2.9 | + 24.6 | 222.1 |

## Table B-1—Continued

| Year | Exports | Imports | Trade Balance Deficit(—)b | Net Specie Import(+)b | Net Capital Inflow (+) | Cumulative Balance |
|------|---------|---------|---------------------------|------------------------|-------------------------|---------------------|
| 1851 | 188.9 | 219.2 | — 30.3 | — 24.0 | + 4.1 | 229.6 |
| 1852 | 167.0 | 215.7 | — 48.8 | — 37.2 | + 13.0 | 245.8 |
| 1853 | 203.5 | 274.3 | — 70.8 | — 23.3 | + 55.6 | 301.3 |
| 1854 | 237.0 | 309.7 | — 72.7 | — 34.4 | + 35.1 | 343.3 |
| 1855 | 218.9 | 268.1 | — 49.2 | — 52.6 | + 12.8 | 356.3 |
| 1856 | 281.2 | 322.8 | — 41.6 | — 41.5 | + 10.7 | 366.9 |
| 1857 | 293.8 | 362.4 | — 68.5 | — 56.7 | + 16.4 | 383.3 |
| 1858 | 272.0 | 273.9 | — 1.9 | — 33.4 | — 23.1 | 360.2 |
| 1859 | 292.9 | 344.6 | — 51.7 | — 56.5 | + 26.2 | 386.5 |
| 1860 | 333.6 | 367.8 | — 34.2 | — 58.0 | — 7.3 | 379.2 |
| 1861 | 228.5 | 298.0 | — 68.2 | + 15.7 | + 104.4 | 483.6 |
| 1862 | 203.6 | 195.0 | + 14.4 | — 22.5 | — 1.1 | 482.5 |
| 1863 | 210.6 | 250.6 | — 28.9 | — 55.5 | + 12.6 | 495.1 |
| 1864 | 167.4 | 325.9 | — 143.5 | — 92.4 | + 110.6 | 605.7 |
| 1865 | 174.5 | 245.9 | — 64.7 | — 59.8 | + 68.7 | 674.4 |
| 1866 | 357.8 | 447.9 | — 88.8 | — 76.2 | + 94.4 | 768.8 |
| 1867 | 304.2 | 407.7 | — 102.9 | — 41.9 | + 145.6 | 914.4 |
| 1868 | 297.5 | 368.2 | — 69.8 | — 82.6 | + 72.7 | 987.1 |
| 1869 | 303.1 | 430.0 | — 125.7 | — 40.8 | + 169.2 | 1,156.3 |
| 1870 | 412.3 | 449.0 | — 35.6 | — 33.4 | + 99.4 | 1,255.7 |
| 1871 | 464.3 | 535.8 | — 70.6 | — 77.2 | + 100.9 | 1,356.6 |
| 1872 | 457.9 | 648.5 | — 189.3 | — 66.1 | + 242.8 | 1,599.4 |
| 1873 | 544.6 | 661.4 | — 114.9 | — 63.2 | + 182.9 | 1,782.3 |
| 1874 | 606.8 | 584.4 | + 26.6 | — 38.1 | + 82.2 | 1,864.5 |
| 1875 | 536.8 | 549.0 | — 10.5 | — 71.3 | + 86.9 | 1,951.4 |
| 1876 | 559.5 | 470.0 | + 91.7 | — 40.6 | + 1.8 | 1,953.2 |
| 1877 | 622.3 | 460.3 | + 163.6 | — 15.8 | — 57.3 | 1,895.9 |
| 1878 | 712.3 | 445.8 | + 269.4 | — 3.9 | — 161.9 | 1,734.0 |
| 1879 | 728.5 | 454.7 | + 276.4 | — 5.0 | — 160.2 | 1,573.8 |
| 1880 | 851.1 | 681.3 | + 171.4 | + 75.7 | + 29.4 | 1,603.2 |
| 1881 | 917.7 | 655.5 | + 263.9 | + 91.2 | — 40.8 | 1,562.4 |
| 1882 | 766.7 | 739.1 | + 28.7 | — 6.9 | + 109.5 | 1,671.9 |
| 1883 | 841.7 | 737.6 | + 106.3 | — 3.4 | + 51.1 | 1,723.0 |
| 1884 | 752.6 | 715.1 | + 39.1 | — 29.8 | + 105.3 | 1,828.3 |
| 1885 | 755.9 | 618.5 | + 138.4 | + .0 | + 32.9 | 1,861.2 |
| 1886 | 696.7 | 680.6 | + 17.3 | — 34.8 | + 135.9 | 1,997.1 |
| 1887 | 734.3 | 741.5 | — 6.3 | + 23.9 | + 230.2 | 2,227.3 |
| 1888 | 716.7 | 775.4 | — 58.3 | + 11.0 | + 285.0 | 2,512.3 |
| 1889 | 762.7 | 798.0 | — 34.8 | — 68.2 | + 201.6 | 2,713.9 |
| 1890 | 881.6 | 845.4 | + 36.9 | — 19.0 | + 192.6 | 2,906.5 |
| 1891 | 909.8 | 857.2 | + 53.0 | — 74.4 | + 134.5 | 3,041.0 |
| 1892 | 1,050.9 | 835.7 | + 215.7 | — 13.5 | + 40.8 | 3,081.8 |
| 1893 | 862.3 | 875.1 | — 12.3 | — 105.4 | + 145.4 | 3,227.2 |
| 1894 | 892.1 | 661.5 | + 231.2 | — 41.7 | — 66.0 | 3,161.2 |
| 1895 | 807.5 | 739.3 | + 68.6 | — 57.2 | + 137.0 | 3,298.2 |
| 1896 | 882.6 | 787.5 | + 95.8 | — 110.7 | + 39.8 | 3,338.0 |
| 1897 | 1,051.0 | 772.4 | + 278.9 | + 13.3 | — 23.1 | 3,314.9 |

## Table B-1—Continued

| Year | Exports | Imports | Trade Balance Deficit(—)b | Net Specie Import(+)b | Net Capital Inflow (+) | Cumulative Balance |
|---|---|---|---|---|---|---|
| 1898 | 1,231.5 | 622.2 | + 610.7 | + 80.8 | — 278.5 | 3,036.4 |
| 1899 | 1,227.0 | 704.1 | + 523.8 | + 25.8 | — 249.1 | 2,787.3 |
| 1900 | 1,394.5 | 858.4 | + 536.6 | — 25.2 | — 296.4 | 2,490.9 |
| 1901 | 1,487.8 | 823.2 | + 644.6 | + 12.9 | — 273 | |
| 1902 | 1,381.7 | 903.3 | + 478.4 | + 3.4 | — 82 | |
| 1903 | 1,420.1 | 1,025.7 | + 394.4 | — 2.1 | — 154 | |
| 1904 | 1,460.8 | 991.1 | + 469.7 | + 17.6 | — 127 | |
| 1905 | 1,518.6 | 1,117.5 | + 401.0 | — 38.9 | — 94 | |
| 1906 | 1,743.9 | 1,226.6 | + 517.3 | + 57.6 | + 22 | |
| 1907 | 1,880.9 | 1,434.4 | + 446.4 | + 63.1 | + 35 | |
| 1908 | 1,860.8 | 1,194.3 | + 666.4 | + 75.9 | — 191 | |
| 1909 | 1,663.0 | 1,311.9 | + 351.1 | — 47.5 | + 143 | |
| 1910 | 1,745.0 | 1,556.9 | + 188.0 | — 75.2 | + 229 | |
| 1911 | 2,049.3 | 1,527.2 | + 522.1 | + 51.1 | + 40 | |
| 1912 | 2,204.3 | 1,653.3 | + 555.1 | — 8.4 | + 36 | |
| 1913 | 2,465.9 | 1,813.0 | + 652.9 | — 8.6 | — 142 | |
| 1914 | 2,364.6 | 1,893.9 | + 470.7 | — 45.5 | + 14 | |
| 1915 | 2,768.6 | 1,674.2 | +1,094.4 | + 25.3 | —1,099 | |
| 1916 | 5,482.6 | 2,391.6 | +3,091.0 | + 530.2 | —2,421 | |
| 1917 | 6,233.5 | 2,952.5 | +3,281.0 | + 180.6 | —2,983 | |
| 1918 | 6,149.1 | 3,031.2 | +3,117.9 | + 21.0 | —2,185 | |
| 1919 | 7,920.4 | 3,904.4 | +4,016.1 | — 291.7 | —2,712 | |
| 1920 | 8,228.0 | 5,278.5 | +2,949.5 | + 95.0 | —1,007 | |
| 1921 | 4,485.0 | 2,509.1 | +1,975.9 | + 667.4 | — 562 | |
| 1922 | 3,831.8 | 3,112.7 | + 719.0 | + 238.3 | — 784 | |
| 1923 | 4,167.5 | 3,792.1 | + 375.4 | + 294.1 | + 13 | |
| 1924 | 4,591.0 | 3,610.0 | + 981.0 | + 258.1 | — 553 | |
| 1925 | 4,909.8 | 4,226.6 | + 683.3 | — 134.4 | — 649 | |
| 1926 | 4,808.7 | 4,430.9 | + 377.8 | + 97.8 | — 277 | |
| 1927 | 4,865.4 | 4,184.7 | + 680.6 | + 6.1 | — 406 | |
| 1928 | 5,128.4 | 4,091.4 | +1,036.9 | — 391.9 | —1,146 | |
| 1929 | 5,241.0 | 4,399.4 | + 841.6 | + 175.1 | — 244 | |
| 1930 | 3,843.2 | 3,060.9 | + 782.3 | + 280.1 | — 700 | |
| 1931 | 2,424.3 | 2,090.6 | + 333.7 | + 145.3 | — 429 | |
| 1932 | 1,611.0 | 1,322.8 | + 288.2 | — 446.2 | — 195 | |
| 1933 | 1,675.0 | 1,449.6 | + 225.4 | — 173.5 | — 342 | |
| 1934 | 2,132.8 | 1,655.1 | + 477.7 | +1,133.9 | + 425 | |
| 1935 | 2,282.9 | 2,047.5 | + 235.4 | +1,739.0 | +1,512 | |

aExports, imports, and the trade balance are taken from the following sources: 1820-1860, Douglas C. North, "The United States Balance of Payments, 1790-1860," *Trends in the American Economy in the Nineteenth Century* ("Studies in Income and Wealth," Vol. XXIV [Princeton, N. J.: Princeton University Press, 1960]), Table B-1, Cols. 1, 2, 3, p. 605 (this volume is hereafter cited as *Trends*); 1861-1900, Matthew Simon, *Trends*, Table 27, Rows 1, 3, 4, pp. 699-705; 1901-1935, U. S. Bureau of the Census, *Historical Statistics of the United States, 1789-1945*

(Washington, D. C.: U. S. Government Printing Office, 1949), M 51, 54, 55, pp. 244-245.

The net specie balance is taken from the following sources: 1820-1860, North, *Trends,* Table B-1, Col. 6, p. 605; 1861-1900, Simon, *Trends,* Table 27, Rows 28, 29, pp. 699-705; 1901-1935, U. S. Bureau of the Census, *Historical Statistics of the United States, 1789-1945,* M 47, pp. 243-245.

Net capital movements and the cumulative balance are taken from the following sources: 1820-1860, North, *Trends,* Table B-5, Cols. 8, 9, p. 621; Simon, *Trends,* Table 27, Row 30, 31, pp. 699-705; 1901-1918, Raymond W. Goldsmith, *A Study of Saving in the United States* (Princeton, N.J.: Princeton University Press, 1955), Vol. I, Table K-1, Col. 7, p. 1079 less Table K-3, Col. 9, p. 1085; 1919-1935, U. S. Department of Commerce, *Balance of Payments, Statistical Supplement,* (Washington, D. C.: U. S. Government Printing Office, 1958), pp. 11-13.

ᵇThe trade balance may not equal the difference between merchandise exports and imports due to rounding off and the inclusion of net sales of ships in that balance. The cumulative balance of indebtedness may not seem consistent with estimates of net capital movements due to allowances for default and war indemnities. Whereas the specie balance includes both gold and silver 1820-1900, from 1901 to 1935 the figures are for net gold flows. If the reader wishes further clarification of these estimates, see the indicated sources and Appendix A.

**Table B-2** Foreign Long-Term Investments in the United States by Type of Investment for Selected Years: 1853, 1866, 1868, 1869, 1914, and 1919 (in Millions of Dollars)[a]

| Year | Direct Investment | Corporate Stocks | | | Government and Corporate Bonds | | | | | | | Total | Total Excluding Federal |
|---|---|---|---|---|---|---|---|---|---|---|---|---|---|
| | | Total | Railroad | Other | Total | Federal | State and Local | Corporate Bonds | Of Which Railroads | Other | Miscellaneous | | |
| 1853 | (1) | 16.6 (7%) (9%) * ** | 8.2 (4%) (4%) | 8.4 (4%) (5%) | 204.6 (92%) | 27.0 (12%) | 132.0 (59%) (68%) | 46.2 (21%) (24%) | 43.9 (20%) (22%) | 2.3 (1%) | (N. A.) | 222.2 | 195.2 |
| 1866 | (1) | (N. A.) | 48.8 (8%) (20%) | (N. A.) | (N. A.) | 350.0 (58%) | 150.0 (25%) (60%) | (N. A.) | 50.7 (8%) (20%) | (N. A.) | (N. A.) | 599.5 | 249.5 |
| 1868 | (1) | 76.0 (8%) (32%) | 56.0 (6%) (23%) | 20.0 (2%) (8%) | 862.4 (92%) | 700.0 (75%) | 60.0 (6%) (25%) | 102.4 (11%) (43%) | 93.5 (10%) (39%) | 8.9 (1%) | (N. A.) | 938.4 | 238.4 |
| 1869 | (1) | 128.0 (9%) (32%) | 113.0 (8%) (29%) | 15.0 (1%) (4%) | (N. A.) | 1,000.0 (72%) | 107.5 (7%) (28%) | (N. A.) | 130.0 (9%) (33%) | (N. A.) | 25 (1%) | 1,390.5 | 390.5 |
| 1914 | 1,310.0 (19%) | (N. A.) | 1068.0 (16%) | (2) | (N. A.) | (2) | (2) | (N. A.) | 2,765.0 (41%) | (2) | 1,607 (24%) | 6,750.0 | |
| 1919 | 900 (36%) | (N. A.) | 232 (9%) | (2) | (N. A.) | (2) | (2) | (N. A.) | 847.0 (34%) | (2) | 544 (22%) | 2,523.0 | |

[a]Data for 1853 are as of June 30, the source of which is a report by the Secretary of the Treasury: U. S. Senate, *Senate Executive Document, No. 42*, 33rd Cong., 1st Sess., 1854, quoted by Cleona Lewis in *America's Stake in International Investments* (Washington, D.C.: The Brookings Institution, 1938), pp. 518, 521-522.

Figures for 1866 and 1868 are from *Hunt's Merchants' Magazine and Commercial Review*, October, 1868, no page given, and are quoted in Paul H. Dickens, "The Transition Period in American International Financing: 1897-1914," (unpublished Ph.D. dissertation, George Washington University, 1933).

Data for 1869 are from a Report by David A. Wells, Special Commissioner for the Revenue: U. S. House of Representatives, *House Executive Document, No. 27*, 41st Cong., 2nd Sess., 1870.

Figures for 1914 and 1919 are from Lewis, pp. 447, 450, 454, 558.

All these figures were assembled together in an unpublished research manuscript by the National Bureau of Economic Research.

(N.A.) Not available.
(1) Not estimated but probably small.
(2) Included in miscellaneous.

*The uppermost percentage figure in brackets refers to the share in total foreign holdings; the lower percentage figure in brackets refers to the share in total foreign holdings *less* federal bonds.

**Table B-3** United States Imports in Current Prices, Original Data and Original Data as Deviation from Trend, 1820-1934 (in Millions of Dollars)

| Year | Imports[a] | Imports (trend removed)[b] | Year | Imports[a] | Imports (trend removed)[b] |
|---|---|---|---|---|---|
| 1820 | 74.5 | 123.8 | 1865 | 245.9 | 84.6 |
| 1821 | 54.5 | 87.5 | 1866 | 447.9 | 148.0 |
| 1822 | 79.9 | 123.9 | 1867 | 407.7 | 130.2 |
| 1823 | 72.5 | 108.5 | 1868 | 368.2 | 113.3 |
| 1824 | 72.2 | 104.6 | 1869 | 430.0 | 127.6 |
| 1825 | 90.2 | 126.2 | 1870 | 449.0 | 128.0 |
| 1826 | 78.1 | 105.7 | 1871 | 535.8 | 147.5 |
| 1827 | 71.3 | 93.3 | 1872 | 648.5 | 172.1 |
| 1828 | 81.1 | 102.5 | 1873 | 661.4 | 169.2 |
| 1829 | 67.1 | 81.9 | 1874 | 584.4 | 144.2 |
| 1830 | 62.7 | 74.0 | 1875 | 549.0 | 130.6 |
| 1831 | 95.9 | 190.4 | 1876 | 470.0 | 107.7 |
| 1832 | 97.0 | 106.8 | 1877 | 460.3 | 101.7 |
| 1833 | 103.1 | 109.7 | 1878 | 445.8 | 94.9 |
| 1834 | 110.8 | 114.9 | 1879 | 454.7 | 93.3 |
| 1835 | 139.5 | 138.5 | 1880 | 681.3 | 134.7 |
| 1836 | 180.1 | 172.7 | 1881 | 655.5 | 124.9 |
| 1837 | 133.1 | 123.2 | 1882 | 739.1 | 135.7 |
| 1838 | 97.9 | 87.6 | 1883 | 737.6 | 130.5 |
| 1839 | 159.6 | 137.8 | 1884 | 715.1 | 121.9 |
| 1840 | 100.2 | 83.6 | 1885 | 618.5 | 101.6 |
| 1841 | 125.4 | 101.0 | 1886 | 680.6 | 107.7 |
| 1842 | 98.0 | 76.2 | 1887 | 741.5 | 113.0 |
| 1843 | 43.3 | 32.5 | 1888 | 775.4 | 113.9 |
| 1844 | 104.7 | 75.8 | 1889 | 798.0 | 112.9 |
| 1845 | 115.4 | 80.8 | 1890 | 845.4 | 115.2 |
| 1846 | 122.6 | 82.1 | 1891 | 857.2 | 112.5 |
| 1847 | 127.3 | 83.0 | 1892 | 835.7 | 105.6 |
| 1848 | 154.6 | 97.3 | 1893 | 875.1 | 106.5 |
| 1849 | 146.9 | 89.2 | 1894 | 661.5 | 77.5 |
| 1850 | 180.5 | 105.9 | 1895 | 739.3 | 83.5 |
| 1851 | 219.2 | 124.1 | 1896 | 787.5 | 85.6 |
| 1852 | 215.7 | 117.8 | 1897 | 772.4 | 80.8 |
| 1853 | 274.3 | 144.6 | 1898 | 622.2 | 62.7 |
| 1854 | 309.7 | 157.5 | 1899 | 704.1 | 68.3 |
| 1855 | 268.1 | 131.6 | 1900 | 858.4 | 80.2 |
| 1856 | 322.8 | 152.8 | 1901 | 823.2 | 74.0 |
| 1857 | 362.4 | 165.6 | 1902 | 903.3 | 78.2 |
| 1858 | 273.9 | 120.7 | 1903 | 1,025.7 | 85.5 |
| 1859 | 344.6 | 146.5 | 1904 | 991.1 | 79.5 |
| 1860 | 367.8 | 150.9 | 1905 | 1,117.5 | 86.2 |
| 1861 | 298.0 | 118.4 | 1906 | 1,226.6 | 90.8 |
| 1862 | 195.0 | 74.3 | 1907 | 1,434.4 | 103.1 |
| 1863 | 250.6 | 92.5 | 1908 | 1,194.3 | 82.2 |
| 1864 | 325.9 | 116.1 | 1909 | 1,311.9 | 86.9 |

## Table B-3—Continued

| Year | Imports[a] | Imports (trend removed)[b] | Year | Imports[a] | Imports (trend removed)[b] |
|------|-----------|---------------------------|------|-----------|---------------------------|
| 1910 | 1,556.9 | 99.2 | 1923 | 3,792.1 | 145.8 |
| 1911 | 1,527.2 | 93.6 | 1924 | 3,609.9 | 133.5 |
| 1912 | 1,653.3 | 97.5 | 1925 | 4,226.6 | 150.3 |
| 1913 | 1,813.0 | 102.9 | 1926 | 4,430.9 | 151.5 |
| 1914 | 1,893.9 | 103.4 | 1927 | 4,184.7 | 137.5 |
| 1915 | 1,674.2 | 87.9 | 1928 | 4,091.4 | 129.3 |
| 1916 | 2,391.6 | 120.8 | 1929 | 4,399.4 | 133.6 |
| 1917 | 2,952.5 | 143.5 | 1930 | 3,060.9 | 89.4 |
| 1918 | 3,031.2 | 141.7 | 1931 | 2,090.6 | 58.7 |
| 1919 | 3,904.4 | 175.5 | 1932 | 1,322.8 | 35.7 |
| 1920 | 5,278.5 | 228.2 | 1933 | 1,449.6 | 37.6 |
| 1921 | 2,509.1 | 104.3 | 1934 | 1,655.0 | 41.5 |
| 1922 | 3,112.7 | 124.5 | | | |

[a]Imports in current prices are taken from Table B-1.
[b]Trend line: $\log y = 2.6558 + .0160t + .000011t^2$, $t = 0 = 1877$.

**Table B-4** United States Import and Export Price Indices, 1820-1935[a]

| Year | Export Prices[b] | Import Prices[b] | Year | Export Prices[b] | Import Prices[b] |
|------|-----------------|------------------|------|-----------------|------------------|
| 1820 | 155 | 166 | 1842 | 71 | 92 |
| 1821 | 130 | 154 | 1843 | 66 | 89 |
| 1822 | 130 | 153 | 1844 | 70 | 88 |
| 1823 | 104 | 138 | 1845 | 51 | 89 |
| 1824 | 134 | 131 | 1846 | 72 | 88 |
| 1825 | 169 | 134 | 1847 | 102 | 89 |
| 1826 | 111 | 128 | 1848 | 73 | 83 |
| 1827 | 84 | 126 | 1849 | 69 | 80 |
| 1828 | 94 | 123 | 1850 | 112 | 89 |
| 1829 | 90 | 120 | 1851 | 110 | 83 |
| 1830 | 91 | 113 | 1852 | 86 | 80 |
| 1831 | 88 | 109 | 1853 | 100 | 87 |
| 1832 | 85 | 109 | 1854 | 100 | 93 |
| 1833 | 112 | 109 | 1855 | 94 | 101 |
| 1834 | 117 | 104 | 1856 | 94 | 106 |
| 1835 | 159 | 110 | 1857 | 123 | 106 |
| 1836 | 150 | 117 | 1858 | 111 | 98 |
| 1837 | 120 | 109 | 1859 | 110 | 94 |
| 1838 | 92 | 110 | 1860 | 100 (80) | 98 |
| 1839 | 121 | 107 | 1861 | 80 | 95 |
| 1840 | 81 | 98 | 1862 | 83 | 93 |
| 1841 | 86 | 102 | 1863 | 69 | 95 |

## Table B-4—Continued

| Year | Export Prices[b] | Import Prices[b] | Year | Export Prices[b] | Import Prices[b] |
|------|------|------|------|------|------|
| 1864 | 71 | 107 | 1900 | 80 | 87 |
| 1865 | 74 | 112 | 1901 | 78 | 83 |
| 1866 | 86 | 137 | 1902 | 80 | 81 |
| 1867 | 99 | 117 | 1903 | 86 | 84 |
| 1868 | 95 | 113 | 1904 | 86 | 86 |
| 1869 | 98 | 114 | 1905 | 83 | 91 |
| 1870 | 98 | 123 | 1906 | 91 | 95 |
| 1871 | 100 | 127 | 1907 | 95 | 99 |
| 1872 | 98 | 119 | 1908 | 89 | 88 |
| 1873 | 95 | 117 | 1909 | 94 | 88 |
| 1874 | 97 | 111 | 1910 | 102 | 95 |
| 1875 | 102 | 109 | 1911 | 94 | 96 |
| 1876 | 93 | 97 | 1912 | 95 | 101 |
| 1877 | 89 | 107 | 1913 | 100 | 100 |
| 1878 | 86 | 108 | 1914 | 98 | 94 |
| 1879 | 91 | 102 | 1915 | 104 | 97 |
| 1880 | 100 | 113 | 1916 | 135 | 120 |
| 1881 | 102 | 108 | 1917 | 178 | 145 |
| 1882 | 108 | 108 | 1918 | 212 | 161 |
| 1883 | 102 | 102 | 1919 | 221 | 181 |
| 1884 | 95 | 95 | 1920 | 238 | 219 |
| 1885 | 89 | 88 | 1921 | 161 | 125 |
| 1886 | 83 | 88 | 1922 | 147 | 120 |
| 1887 | 85 | 91 | 1923 | 159 | 137 |
| 1888 | 88 | 89 | 1924 | 156 | 135 |
| 1889 | 85 | 94 | 1925 | 170 | 149 |
| 1890 | 85 | 93 | 1926 | 145 | 146 |
| 1891 | 88 | 92 | 1927 | 135 | 133 |
| 1892 | 82 | 89 | 1928 | 139 | 129 |
| 1893 | 80 | 92 | 1929 | 137 | 122 |
| 1894 | 69 | 84 | 1930 | 123 | 100 |
| 1895 | 71 | 80 | 1931 | 94 | 77 |
| 1896 | 69 | 81 | 1932 | 80 | 60 |
| 1897 | 68 | 76 | 1933 | 85 | 60 |
| 1898 | 68 | 76 | 1934 | 99 | 70 |
| 1899 | 71 | 82 | 1935 | 102 | 70 |

[a]Export prices: 1820-1860, a cotton price index quoted in M. B. Hammond, *The Cotton Industry*, American Economic Association, New Series No. 1 (New York: Macmillan Co., 1897), Appendix 1; 1861-1878, from Simon, *Trends*, Table 6, Col. 1, p. 650; 1879-1923, from estimates done by Robert E. Lipsey at the National Bureau of Economic Research; 1924-1935, from official Department of Commerce estimates.

Import prices: 1820-1860, from North, *Trends*, Table B-2, Col. 9, pp. 607-608; 1861-1878, Simon, *Trends*, Table 7, Col. 1, p. 652; 1879-1923, from estimates by Lipsey at the National Bureau of Economic Research; 1924-1935, from official Department of Commerce estimates.

[b]Imports prices are for the base year 1913 = 100. Export prices are for the base year 1860 = 100 (1820-1860), and for 1913 = 100 (1861-1935).

**Table B-5** United States Deflated Imports, Original Data and Original Data as Deviation from Trend, 1820-1934 (in Millions of Dollars)

| Year | Deflated Imports[a] | Deflated Imports[b] (trend removed) | Year | Deflated Imports[a] | Deflated Imports[b] (trend removed) |
|---|---|---|---|---|---|
| 1820 | 44.7 | 76.2 | 1864 | 303.4 | 103.2 |
| 1821 | 35.4 | 58.2 | 1865 | 220.1 | 72.1 |
| 1822 | 52.3 | 82.8 | 1866 | 327.9 | 103.6 |
| 1823 | 52.5 | 80.2 | 1867 | 347.6 | 105.9 |
| 1824 | 55.0 | 81.0 | 1868 | 327.3 | 96.1 |
| 1825 | 67.6 | 96.0 | 1869 | 376.5 | 106.6 |
| 1826 | 61.1 | 83.6 | 1870 | 365.0 | 99.6 |
| 1827 | 56.8 | 74.9 | 1871 | 422.2 | 111.1 |
| 1828 | 65.8 | 83.7 | 1872 | 547.3 | 138.8 |
| 1829 | 56.0 | 68.6 | 1873 | 565.8 | 138.4 |
| 1830 | 55.5 | 65.6 | 1874 | 525.6 | 123.9 |
| 1831 | 88.3 | 100.6 | 1875 | 504.6 | 114.7 |
| 1832 | 89.3 | 98.0 | 1876 | 483.0 | 105.8 |
| 1833 | 94.9 | 100.4 | 1877 | 429.8 | 90.8 |
| 1834 | 106.4 | 106.6 | 1878 | 411.6 | 83.8 |
| 1835 | 127.2 | 125.2 | 1879 | 444.0 | 87.2 |
| 1836 | 154.6 | 146.7 | 1880 | 602.4 | 114.0 |
| 1837 | 122.5 | 112.0 | 1881 | 608.6 | 111.1 |
| 1838 | 89.2 | 78.7 | 1882 | 682.5 | 120.1 |
| 1839 | 148.6 | 126.3 | 1883 | 724.6 | 122.9 |
| 1840 | 101.9 | 83.5 | 1884 | 749.6 | 122.6 |
| 1841 | 123.2 | 97.3 | 1885 | 705.3 | 111.2 |
| 1842 | 106.2 | 80.9 | 1886 | 777.8 | 118.2 |
| 1843 | 48.5 | 35.6 | 1887 | 815.7 | 119.5 |
| 1844 | 118.7 | 83.9 | 1888 | 873.2 | 123.3 |
| 1845 | 129.3 | 88.2 | 1889 | 849.8 | 115.7 |
| 1846 | 139.0 | 91.4 | 1890 | 907.1 | 119.1 |
| 1847 | 142.6 | 90.4 | 1891 | 931.8 | 117.9 |
| 1848 | 187.1 | 114.4 | 1892 | 944.3 | 115.2 |
| 1849 | 182.9 | 107.7 | 1893 | 951.2 | 111.9 |
| 1850 | 202.1 | 114.8 | 1894 | 792.3 | 89.8 |
| 1851 | 265.4 | 145.3 | 1895 | 929.9 | 101.7 |
| 1852 | 268.7 | 141.8 | 1896 | 975.9 | 102.8 |
| 1853 | 315.0 | 160.2 | 1897 | 1,017.6 | 103.4 |
| 1854 | 331.6 | 162.6 | 1898 | 821.9 | 80.5 |
| 1855 | 266.3 | 125.9 | 1899 | 864.0 | 81.7 |
| 1856 | 303.7 | 138.4 | 1900 | 990.1 | 90.1 |
| 1857 | 340.9 | 151.2 | 1901 | 996.6 | 87.5 |
| 1858 | 278.3 | 117.9 | 1902 | 1,118.0 | 94.5 |
| 1859 | 367.0 | 147.7 | 1903 | 1,221.1 | 99.6 |
| 1860 | 373.7 | 147.1 | 1904 | 1,155.1 | 90.9 |
| 1861 | 315.3 | 119.7 | 1905 | 1,233.5 | 93.5 |
| 1862 | 209.0 | 76.5 | 1906 | 1,295.2 | 94.7 |
| 1863 | 264.6 | 93.3 | 1907 | 1,446.0 | 101.9 |

## Table B-5—Continued

| Year | Deflated Imports[a] | Deflated Imports[b] (trend removed) | Year | Deflated Imports[a] | Deflated Imports[b] (trend removed) |
|------|---------|---------|------|---------|---------|
| 1908 | 1,355.7 | 92.1 | 1922 | 2,600.4 | 105.9 |
| 1909 | 1,490.8 | 97.6 | 1923 | 2,776.0 | 108.9 |
| 1910 | 1,645.8 | 104.5 | 1924 | 2,678.0 | 101.3 |
| 1911 | 1,589.2 | 96.7 | 1925 | 2,838.5 | 103.6 |
| 1912 | 1,636.7 | 96.1 | 1926 | 3,032.8 | 106.7 |
| 1913 | 1,813.0 | 102.6 | 1927 | 3,137.0 | 106.4 |
| 1914 | 2,021.3 | 110.3 | 1928 | 3,166.8 | 103.5 |
| 1915 | 1,722.4 | 90.6 | 1929 | 3,600.1 | 113.5 |
| 1916 | 1,989.7 | 100.9 | 1930 | 3,070.1 | 93.3 |
| 1917 | 2,031.9 | 99.3 | 1931 | 2,708.1 | 79.3 |
| 1918 | 1,879.2 | 88.6 | 1932 | 2,190.0 | 61.9 |
| 1919 | 2,157.1 | 98.0 | 1933 | 2,399.9 | 64.7 |
| 1920 | 2,409.2 | 105.5 | 1934 | 2,357.6 | 61.9 |
| 1921 | 2,004.1 | 85.2 | | | |

[a]Imports in current prices are from Table B-1, and import prices are from Table B-4.

[b]Trend line: $\log y = 2.6292 + .0159t - .000021t^2$, $t = 0 = 1877$.

**Table B-6** United States Import Components, Five Groups, 1850-1935 (in Millions of Dollars)[a]

| Year | Crude Materials | Crude Foodstuffs | Manufactured Foodstuffs | Semi-Manufactures | Finished Manufactures |
|------|-----------------|------------------|-------------------------|-------------------|-----------------------|
| 1850 | 12 | 18 | 21 | 26 | 95 |
| 1851 | 16 | 19 | 29 | 26 | 118 |
| 1852 | 13 | 23 | 29 | 21 | 119 |
| 1853 | 18 | 26 | 32 | 42 | 144 |
| 1854 | 22 | 25 | 32 | 44 | 172 |
| 1855 | 27 | 32 | 34 | 34 | 128 |
| 1856 | 27 | 39 | 46 | 40 | 157 |
| 1857 | 34 | 40 | 71 | 38 | 163 |
| 1858 | 34 | 35 | 45 | 31 | 116 |
| 1859 | 38 | 43 | 57 | 40 | 151 |
| 1860 | 39 | 45 | 59 | 34 | 172 |
| 1861 | 30 | 40 | 53 | 32 | 132 |
| 1862 | 32 | 32 | 34 | 23 | 65 |
| 1863 | 47 | 30 | 35 | 35 | 95 |
| 1864 | 39 | 44 | 51 | 52 | 128 |
| 1865 | 29 | 35 | 48 | 29 | 96 |
| 1866 | 47 | 60 | 72 | 55 | 198 |
| 1867 | 43 | 50 | 65 | 55 | 180 |
| 1868 | 40 | 51 | 77 | 53 | 133 |
| 1869 | 50 | 52 | 95 | 62 | 156 |
| 1870 | 56 | 54 | 96 | 55 | 173 |
| 1871 | 77 | 63 | 103 | 72 | 203 |
| 1872 | 102 | 76 | 121 | 87 | 237 |
| 1873 | 107 | 83 | 122 | 96 | 232 |
| 1874 | 89 | 94 | 119 | 71 | 192 |
| 1875 | 88 | 90 | 113 | 63 | 177 |
| 1876 | 77 | 94 | 91 | 51 | 145 |
| 1877 | 76 | 86 | 114 | 48 | 125 |
| 1878 | 79 | 84 | 102 | 46 | 124 |
| 1879 | 80 | 82 | 102 | 49 | 130 |
| 1880 | 142 | 100 | 118 | 110 | 196 |
| 1881 | 125 | 102 | 123 | 87 | 203 |
| 1882 | 142 | 104 | 139 | 98 | 238 |
| 1883 | 146 | 93 | 142 | 98 | 242 |
| 1884 | 131 | 103 | 130 | 94 | 207 |
| 1885 | 120 | 93 | 102 | 78 | 182 |
| 1886 | 144 | 91 | 112 | 91 | 194 |
| 1887 | 151 | 106 | 111 | 120 | 202 |
| 1888 | 163 | 116 | 111 | 121 | 211 |
| 1889 | 172 | 123 | 122 | 115 | 212 |
| 1890 | 179 | 128 | 133 | 116 | 230 |
| 1891 | 192 | 150 | 147 | 136 | 217 |
| 1892 | 194 | 175 | 139 | 112 | 204 |
| 1893 | 216 | 131 | 153 | 135 | 228 |
| 1894 | 134 | 133 | 155 | 82 | 148 |

## Table B-6—Continued

| Year | Crude Materials | Crude Foodstuffs | Manufactured Foodstuffs | Semi-Manufactures | Finished Manufactures |
|------|-----------------|------------------|-------------------------|-------------------|-----------------------|
| 1895 | 187   | 141 | 107   | 96  | 199 |
| 1896 | 203   | 130 | 118   | 101 | 226 |
| 1897 | 200   | 128 | 129   | 88  | 217 |
| 1898 | 193   | 103 | 86    | 79  | 153 |
| 1899 | 213   | 98  | 123   | 91  | 169 |
| 1900 | 281   | 97  | 133   | 134 | 203 |
| 1901 | 254   | 110 | 125   | 127 | 205 |
| 1902 | 308   | 120 | 95    | 147 | 231 |
| 1903 | 336   | 119 | 116   | 195 | 257 |
| 1904 | 327   | 132 | 118   | 160 | 252 |
| 1905 | 395   | 146 | 145   | 177 | 252 |
| 1906 | 423   | 134 | 140   | 220 | 307 |
| 1907 | 487   | 149 | 158   | 274 | 364 |
| 1908 | 373   | 145 | 147   | 196 | 331 |
| 1909 | 460   | 164 | 165   | 222 | 299 |
| 1910 | 577   | 144 | 181   | 285 | 367 |
| 1911 | 524   | 181 | 172   | 287 | 361 |
| 1912 | 573   | 230 | 196   | 293 | 360 |
| 1913 | 649   | 211 | 194   | 349 | 408 |
| 1914 | 649   | 247 | 227   | 319 | 449 |
| 1915 | 591   | 223 | 285   | 237 | 335 |
| 1916 | 1,029 | 260 | 338   | 417 | 345 |
| 1917 | 1,286 | 385 | 351   | 536 | 392 |
| 1918 | 1,233 | 345 | 397   | 649 | 404 |
| 1919 | 1,701 | 545 | 555   | 608 | 493 |
| 1920 | 1,783 | 577 | 1,238 | 802 | 876 |
| 1921 | 858   | 300 | 368   | 361 | 620 |
| 1922 | 1,179 | 329 | 387   | 552 | 662 |
| 1923 | 1,406 | 363 | 530   | 720 | 771 |
| 1924 | 1,258 | 424 | 521   | 655 | 749 |
| 1925 | 1,748 | 494 | 432   | 755 | 795 |
| 1926 | 1,792 | 539 | 417   | 804 | 876 |
| 1927 | 1,600 | 504 | 450   | 749 | 878 |
| 1928 | 1,466 | 549 | 405   | 762 | 906 |
| 1929 | 1,558 | 538 | 423   | 685 | 993 |
| 1930 | 1,002 | 400 | 293   | 608 | 757 |
| 1931 | 642   | 304 | 222   | 372 | 549 |
| 1932 | 358   | 232 | 173   | 216 | 340 |
| 1933 | 418   | 215 | 201   | 292 | 322 |
| 1934 | 460   | 254 | 263   | 307 | 350 |
| 1935 | 582   | 322 | 318   | 409 | 405 |

aU. S. Bureau of the Census, *Historical Statistics of the United States, 1789-1945,* M 63, 64, 65, 66, 67, pp. 246-247.

**Table B-7** United States Export Components, Five Groups, 1850-1935 (in Millions of Dollars)[a]

| Year | Crude Materials | Crude Foodstuffs | Manufactured Foodstuffs | Semi-Manufactures | Finished Manufactures |
|------|------|------|------|------|------|
| 1850 | 84 | 7 | 20 | 6 | 17 |
| 1851 | 124 | 5 | 19 | 6 | 22 |
| 1852 | 100 | 7 | 19 | 6 | 21 |
| 1853 | 124 | 8 | 26 | 6 | 24 |
| 1854 | 107 | 22 | 46 | 10 | 26 |
| 1855 | 108 | 10 | 33 | 11 | 28 |
| 1856 | 145 | 28 | 53 | 8 | 31 |
| 1857 | 158 | 31 | 48 | 11 | 30 |
| 1858 | 155 | 17 | 38 | 9 | 30 |
| 1859 | 190 | 10 | 32 | 10 | 35 |
| 1860 | 216 | 12 | 38 | 12 | 35 |
| 1861 | 58 | 48 | 53 | 8 | 35 |
| 1862 | 18 | 55 | 70 | 8 | 26 |
| 1863 | 29 | 45 | 66 | 11 | 33 |
| 1864 | 28 | 24 | 54 | 9 | 25 |
| 1865 | 34 | 13 | 47 | 10 | 30 |
| 1866 | 228 | 16 | 40 | 12 | 39 |
| 1867 | 166 | 20 | 34 | 15 | 43 |
| 1868 | 132 | 34 | 42 | 17 | 42 |
| 1869 | 145 | 25 | 43 | 13 | 47 |
| 1870 | 213 | 41 | 50 | 13 | 56 |
| 1871 | 223 | 48 | 66 | 13 | 75 |
| 1872 | 198 | 59 | 84 | 21 | 65 |
| 1873 | 333 | 69 | 100 | 24 | 76 |
| 1874 | 229 | 119 | 114 | 26 | 81 |
| 1875 | 207 | 79 | 110 | 27 | 74 |
| 1876 | 203 | 94 | 121 | 31 | 74 |
| 1877 | 204 | 90 | 150 | 31 | 112 |
| 1878 | 216 | 154 | 170 | 28 | 110 |
| 1879 | 202 | 188 | 174 | 30 | 103 |
| 1880 | 242 | 266 | 193 | 29 | 92 |
| 1881 | 280 | 241 | 226 | 32 | 102 |
| 1882 | 238 | 155 | 178 | 37 | 124 |
| 1883 | 294 | 163 | 186 | 37 | 122 |
| 1884 | 243 | 130 | 194 | 37 | 118 |
| 1885 | 251 | 123 | 201 | 39 | 110 |
| 1886 | 256 | 100 | 162 | 34 | 111 |
| 1887 | 252 | 125 | 175 | 36 | 112 |
| 1888 | 273 | 86 | 169 | 40 | 113 |
| 1889 | 291 | 98 | 174 | 42 | 123 |
| 1890 | 309 | 132 | 224 | 46 | 132 |
| 1891 | 351 | 106 | 226 | 47 | 140 |
| 1892 | 319 | 262 | 250 | 50 | 132 |
| 1893 | 251 | 153 | 247 | 49 | 129 |
| 1894 | 283 | 133 | 249 | 67 | 135 |
| 1895 | 269 | 99 | 219 | 62 | 143 |
| 1896 | 257 | 128 | 219 | 76 | 181 |

## Table B-7—Continued

| Year | Crude Materials | Crude Foodstuffs | Manufactured Foodstuffs | Semi-Manufactures | Finished Manufactures |
|------|-----------------|------------------|-------------------------|-------------------|-----------------------|
| 1897 | 304 | 181 | 235 | 98 | 212 |
| 1898 | 295 | 305 | 284 | 101 | 222 |
| 1899 | 285 | 232 | 304 | 117 | 262 |
| 1900 | 340 | 225 | 319 | 153 | 331 |
| 1901 | 411 | 245 | 337 | 148 | 317 |
| 1902 | 387 | 184 | 328 | 132 | 321 |
| 1903 | 415 | 185 | 323 | 140 | 327 |
| 1904 | 466 | 135 | 308 | 174 | 348 |
| 1905 | 478 | 118 | 283 | 209 | 402 |
| 1906 | 507 | 177 | 347 | 226 | 459 |
| 1907 | 600 | 167 | 345 | 259 | 480 |
| 1908 | 563 | 189 | 331 | 261 | 489 |
| 1909 | 528 | 135 | 302 | 231 | 440 |
| 1910 | 574 | 109 | 259 | 267 | 499 |
| 1911 | 720 | 103 | 282 | 309 | 598 |
| 1912 | 731 | 99 | 318 | 348 | 672 |
| 1913 | 740 | 181 | 321 | 408 | 776 |
| 1914 | 799 | 137 | 293 | 374 | 724 |
| 1915 | 591 | 506 | 454 | 355 | 807 |
| 1916 | 815 | 421 | 648 | 912 | 2,625 |
| 1917 | 832 | 508 | 806 | 1,315 | 2,705 |
| 1918 | 972 | 547 | 1,405 | 1,053 | 2,069 |
| 1919 | 1,623 | 678 | 1,962 | 922 | 2,563 |
| 1920 | 1,882 | 917 | 1,116 | 958 | 3,204 |
| 1921 | 983 | 673 | 685 | 410 | 1,626 |
| 1922 | 988 | 458 | 587 | 437 | 1,292 |
| 1923 | 1,208 | 257 | 583 | 563 | 1,477 |
| 1924 | 1,332 | 392 | 573 | 610 | 1,588 |
| 1925 | 1,422 | 317 | 573 | 661 | 1,843 |
| 1926 | 1,261 | 335 | 503 | 655 | 1,956 |
| 1927 | 1,192 | 421 | 463 | 699 | 1,981 |
| 1928 | 1,293 | 294 | 465 | 716 | 2,260 |
| 1929 | 1,142 | 269 | 484 | 729 | 2,531 |
| 1930 | 829 | 178 | 362 | 512 | 1,898 |
| 1931 | 566 | 127 | 246 | 317 | 1,119 |
| 1932 | 513 | 89 | 152 | 196 | 624 |
| 1933 | 590 | 48 | 154 | 237 | 616 |
| 1934 | 652 | 59 | 167 | 341 | 878 |
| 1935 | 682 | 58 | 157 | 349 | 994 |

aU. S. Bureau of the Census, *Historical Statistics of the United States, 1789-1945,* M 57, 58, 59, 60, 61, pp. 246-247.

**Table B-8** United States Cotton: Revenue Exported, Prices, and Production, 1820-1860[a]

| Year | (1)<br>Cotton Exports<br>(in thousands of<br>bales) | (2)<br>Cotton Prices<br>(cents/lb) | Cotton Revenue<br>Index<br>(1) x (2) x 100 | Total Cotton<br>Production<br>(in thousands of<br>bales) |
|---|---|---|---|---|
| 1820 | 484 | .1700 | 8,228 | 606 |
| 1821 | 449 | .1432 | 6,430 | 647 |
| 1822 | 511 | .1432 | 7,318 | 742 |
| 1823 | 583 | .1140 | 6,646 | 621 |
| 1824 | 505 | .1475 | 7,449 | 762 |
| 1825 | 617 | .1859 | 11,470 | 892 |
| 1826 | 656 | .1219 | 7,997 | 1,121 |
| 1827 | 854 | .0926 | 7,908 | 957 |
| 1828 | 600 | .1032 | 6,192 | 721 |
| 1829 | 749 | .0988 | 7,400 | 870 |
| 1830 | 839 | .1004 | 8,423 | 976 |
| 1831 | 773 | .0971 | 7,505 | 1,038 |
| 1832 | 892 | .0938 | 8,367 | 987 |
| 1833 | 867 | .1232 | 10,681 | 1,070 |
| 1834 | 1,028 | .1290 | 13,261 | 1,205 |
| 1835 | 1,023 | .1745 | 17,851 | 1,254 |
| 1836 | 1,117 | .1650 | 18,430 | 1,361 |
| 1837 | 1,168 | .1325 | 15,476 | 1,424 |
| 1838 | 1,576 | .1014 | 15,981 | 1,801 |
| 1839 | 1,075 | .1336 | 14,362 | 1,361 |
| 1840 | 1,876 | .0892 | 16,734 | 2,178 |
| 1841 | 1,313 | .0950 | 12,474 | 1,635 |
| 1842 | 1,465 | .0785 | 11,500 | 1,684 |
| 1843 | 2,010 | .0725 | 14,573 | 2,379 |
| 1844 | 1,629 | .0773 | 12,592 | 2,030 |
| 1845 | 2,084 | .0563 | 11,733 | 2,395 |
| 1846 | 1,667 | .0787 | 13,119 | 2,101 |
| 1847 | 1,241 | .1121 | 13,912 | 1,779 |
| 1848 | 1,858 | .0803 | 14,920 | 2,440 |
| 1849 | 2,228 | .0775 | 16,821 | 2,867 |
| 1850 | 1,590 | .1234 | 19,621 | 2,334 |
| 1851 | 1,989 | .1214 | 24,146 | 2,454 |
| 1852 | 2,444 | .0950 | 23,218 | 3,126 |
| 1853 | 2,528 | .1102 | 27,859 | 3,416 |
| 1854 | 2,319 | .1097 | 25,439 | 3,075 |
| 1855 | 2,244 | .1039 | 23,315 | 2,983 |
| 1856 | 2,955 | .1030 | 30,437 | 3,656 |
| 1857 | 2,253 | .1351 | 30,438 | 3,094 |
| 1858 | 3,590 | .1223 | 43,906 | 3,257 |
| 1859 | 3,021 | .1208 | 36,494 | 4,019 |
| 1860 | 3,774 | .1100 | 41,514 | 4,861 |

[a]Hammond, *Cotton Industry*, Appendix 1. Cotton prices are for middling uplands in the New York market.

**Table B-9** Grain and Wheat Exports from the United States and
Wheat Prices, 1850-1890[a]

| Year | Total Grain Exports (in thousands of dollars) | Total Wheat Exports (in thousands of bushels) | Wheat Prices per Bushel |
|------|------|------|------|
| 1850 | | | |
| 1851 | 2,908 | 1,026 | .999 |
| 1852 | 4,429 | 2,694 | .948 |
| 1853 | 5,894 | 3,890 | 1.119 |
| 1854 | 19,070 | 8,036 | 1.545 |
| 1855 | 8,529 | 798 | 1.664 |
| 1856 | 25,456 | 8,154 | 1.854 |
| 1857 | 28,105 | 14,570 | 1.526 |
| 1858 | 12,963 | 8,926 | 1.015 |
| 1859 | 5,353 | 3,002 | .949 |
| 1860 | 7,534 | 4,155 | .981 |
| 1861 | 46,329 | 31,238 | 1.227 |
| 1862 | 55,325 | 37,289 | 1.126 |
| 1863 | 59,180 | 36,160 | .957 |
| 1864 | 35,268 | 23,681 | .875 |
| 1865 | 23,565 | 9,937 | .972 |
| 1866 | 19,998 | 5,579 | 1.001 |
| 1867 | 23,293 | 6,146 | 1.158 |
| 1868 | 44,294 | 15,940 | 1.492 |
| 1869 | 31,612 | 17,557 | 1.108 |
| 1870 | 48,854 | 36,584 | 1.088 |
| 1871 | 52,930 | 34,304 | 1.192 |
| 1872 | 63,801 | 26,423 | 1.332 |
| 1873 | 76,330 | 39,204 | 1.205 |
| 1874 | 128,354 | 71,039 | 1.300 |
| 1875 | 84,621 | 53,047 | 1.030 |
| 1876 | 102,927 | 55,073 | 1.123 |
| 1877 | 92,438 | 40,325 | 1.121 |
| 1878 | 151,797 | 72,404 | 1.310 |
| 1879 | 176,479 | 122,353 | 1.066 |
| 1880 | 247,300 | 153,252 | 1.243 |
| 1881 | 221,023 | 150,565 | 1.114 |
| 1882 | 143,171 | 95,271 | 1.185 |
| 1883 | 149,826 | 106,385 | 1.127 |
| 1884 | 108,102 | 70,349 | 1.066 |
| 1885 | 104,873 | 84,653 | .862 |
| 1886 | 84,237 | 57,759 | .870 |
| 1887 | 111,213 | 101,971 | .890 |
| 1888 | 70,108 | 65,789 | .855 |
| 1889 | 75,892 | 46,414 | .897 |
| 1890 | 94,478 | 54,387 | .832 |

[a]Total grain and wheat exports are taken from U. S. Department of Commerce, *Exports of Farm Products from the United States, 1851-1908*, Bureau of Statistics Bulletin No. 75 (Washington, D. C.: U. S. Government Printing Office, 1910), p. 14. Wheat prices, *ibid.*, Table 13, p. 16.

**Table B-10** Riggleman Building Index of United States Building, Original Data and Original Data as Deviation from Trend, 1831-1913[a]

| Year | Riggleman Index | Riggleman Index (trend removed) | Year | Riggleman Index | Riggleman Index (trend removed) |
|------|----------------|-------------------------------|------|----------------|-------------------------------|
| 1831 | 19 | 64.30 | 1873 | 29 | 96.93 |
| 1832 | 28 | 95.01 | 1874 | 24.5 | 81.61 |
| 1833 | 35 | 119.05 | 1875 | 24.5 | 81.31 |
| 1834 | 37 | 126.19 | 1876 | 20 | 66.14 |
| 1835 | 39 | 133.33 | 1877 | 18 | 59.29 |
| 1836 | 52 | 178.14 | 1878 | 17 | 55.77 |
| 1837 | 25 | 85.82 | 1879 | 20 | 65.36 |
| 1838 | 22 | 75.62 | 1880 | 21.5 | 69.96 |
| 1839 | 19 | 65.45 | 1881 | 25 | 81.01 |
| 1840 | 16.5 | 56.94 | 1882 | 28 | 90.32 |
| 1841 | 17.5 | 60.47 | 1883 | 30 | 96.31 |
| 1842 | 14.5 | 50.17 | 1884 | 32 | 102.27 |
| 1843 | 13 | 45.03 | 1885 | 36 | 114.50 |
| 1844 | 14.5 | 50.28 | 1886 | 37.5 | 118.67 |
| 1845 | 17.5 | 60.74 | 1887 | 38.5 | 121.22 |
| 1846 | 24 | 83.36 | 1888 | 37 | 115.88 |
| 1847 | 30 | 104.24 | 1889 | 44.5 | 138.63 |
| 1848 | 30 | 104.28 | 1890 | 48 | 148.74 |
| 1849 | 34 | 118.22 | 1891 | 42.5 | 130.97 |
| 1850 | 42 | 146.04 | 1892 | 43 | 131.78 |
| 1851 | 44 | 152.99 | 1893 | 31.5 | 95.98 |
| 1852 | 48.5 | 168.58 | 1894 | 29 | 87.85 |
| 1853 | 50.5 | 175.47 | 1895 | 35.5 | 106.93 |
| 1854 | 47.5 | 164.99 | 1896 | 30 | 89.82 |
| 1855 | 44.5 | 154.46 | 1897 | 31.5 | 93.72 |
| 1856 | 45 | 156.09 | 1898 | 27 | 79.83 |
| 1857 | 42 | 145.53 | 1899 | 31 | 91.10 |
| 1858 | 27 | 93.43 | 1900 | 22.5 | 65.69 |
| 1859 | 28 | 96.79 | 1901 | 30.5 | 88.48 |
| 1860 | 30.5 | 105.28 | 1902 | 30 | 86.46 |
| 1861 | 20 | 68.92 | 1903 | 29.5 | 84.45 |
| 1862 | 18 | 61.92 | 1904 | 33.5 | 95.28 |
| 1863 | 20.5 | 70.37 | 1905 | 42 | 118.64 |
| 1864 | 13.5 | 46.25 | 1906 | 42 | 117.85 |
| 1865 | 17.5 | 59.83 | 1907 | 35.5 | 98.91 |
| 1866 | 25 | 85.27 | 1908 | 33 | 91.29 |
| 1867 | 29.5 | 100.37 | 1909 | 43.5 | 119.51 |
| 1868 | 33 | 111.98 | 1910 | 39.5 | 107.75 |
| 1869 | 35.5 | 120.14 | 1911 | 38 | 102.90 |
| 1870 | 35.5 | 119.81 | 1912 | 40.5 | 108.87 |
| 1871 | 37.5 | 126.18 | 1913 | 33 | 88.05 |
| 1872 | 30 | 100.60 | | | |

[a]Original data taken from J. R. Riggleman, "Building Cycles in the United States, 1830-1935" (unpublished Ph.D. dissertation, The Johns Hopkins University), as listed in Brinley Thomas, *Migration and Economic Growth* (Cambridge: Cambridge University Press, 1954), Appendix 4, Table 108, p. 298, with the trendless index.

**Table B-11** Frickey Index for United States Manufacturing Production, Original Data and Original Data as Deviation from Trend, 1860-1914[a]

| Year | Frickey Index | Frickey Index (trend removed) | Year | Frickey Index | Frickey Index (trend removed) |
|------|------|------|------|------|------|
| 1860 | 16 | 106 | 1888 | 62 | 104 |
| 1861 | 16 | 99 | 1889 | 66 | 106 |
| 1862 | 15 | 87 | 1890 | 71 | 110 |
| 1863 | 17 | 94 | 1891 | 73 | 107 |
| 1864 | 18 | 98 | 1892 | 79 | 110 |
| 1865 | 17 | 88 | 1893 | 70 | 93 |
| 1866 | 21 | 104 | 1894 | 68 | 86 |
| 1867 | 22 | 102 | 1895 | 81 | 98 |
| 1868 | 23 | 102 | 1896 | 74 | 85 |
| 1869 | 25 | 107 | 1897 | 80 | 88 |
| 1870 | 25 | 101 | 1898 | 91 | 95 |
| 1871 | 26 | 102 | 1899 | 100 | 99 |
| 1872 | 31 | 114 | 1900 | 100 | 95 |
| 1873 | 30 | 106 | 1901 | 111 | 100 |
| 1874 | 29 | 98 | 1902 | 127 | 109 |
| 1875 | 28 | 90 | 1903 | 126 | 103 |
| 1876 | 28 | 86 | 1904 | 121 | 94 |
| 1877 | 30 | 87 | 1905 | 140 | 104 |
| 1878 | 32 | 88 | 1906 | 152 | 108 |
| 1879 | 36 | 95 | 1907 | 156 | 106 |
| 1880 | 42 | 106 | 1908 | 127 | 82 |
| 1881 | 46 | 110 | 1909 | 166 | 102 |
| 1882 | 49 | 111 | 1910 | 172 | 101 |
| 1883 | 50 | 109 | 1911 | 162 | 90 |
| 1884 | 47 | 97 | 1912 | 194 | 103 |
| 1885 | 47 | 92 | 1913 | 203 | 102 |
| 1886 | 57 | 106 | 1914 | 192 | 93 |
| 1887 | 60 | 107 | | | |

[a]Edwin Frickey, *Production in the United States, 1860-1914* (Cambridge, Mass.: Harvard University Press, 1947), Tables 6 and 7, pp. 54, 60. Original data is for the base year 1899 = 100.

**Table B-12** Bituminous Coal Output in the United States, Original Data and Original Data as Deviation from Trend, 1841-1913ᵃ (Thousands Net Tons of 2,000 Pounds)

| Year | Output | Output (trend removed) | Year | Output | Output (trend removed) |
|------|--------|------------------------|------|--------|------------------------|
| 1841 | 1,109  | 103.84 | 1878 | 36,246  | 92.36  |
| 1842 | 1,244  | 104.36 | 1879 | 37,898  | 88.76  |
| 1843 | 1,504  | 113.08 | 1880 | 42,832  | 92.27  |
| 1844 | 1,672  | 112.82 | 1881 | 53,961  | 107.00 |
| 1845 | 1,830  | 110.84 | 1882 | 68,430  | 124.98 |
| 1846 | 1,978  | 107.68 | 1883 | 77,251  | 130.05 |
| 1847 | 1,735  | 84.88  | 1884 | 82,999  | 128.88 |
| 1848 | 1,968  | 86.66  | 1885 | 72,824  | 104.37 |
| 1849 | 2,453  | 97.23  | 1886 | 74,645  | 98.81  |
| 1850 | 2,880  | 102.86 | 1887 | 88,562  | 108.36 |
| 1851 | 3,253  | 104.73 | 1888 | 102,040 | 115.47 |
| 1852 | 3,665  | 106.45 | 1889 | 95,683  | 100.22 |
| 1853 | 4,170  | 109.36 | 1890 | 111,302 | 107.97 |
| 1854 | 4,582  | 108.58 | 1891 | 117,901 | 106.01 |
| 1855 | 4,785  | 102.48 | 1892 | 126,857 | 105.78 |
| 1856 | 5,012  | 97.11  | 1893 | 128,385 | 99.36  |
| 1857 | 5,154  | 90.42  | 1894 | 118,820 | 85.41  |
| 1858 | 5,548  | 88.18  | 1895 | 135,118 | 90.26  |
| 1859 | 6,013  | 86.63  | 1896 | 137,640 | 85.52  |
| 1860 | 6,494  | 84.88  | 1897 | 147,618 | 85.36  |
| 1861 | 6,688  | 79.35  | 1898 | 166,594 | 89.71  |
| 1862 | 7,791  | 83.98  | 1899 | 193,323 | 97.02  |
| 1863 | 9,534  | 93.42  | 1900 | 212,316 | 99.38  |
| 1864 | 11,067 | 98.65  | 1901 | 225,828 | 98.67  |
| 1865 | 11,900 | 96.57  | 1902 | 260,217 | 106.15 |
| 1866 | 13,352 | 98.71  | 1903 | 282,749 | 107.80 |
| 1867 | 14,722 | 99.21  | 1904 | 278,660 | 99.35  |
| 1868 | 15,859 | 97.49  | 1905 | 315,063 | 105.12 |
| 1869 | 15,821 | 88.78  | 1906 | 342,875 | 107.14 |
| 1870 | 17,371 | 89.05  | 1907 | 394,759 | 115.59 |
| 1871 | 27,543 | 129.07 | 1908 | 332,574 | 91.32  |
| 1872 | 27,220 | 116.68 | 1909 | 379,744 | 97.86  |
| 1873 | 31,450 | 123.40 | 1910 | 417,111 | 100.94 |
| 1874 | 27,787 | 99.87  | 1911 | 405,907 | 92.30  |
| 1875 | 29,863 | 98.39  | 1912 | 450,105 | 96.25  |
| 1876 | 30,487 | 92.13  | 1913 | 478,435 | 96.28  |
| 1877 | 34,841 | 96.65  |      |         |        |

ᵃOriginal data is from U. S. Bureau of the Census, *Historical Statistics of the United States, 1789-1945*, G 13, as listed in Thomas, *Migration*, Appendix 4, Table 97, p. 287, with trend removed index.

**Table B-13** Miles of Railroad Track Added in the United States, Original Data and Original Data as Deviation from Trend, 1831-1913 (1913 Dollars)[a]

| Year | Miles Added | Miles Added (trend removed) | Year | Miles Added | Miles Added (trend removed) |
|---|---|---|---|---|---|
| 1831 | 72 | 51.80 | 1873 | 4,097 | 120.89 |
| 1832 | 134 | 85.90 | 1874 | 2,117 | 60.23 |
| 1833 | 151 | 86.29 | 1875 | 1,711 | 47.03 |
| 1834 | 253 | 129.74 | 1876 | 2,712 | 72.14 |
| 1835 | 465 | 214.29 | 1877 | 2,274 | 58.65 |
| 1836 | 175 | 72.31 | 1878 | 2,665 | 66.78 |
| 1837 | 224 | 83.58 | 1879 | 4,809 | 117.26 |
| 1838 | 416 | 140.07 | 1880 | 6,711 | 159.56 |
| 1839 | 389 | 118.24 | 1881 | 9,846 | 228.66 |
| 1840 | 516 | 142.15 | 1882 | 11,569 | 262.87 |
| 1841 | 717 | 179.25 | 1883 | 6,745 | 150.26 |
| 1842 | 491 | 111.59 | 1884 | 3,923 | 85.84 |
| 1843 | 159 | 32.92 | 1885 | 2,975 | 64.06 |
| 1844 | 192 | 36.29 | 1886 | 8,018 | 170.20 |
| 1845 | 256 | 44.21 | 1887 | 12,876 | 269.94 |
| 1846 | 297 | 46.92 | 1888 | 6,900 | 143.12 |
| 1847 | 668 | 96.95 | 1889 | 5,162 | 106.15 |
| 1848 | 398 | 53.07 | 1890 | 5,915 | 120.79 |
| 1849 | 1,369 | 167.98 | 1891 | 4,844 | 98.42 |
| 1850 | 1,656 | 187.54 | 1892 | 3,656 | 74.04 |
| 1851 | 1,961 | 205.34 | 1893 | 4,143 | 83.80 |
| 1852 | 1,926 | 186.63 | 1894 | 2,899 | 58.66 |
| 1853 | 2,452 | 220.50 | 1895 | 1,895 | 38.43 |
| 1854 | 1,360 | 113.71 | 1896 | 2,053 | 41.81 |
| 1855 | 1,654 | 128.72 | 1897 | 2,163 | 44.31 |
| 1856 | 3,642 | 264.30 | 1898 | 2,026 | 41.83 |
| 1857 | 2,487 | 168.72 | 1899 | 3,466 | 72.27 |
| 1858 | 2,465 | 156.61 | 1900 | 4,628 | 97.62 |
| 1859 | 1,821 | 108.46 | 1901 | 3,324 | 71.06 |
| 1860 | 1,837 | 102.86 | 1902 | 4,965 | 107.75 |
| 1861 | 660 | 34.79 | 1903 | 6,169 | 136.18 |
| 1862 | 834 | 41.47 | 1904 | 6,690 | 150.51 |
| 1863 | 1,050 | 49.32 | 1905 | 5,084 | 116.77 |
| 1864 | 738 | 32.81 | 1906 | 5,565 | 130.73 |
| 1865 | 1,177 | 49.64 | 1907 | 6,188 | 148.96 |
| 1866 | 1,716 | 68.78 | 1908 | 3,897 | 96.29 |
| 1867 | 2,249 | 85.81 | 1909 | 3,238 | 82.29 |
| 1868 | 2,979 | 108.37 | 1910 | 5,908 | 154.70 |
| 1869 | 4,615 | 160.41 | 1911 | 4,740 | 128.14 |
| 1870 | 6,078 | 202.26 | 1912 | 3,301 | 92.28 |
| 1871 | 7,379 | 235.45 | 1913 | 3,003 | 86.99 |
| 1872 | 5,870 | 179.95 | | | |

[a]Original data are from Simon Kuznets, *Secular Movements in Production and Prices* (New York: Houghton Mifflin, 1930), pp. 526-27, which are based mainly on Poor's estimates. The trend removal data come from Thomas, *Migration*, Appendix 4, Table 98, p. 288.

**Table B-14** Net Capital Expenditure in United States Railroads, Original Data and Original Data as Deviation from Trend, 1870-1915 (in Millions of Dollars)

| Year | Net Capital Expenditure in Steam Rails[a] (current prices) | Net Capital Expenditure (trend removed)[b] | Year | Net Capital Expenditure in Steam Rails[a] (current prices) | Net Capital Expenditure (trend removed)[b] |
|---|---|---|---|---|---|
| 1870 | 324 | | 1893 | 310 | 65.8 |
| 1871 | 358 | | 1894 | 65 | 20.8 |
| 1872 | 306 | | 1895 | − 58 | − 58.4 |
| 1873 | 181 | − 15.6 | 1896 | − 82 | −137.0 |
| 1874 | 68 | − 65.4 | 1897 | − 79 | −151.5 |
| 1875 | 27 | −102.5 | 1898 | − 50 | −138.6 |
| 1876 | 29 | −115.4 | 1899 | 31 | −125.9 |
| 1877 | 46 | −104.7 | 1900 | 50 | −113.6 |
| 1878 | 47 | − 57.4 | 1901 | 30 | −106.6 |
| 1879 | 57 | 18.8 | 1902 | 36 | −110.6 |
| 1880 | 204 | 80.2 | 1903 | 44 | −105.8 |
| 1881 | 356 | 116.6 | 1904 | 75 | − 72.9 |
| 1882 | 304 | 133.2 | 1905 | 143 | − 26.0 |
| 1883 | 185 | 109.1 | 1906 | 269 | 17.9 |
| 1884 | 101 | 64.2 | 1907 | 350 | 62.0 |
| 1885 | 50 | 41.9 | 1908 | 348 | 105.6 |
| 1886 | 103 | 36.7 | 1909 | 385 | 108.8 |
| 1887 | 169 | 41.9 | 1910 | 456 | 88.8 |
| 1888 | 141 | 56.5 | 1911 | 385 | 74.5 |
| 1889 | 114 | 60.5 | 1912 | 355 | |
| 1890 | 115 | 84.0 | 1913 | 386 | |
| 1891 | 120 | 116.3 | 1914 | 168 | |
| 1892 | 289 | 104.0 | 1915 | − 26 | |

[a]Melville Ulmer, *Capital in Transportation, Communications, and Public Utilities: Its Formation and Financing*, National Bureau of Economic Research (Princeton, N. J.: Princeton University Press, 1960), Table C-1, pp. 256-257.

[b]Trend line: log $y = 75.8410 + 3.0381t + .5138t^2$, $t = 0 = 1892$. The figures for the Ulmer series after trend removal have been smoothed by a five-year moving average.

**Table B-15** Net Changes in the Money Supply and Domestic Gold Stock in the United States, 1875-1915 (in Millions of Dollars)[a]

| Year | Net Changes in Money Supply | Net Changes in Domestic Gold Stock | Year | Net Changes in Money Supply | Net Changes in Domestic Gold Stock |
|------|-----|-----|------|-----|-----|
| 1875 |       |      | 1896 | — 211 | — 37 |
| 1876 | — 37  | 9    | 1897 | 216   | 97   |
| 1877 | — 41  | 37   | 1898 | 655   | 165  |
| 1878 | — 62  | 46   | 1899 | 897   | 102  |
| 1879 | 220   | 32   | 1900 | 344   | 71   |
| 1880 | 267   | 106  | 1901 | 958   | 90   |
| 1881 | 457   | 127  | 1902 | 673   | 68   |
| 1882 | 95    | 28   | 1903 | 513   | 56   |
| 1883 | 217   | 36   | 1904 | 462   | 79   |
| 1884 | — 47  | 3    | 1905 | 1,088 | 30   |
| 1885 | 73    | 43   | 1906 | 792   | 118  |
| 1886 | 246   | 2    | 1907 | 710   | — 9  |
| 1887 | 196   | 64   | 1908 | — 454 | 152  |
| 1888 | 83    | 51   | 1909 | 1,301 | 24   |
| 1889 | 181   | — 25 | 1910 | 505   | — 6  |
| 1890 | 365   | 15   | 1911 | 815   | 117  |
| 1891 | 111   | — 49 | 1912 | 1,005 | 65   |
| 1892 | 451   | 18   | 1913 | 378   | 52   |
| 1893 | — 282 | — 67 | 1914 | 730   | 20   |
| 1894 | 36    | 30   | 1915 | 991   | 95   |
| 1895 | 253   | 9    |      |       |      |

[a]Estimates of the money supply, currency outside banks, and total demand and time deposits at commercial banks are from Milton Friedman and Anna J. Schwartz, "The Stock of Money in the United States, 1875-1955" (New York: National Bureau of Economic Research, 1958; mimeographed), Table I-1, Col. 9. The monetary gold stock comes from the Secretary of the Treasury, *Annual Report of the Director of the Mint, 1921* (Washington, D. C.: U. S. Government Printing Office, 1921), p. 130, and includes coin and bullion in the Treasury, coin and bullion in the national banks, and coin in circulation. The money supply estimates are for fiscal years ending August, 1875-1881, and ending June, 1882-1915. Estimates of the monetary gold stock are for fiscal years ending June, 1875-1915.

**Table B-16** Money Supply in the Hands of the Public in the United States and Specie in Banks, 1834-1863 (in Thousands of Dollars)[a]

| Year | Money Supply | Net Change in Money Supply | Specie in Banks |
|------|------|------|------|
| 1834 | 113,019 | | |
| 1835 | 123,787 | 10,768 | 43,938 |
| 1836 | 160,864 | 37,077 | 40,020 |
| 1837 | 160,048 | — 816 | 37,915 |
| 1838 | 158,304 | — 1,744 | 35,184 |
| 1839 | 175,563 | 17,259 | 45,133 |
| 1840 | 159,344 | — 16,219 | 33,105 |
| 1841 | 139,400 | — 19,944 | 34,814 |
| 1842 | 144,003 | 4,603 | 28,440 |
| 1843 | 127,518 | — 16,485 | 33,516 |
| 1844 | 137,176 | 9,658 | 49,898 |
| 1845 | 165,063 | 27,887 | 44,241 |
| 1846 | 195,337 | 30,274 | 42,012 |
| 1847 | 221,788 | 26,451 | 35,133 |
| 1848 | 223,438 | 1,650 | 46,370 |
| 1849 | 226,502 | 3,064 | 43,619 |
| 1850 | 273,432 | 46,930 | 45,379 |
| 1851 | 327,285 | 53,853 | 48,671 |
| 1852 | 346,368 | 19,083 | 47,000 |
| 1853 | 408,957 | 62,589 | 53,000 |
| 1854 | 450,576 | 41,619 | 59,410 |
| 1855 | 453,370 | 2,794 | 53,945 |
| 1856 | 471,882 | 18,512 | 59,314 |
| 1857 | 510,015 | 38,133 | 58,350 |
| 1858 | 424,449 | — 85,566 | 74,413 |
| 1859 | 470,086 | 45,637 | 104,538 |
| 1860 | 493,544 | 23,458 | 83,595 |
| 1861 | 543,965 | 50,421 | 87,675 |
| 1862 | 681,535 | 137,570 | 102,146 |
| 1863 | 1,022,461 | 340,926 | 101,227 |

[a]The money supply data, estimated as of the first of each year, are taken from unpublished research by Moses Abramovitz: 1834-1859 is from Secretary of the Treasury, *Report of the Comptroller of the Currency, 1896* (Washington, D. C.: U. S. Government Printing Office, 1896), Vol. I, p. 544, except for 1835 which was corrected by George Macesich; 1860-1863 are from the Secretary of the Treasury, *Annual Report of the Comptroller of the Currency, 1928* (Washington, D. C.: U. S. Government Printing Office, 1929), p. 554. Estimates of specie in banks were taken from Secretary of the Treasury, *Report of the Comptroller of the Currency, 1876* (Washington, D. C.: U. S. Government Printing Office, 1876), p. 204, except for 1852 and 1853 which were estimated independently by Abramovitz.

**Table B-17** United States Railroad Stock Prices, Original Data and Original Data as Deviation from Trend, 1843-1862 and 1871-1915[a]

| Year | Railroad Stock Prices | Railroad Stock Prices (trend removed)[b] | Year | Railroad Stock Prices | Railroad Stock Prices (trend removed)[b] |
|---|---|---|---|---|---|
| 1843 | 42.3 | | 1884 | 14.68 | 104 |
| 1844 | 67.3 | | 1885 | 14.14 | 99 |
| 1845 | 65.6 | | 1886 | 16.57 | 115 |
| 1846 | 69.3 | | 1887 | 17.11 | 117 |
| 1847 | 75.3 | | 1888 | 15.78 | 106 |
| 1848 | 67.8 | | 1889 | 15.70 | 104 |
| 1849 | 71.4 | | 1890 | 15.80 | 103 |
| 1850 | 79.0 | | 1891 | 15.22 | 97 |
| 1851 | 87.3 | | 1892 | 16.58 | 104 |
| 1852 | 98.3 | | 1893 | 14.15 | 86 |
| 1853 | 100.0 | | 1894 | 12.95 | 77 |
| 1854 | 82.4 | | 1895 | 13.29 | 77 |
| 1855 | 72.1 | | 1896 | 12.48 | 71 |
| 1856 | 68.9 | | 1897 | 13.06 | 72 |
| 1857 | 57.5 | | 1898 | 14.71 | 79 |
| 1858 | 52.4 | | 1899 | 18.21 | 95 |
| 1859 | 46.4 | | 1900 | 18.62 | 94 |
| 1860 | 56.5 | | 1901 | 25.01 | 122 |
| 1861 | 51.8 | | 1902 | 28.37 | 134 |
| 1862 | 66.8 | | 1903 | 24.71 | 112 |
| 1871 | 14.26 | 102 | 1904 | 24.61 | 108 |
| 1872 | 15.02 | 109 | 1905 | 31.85 | 134 |
| 1873 | 14.34 | 104 | 1906 | 34.06 | 138 |
| 1874 | 13.53 | 99 | 1907 | 28.09 | 109 |
| 1875 | 13.16 | 96 | 1908 | 28.18 | 105 |
| 1876 | 12.00 | 88 | 1909 | 34.79 | 124 |
| 1877 | 9.22 | 68 | 1910 | 32.90 | 112 |
| 1878 | 10.00 | 73 | 1911 | 32.43 | 106 |
| 1879 | 12.44 | 91 | 1912 | 32.83 | 102 |
| 1880 | 16.08 | 117 | 1913 | 29.48 | 87 |
| 1881 | 19.38 | 141 | 1914 | 27.39 | 77 |
| 1882 | 18.18 | 131 | 1915 | 26.38 | 70 |
| 1883 | 17.44 | 125 | | | |

[a]1843-1862, from W. B. Smith and A. H. Cole, *Fluctuations in American Business, 1790-1860* (Cambridge, Mass.: Harvard University Press, 1935), pp. 180-182 and 1853 is the base year; 1871-1915, from U. S. Bureau of the Census, *Historical Statistics of the United States, Colonial Times to 1957* (Washington, D. C.: U. S. Government Printing Office, 1960), X 353, p. 657 and 1941-1943 = 100.

[b]Trend line: $\log y = 1.2140 + .0098t + .0003t^2$, t = 0 = 1893.

**Table B-18** Four Economic Indices of United States Development, 1820-1860

| Year | Public Land Sales[a] (in thousands of dollars) | Canal Investment[b] (in millions of dollars) | Immigration to U.S.[c] (trend removed) | Index of Business Incorporations[d] |
|------|------|------|------|------|
| 1820 | 1,736 | 1.1 | | |
| 1821 | 1,279 | 1.6 | | |
| 1822 | 1,017 | 2.7 | | |
| 1823 | 807 | 2.8 | | |
| 1824 | 1,500 | 2.5 | | |
| 1825 | 1,292 | 2.7 | | |
| 1826 | 1,130 | 4.0 | | |
| 1827 | 1,405 | 5.6 | | |
| 1828 | 1,219 | 7.8 | | |
| 1829 | 2,163 | 7.0 | | |
| 1830 | 2,409 | 7.5 | | |
| 1831 | 3,366 | 3.7 | 26.97 | |
| 1832 | 2,803 | 4.6 | 67.24 | |
| 1833 | 4,173 | 5.3 | 54.44 | |
| 1834 | 6,064 | 4.4 | 102.34 | |
| 1835 | 16,165 | 3.5 | 71.12 | |
| 1836 | 24,934 | 4.4 | 113.68 | |
| 1837 | 6,941 | 8.2 | 109.19 | |
| 1838 | 4,011 | 12.3 | 49.92 | 183 |
| 1839 | 6,487 | 13.6 | 89.64 | 189 |
| 1840 | 2,747 | 14.3 | 106.82 | 66 |
| 1841 | 1,512 | 11.7 | 96.99 | 80 |
| 1842 | 1,453 | 3.1 | 121.47 | 59 |
| 1843 | 2,050 | 1.0 | 56.91 | 63 |
| 1844 | 2,241 | 1.0 | 82.96 | 110 |
| 1845 | 2,462 | 2.0 | 116.02 | 158 |
| 1846 | 2,881 | 1.8 | 148.59 | 183 |
| 1847 | 3,272 | 4.7 | 222.72 | 146 |
| 1848 | 2,533 | 4.5 | 202.96 | 239 |
| 1849 | 1,743 | 3.4 | 255.52 | 288 |
| 1850 | 1,790 | 4.9 | 263.58 | 453 |
| 1851 | 2,592 | 4.7 | 302.92 | 407 |
| 1852 | 1,392 | 3.4 | 285.09 | 451 |
| 1853 | 5,049 | 3.8 | 272.96 | 668 |
| 1854 | 11,502 | 4.7 | 293.99 | 595 |
| 1855 | 11,282 | 5.3 | 130.75 | 444 |
| 1856 | 4,756 | 4.2 | 124.57 | 360 |
| 1857 | 3,066 | 3.5 | 139.19 | 381 |
| 1858 | 1,793 | 2.8 | 68.96 | 230 |
| 1859 | 1,869 | 1.9 | 66.13 | 421 |
| 1860 | 1,507 | 1.2 | 81.05 | 316 |

[a]Public land sales: A. H. Cole, "Cyclical and Sectional Variations in the Sale of Public Lands, 1816-1860," *Review of Economic Statistics,* IX (January, 1927), 41-53.

[b]Canal investment: H. Jerome Cranmer, "Canal Investment, 1815-1860," *Trends,* Table 3, Col. 1, pp. 555-556.

[c]Immigration: Thomas, *Migration,* Appendix 4, Table 96, p. 286.

[d]Business incorporations: original data in G. H. Evans, *Business Incorporations in the United States, 1800-1943* (New York: National Bureau of Economic Research, 1948) and adjusted by Abramovitz in unpublished research.

**Table B-19** British Balance of Payments, 1820-1913 (in Millions of Pounds Sterling)[a]

| Year | Exports | Imports | Trade Balance Deficit(—) | Net Specie Import (+) | Net Capital Export (+) | Cumulative Balance |
|---|---|---|---|---|---|---|
| 1820 | 36.4 | 43.8 | — 7.4 | + 5.4 | + 3.2 | 46.1 |
| 1821 | 36.7 | 36.1 | + .6 | + 2.2 | + 13.8 | 59.9 |
| 1822 | 37.0 | 36.8 | + .2 | + 2.8 | + 13.3 | 73.2 |
| 1823 | 35.4 | 44.8 | — 9.4 | + 2.5 | + 5.9 | 79.1 |
| 1824 | 38.4 | 43.7 | — 5.3 | — 3.5 | + 16.3 | 95.4 |
| 1825 | 38.9 | 65.4 | — 26.5 | — 5.4 | + 2.4 | 97.8 |
| 1826 | 31.5 | 43.1 | — 11.6 | + 4.0 | + 2.4 | 100.2 |
| 1827 | 37.2 | 52.0 | — 14.8 | + 3.6 | .0 | 100.2 |
| 1828 | 36.8 | 50.8 | — 14.0 | — .3 | + 3.8 | 104.0 |
| 1829 | 35.8 | 47.5 | — 11.7 | — 1.1 | + 6.1 | 110.1 |
| 1830 | 38.3 | 50.3 | — 12.0 | + 3.5 | + .6 | 110.7 |
| 1831 | 37.2 | 55.3 | — 18.1 | — 3.5 | + 2.4 | 113.1 |
| 1832 | 36.5 | 45.2 | — 8.7 | + 1.2 | + 6.1 | 119.2 |
| 1833 | 39.7 | 52.0 | — 12.3 | + 2.4 | + 3.6 | 122.8 |
| 1834 | 41.6 | 56.7 | — 15.1 | — 2.3 | + 7.1 | 129.9 |
| 1835 | 47.4 | 58.7 | — 11.4 | — .8 | + 12.7 | 142.6 |
| 1836 | 53.3 | 75.1 | — 21.8 | — 1.5 | + 5.5 | 148.1 |
| 1837 | 42.1 | 61.1 | — 19.0 | + 2.0 | + 2.3 | 150.4 |
| 1838 | 50.1 | 70.9 | — 20.8 | .0 | + 4.5 | 154.9 |
| 1839 | 52.2 | 80.6 | — 28.4 | — 4.4 | + 3.1 | 158.0 |
| 1840 | 51.4 | 81.2 | — 29.8 | — .9 | — 2.3 | 155.7 |
| 1841 | 51.6 | 74.0 | — 22.4 | + 1.0 | + 1.1 | 156.8 |
| 1842 | 47.4 | 68.0 | — 20.6 | + 2.9 | — .6 | 156.2 |
| 1843 | 52.3 | 63.2 | — 10.9 | + 3.6 | + 9.3 | 165.5 |
| 1844 | 58.6 | 70.9 | — 12.3 | + 3.0 | + 10.4 | 175.9 |
| 1845 | 60.1 | 79.1 | — 19.0 | + 1.0 | + 9.3 | 185.2 |
| 1846 | 57.8 | 78.1 | — 20.3 | + 1.4 | + 8.0 | 193.2 |
| 1847 | 58.8 | 100.3 | — 41.6 | — 5.3 | — 1.1 | 192.1 |
| 1848 | 52.9 | 79.8 | — 26.9 | — 1.0 | + 2.1 | 194.2 |
| 1849 | 63.6 | 89.3 | — 25.7 | — 1.0 | + 3.9 | 198.1 |
| 1850 | 71.4 | 91.0 | — 19.6 | + 1.0 | + 10.6 | 208.7 |
| 1851 | 74.4 | 97.0 | — 22.6 | + 1.2 | + 9.2 | 217.9 |
| 1852 | 78.1 | 97.0 | — 18.9 | + 7.8 | + 7.7 | 225.6 |
| 1853 | 98.9 | 131.6 | — 32.8 | + 6.5 | + 3.3 | 228.9 |
| 1854 | 97.2 | 133.8 | — 36.6 | + 3.6 | + 5.8 | 234.7 |
| 1855 | 95.7 | 122.5 | — 26.8 | + 7.8 | + 13.9 | 248.6 |
| 1856 | 115.8 | 149.1 | — 33.3 | + 1.9 | + 21.8 | 270.4 |
| 1857 | 122.1 | 163.7 | — 41.6 | — 6.5 | + 27.1 | 297.5 |
| 1858 | 116.6 | 141.4 | — 24.8 | + 9.9 | + 22.4 | 319.9 |
| 1859 | 130.4 | 153.9 | — 23.5 | + 1.4 | + 36.1 | 356.0 |
| 1860 | 135.9 | 181.9 | — 46.0 | — 2.5 | + 23.7 | 379.7 |
| 1861 | 125.1 | 183.0 | — 57.9 | — 2.1 | + 14.4 | 394.1 |
| 1862 | 124.0 | 183.5 | — 59.5 | + 2.3 | + 11.5 | 405.6 |
| 1863 | 146.6 | 198.6 | — 52.0 | + 3.5 | + 26.5 | 432.1 |
| 1864 | 160.4 | 222.8 | — 62.4 | + 4.6 | + 22.8 | 454.9 |
| 1865 | 165.8 | 218.1 | — 52.3 | + 6.4 | + 34.9 | 489.8 |
| 1866 | 188.9 | 245.3 | — 56.4 | +12.7 | + 33.0 | 522.8 |
| 1867 | 181.0 | 230.7 | — 49.7 | + 9.5 | + 42.2 | 565.0 |
| 1868 | 179.7 | 246.6 | — 66.9 | + 4.6 | + 36.5 | 601.5 |

## Table B-19—Continued

| Year | Exports | Imports | Trade Balance Deficit(−) | Net Specie Import (+) | Net Capital Export (+) | Cumulative Balance |
|------|---------|---------|--------------------------|-----------------------|------------------------|--------------------|
| 1869 | 190.0 | 248.4 | − 58.4 | + 4.1 | + 46.7 | 648.2 |
| 1870 | 199.6 | 258.8 | − 59.2 | +10.5 | + 44.1 | 692.3 |
| 1871 | 223.1 | 270.5 | − 47.4 | + 4.4 | + 71.3 | 763.6 |
| 1872 | 256.3 | 296.4 | − 40.1 | − .7 | + 98.0 | 861.6 |
| 1873 | 255.2 | 315.4 | − 60.3 | + 4.7 | + 81.3 | 942.9 |
| 1874 | 239.6 | 312.0 | − 72.4 | + 7.5 | + 70.9 | 1,013.8 |
| 1875 | 223.5 | 315.8 | − 92.3 | + 5.6 | + 51.3 | 1,065.1 |
| 1876 | 200.6 | 319.0 | −118.4 | + 7.6 | + 23.2 | 1,088.3 |
| 1877 | 198.9 | 341.0 | −142.1 | − 2.6 | + 13.1 | 1,101.4 |
| 1878 | 192.8 | 316.1 | −123.3 | + 5.7 | + 16.9 | 1,118.3 |
| 1879 | 191.5 | 305.7 | −114.2 | − 4.4 | + 35.5 | 1,153.8 |
| 1880 | 223.1 | 347.9 | −124.8 | − 2.6 | + 35.6 | 1,189.4 |
| 1881 | 234.0 | 334.0 | − 99.9 | − 5.6 | + 65.7 | 1,255.1 |
| 1882 | 241.5 | 347.8 | −106.4 | + 2.6 | + 58.7 | 1,313.8 |
| 1883 | 239.8 | 361.3 | −121.5 | + .8 | + 48.8 | 1,362.6 |
| 1884 | 233.0 | 327.1 | − 94.1 | − 1.6 | + 72.3 | 1,434.9 |
| 1885 | 213.1 | 312.6 | − 99.5 | + .2 | + 62.3 | 1,497.2 |
| 1886 | 212.7 | 293.6 | − 80.9 | − .6 | + 78.9 | 1,576.1 |
| 1887 | 221.9 | 302.9 | − 81.0 | + .6 | + 87.7 | 1,663.8 |
| 1888 | 234.5 | 323.6 | − 89.1 | − .6 | + 91.9 | 1,755.7 |
| 1889 | 248.9 | 361.0 | −112.1 | + 2.0 | + 80.9 | 1,836.6 |
| 1890 | 263.5 | 356.0 | − 92.4 | + 8.8 | + 98.5 | 1,935.1 |
| 1891 | 247.2 | 373.6 | −126.3 | + 2.4 | + 69.4 | 2,004.5 |
| 1892 | 227.1 | 359.2 | −132.2 | + 3.4 | + 59.1 | 2,063.6 |
| 1893 | 218.1 | 345.7 | −127.5 | + 3.7 | + 53.0 | 2,116.6 |
| 1894 | 215.8 | 350.4 | −134.6 | +10.8 | + 38.7 | 2,155.3 |
| 1895 | 225.9 | 356.8 | −130.9 | +14.9 | + 40.0 | 2,195.3 |
| 1896 | 240.2 | 385.6 | −145.4 | − 6.4 | + 56.8 | 2,252.1 |
| 1897 | 234.2 | 391.1 | −156.9 | − .8 | + 41.6 | 2,293.7 |
| 1898 | 233.4 | 409.9 | −176.5 | + 6.2 | + 22.9 | 2,316.6 |
| 1899 | 264.5 | 420.0 | −155.5 | + 9.8 | + 42.4 | 2,359.0 |
| 1900 | 291.2 | 459.9 | −168.7 | + 7.5 | + 37.9 | 2,396.9 |
| 1901 | 280.0 | 454.2 | −174.1 | + 6.2 | + 33.9 | 2,430.8 |
| 1902 | 283.4 | 462.6 | −179.2 | + 5.3 | + 33.3 | 2,464.1 |
| 1903 | 290.8 | 473.0 | −182.2 | − .3 | + 44.8 | 2,508.9 |
| 1904 | 300.7 | 480.7 | −180.0 | − .7 | + 51.7 | 2,560.6 |
| 1905 | 329.8 | 487.2 | −157.4 | + 6.2 | + 81.5 | 2,642.1 |
| 1906 | 375.6 | 522.8 | −147.2 | + 1.8 | +117.5 | 2,759.6 |
| 1907 | 426.0 | 553.9 | −127.8 | + 5.3 | +154.1 | 2,913.7 |
| 1908 | 377.1 | 513.3 | −136.2 | − 6.8 | +154.7 | 3,068.4 |
| 1909 | 378.2 | 533.4 | −155.2 | + 6.5 | +135.6 | 3,204.0 |
| 1910 | 430.4 | 574.5 | −144.1 | + 6.7 | +167.3 | 3,371.3 |
| 1911 | 454.1 | 577.4 | −123.3 | + 6.0 | +196.9 | 3,568.2 |
| 1912 | 487.2 | 632.9 | −145.7 | + 4.6 | +197.1 | 3,765.3 |
| 1913 | 525.3 | 659.2 | −133.9 | +11.9 | +224.3 | 3,989.6 |

aThe trade balance, specie balance, net exports of capital, and the cumulative balance of credit abroad are taken from Albert H. Imlah, *Economic Elements in the Pax Britannica* (Cambridge, Mass.: Harvard University Press, 1958), Table 4, Cols. A, B, J, and K, pp. 70-75; merchandise export and import values are from *ibid.*, Table 8, Cols. A and E, pp. 94-98.

**Table B-20** British Import Values, Original Data and Original Data as Deviation from Trend, 1820-1913 (in Millions of Pounds Sterling)

| Year | Imports[a] | Imports (trend removed)[b] | Year | Imports[a] | Imports (trend removed)[b] |
|------|-----------|----------------------------|------|-----------|----------------------------|
| 1820 | 43.8 | | 1867 | 230.7 | 112 |
| 1821 | 36.1 | 107 | 1868 | 246.6 | 116 |
| 1822 | 36.8 | 104 | 1869 | 248.4 | 114 |
| 1823 | 44.8 | 121 | 1870 | 258.8 | 115 |
| 1824 | 43.7 | 112 | 1871 | 270.5 | 117 |
| 1825 | 65.4 | 163 | 1872 | 296.4 | 124 |
| 1826 | 43.1 | 101 | 1873 | 315.4 | 128 |
| 1827 | 52.0 | 117 | 1874 | 312.0 | 123 |
| 1828 | 50.8 | 109 | 1875 | 315.8 | 121 |
| 1829 | 47.5 | 97 | 1876 | 319.0 | 119 |
| 1830 | 50.3 | 98 | 1877 | 341.0 | 124 |
| 1831 | 55.3 | 104 | 1878 | 316.1 | 112 |
| 1832 | 45.2 | 81 | 1879 | 305.7 | 105 |
| 1833 | 52.0 | 89 | 1880 | 347.9 | 117 |
| 1834 | 56.7 | 95 | 1881 | 334.0 | 109 |
| 1835 | 58.7 | 94 | 1882 | 347.8 | 111 |
| 1836 | 75.1 | 114 | 1883 | 361.3 | 112 |
| 1837 | 61.1 | 88 | 1884 | 327.1 | 99 |
| 1838 | 70.9 | 98 | 1885 | 312.6 | 93 |
| 1839 | 80.6 | 109 | 1886 | 293.6 | 85 |
| 1840 | 81.2 | 104 | 1887 | 302.9 | 86 |
| 1841 | 74.0 | 91 | 1888 | 323.6 | 89 |
| 1842 | 68.0 | 80 | 1889 | 361.0 | 97 |
| 1843 | 63.2 | 72 | 1890 | 356.0 | 94 |
| 1844 | 70.9 | 76 | 1891 | 373.6 | 96 |
| 1845 | 79.1 | 83 | 1892 | 359.2 | 91 |
| 1846 | 78.1 | 79 | 1893 | 345.7 | 85 |
| 1847 | 100.3 | 97 | 1894 | 350.4 | 85 |
| 1848 | 79.8 | 74 | 1895 | 356.8 | 85 |
| 1849 | 89.3 | 80 | 1896 | 385.6 | 90 |
| 1850 | 91.0 | 79 | 1897 | 391.1 | 89 |
| 1851 | 97.0 | 81 | 1898 | 409.9 | 91 |
| 1852 | 97.0 | 78 | 1899 | 420.0 | 92 |
| 1853 | 131.6 | 102 | 1900 | 459.9 | 99 |
| 1854 | 133.8 | 100 | 1901 | 454.2 | 96 |
| 1855 | 122.5 | 89 | 1902 | 462.6 | 96 |
| 1856 | 149.1 | 104 | 1903 | 473.0 | 96 |
| 1857 | 163.7 | 110 | 1904 | 480.7 | 96 |
| 1858 | 141.4 | 92 | 1905 | 487.2 | 95 |
| 1859 | 153.9 | 97 | 1906 | 522.8 | 101 |
| 1860 | 181.9 | 111 | 1907 | 553.9 | 105 |
| 1861 | 183.0 | 108 | 1908 | 513.3 | 96 |
| 1862 | 183.5 | 105 | 1909 | 533.4 | 98 |
| 1863 | 198.6 | 110 | 1910 | 574.5 | 104 |
| 1864 | 222.8 | 119 | 1911 | 577.4 | 103 |
| 1865 | 218.1 | 113 | 1912 | 632.9 | 112 |
| 1866 | 245.3 | 123 | 1913 | 659.2 | 115 |

[a]Table B-19.
[b]Trend line: $\log y = 2.3132 + .01339t - .00008t^2$, $t = 0 = 1867$.

**Table B-21** British Deflated Imports, Original Data and Original Data as Deviation from Trend, 1820-1913 (in Millions of Pounds Sterling)

| Year | Deflated Imports at 1880 Prices[a] | Deflated Imports (trend removed)[b] | Year | Deflated Imports at 1880 Prices[a] | Deflated Imports (trend removed)[b] |
|---|---|---|---|---|---|
| 1820 | 29.2 | | 1867 | 190.9 | 95 |
| 1821 | 26.4 | 98 | 1868 | 202.4 | 98 |
| 1822 | 27.8 | 96 | 1869 | 211.1 | 98 |
| 1823 | 33.6 | 111 | 1870 | 223.4 | 100 |
| 1824 | 34.9 | 110 | 1871 | 250.6 | 108 |
| 1825 | 45.7 | 128 | 1872 | 256.4 | 106 |
| 1826 | 36.6 | 100 | 1873 | 273.3 | 109 |
| 1827 | 43.7 | 118 | 1874 | 276.6 | 107 |
| 1828 | 44.6 | 113 | 1875 | 293.8 | 110 |
| 1829 | 43.4 | 104 | 1876 | 304.3 | 110 |
| 1830 | 47.0 | 107 | 1877 | 316.3 | 111 |
| 1831 | 50.3 | 109 | 1878 | 316.4 | 107 |
| 1832 | 41.5 | 91 | 1879 | 322.4 | 105 |
| 1833 | 45.2 | 91 | 1880 | 347.9 | 109 |
| 1834 | 48.4 | 93 | 1881 | 336.9 | 102 |
| 1835 | 47.0 | 77 | 1882 | 354.4 | 104 |
| 1836 | 58.4 | 101 | 1883 | 377.2 | 108 |
| 1837 | 53.4 | 90 | 1884 | 359.4 | 101 |
| 1838 | 60.9 | 99 | 1885 | 366.6 | 99 |
| 1839 | 65.7 | 95 | 1886 | 366.6 | 96 |
| 1840 | 66.3 | 100 | 1887 | 386.3 | 97 |
| 1841 | 65.3 | 91 | 1888 | 399.7 | 97 |
| 1842 | 62.8 | 89 | 1889 | 439.7 | 104 |
| 1843 | 63.8 | 92 | 1890 | 440.1 | 101 |
| 1844 | 71.6 | 97 | 1891 | 458.2 | 103 |
| 1845 | 80.0 | 103 | 1892 | 459.8 | 99 |
| 1846 | 77.3 | 87 | 1893 | 453.0 | 95 |
| 1847 | 95.5 | 100 | 1894 | 493.0 | 101 |
| 1848 | 91.8 | 100 | 1895 | 518.6 | 103 |
| 1849 | 102.1 | 106 | 1896 | 555.4 | 107 |
| 1850 | 100.3 | 98 | 1897 | 565.7 | 104 |
| 1851 | 107.6 | 103 | 1898 | 588.2 | 108 |
| 1852 | 103.7 | 98 | 1899 | 590.8 | 106 |
| 1853 | 122.8 | 105 | 1900 | 602.1 | 105 |
| 1854 | 116.4 | 100 | 1901 | 614.9 | 104 |
| 1855 | 103.2 | 88 | 1902 | 633.9 | 104 |
| 1856 | 125.9 | 98 | 1903 | 639.5 | 102 |
| 1857 | 127.6 | 98 | 1904 | 646.8 | 100 |
| 1858 | 127.1 | 94 | 1905 | 653.1 | 98 |
| 1859 | 135.6 | 96 | 1906 | 672.3 | 99 |
| 1860 | 156.2 | 104 | 1907 | 681.2 | 97 |
| 1861 | 161.5 | 102 | 1908 | 655.7 | 91 |
| 1862 | 166.1 | 91 | 1909 | 674.2 | 91 |
| 1863 | 165.3 | 93 | 1910 | 687.3 | 90 |
| 1864 | 165.2 | 90 | 1911 | 708.2 | 90 |
| 1865 | 173.4 | 92 | 1912 | 762.7 | 95 |
| 1866 | 193.9 | 100 | 1913 | 790.0 | 95 |

[a]Imlah, *Economic Elements in the Pax Britannica*, Table 8, Col. F, pp. 94-98.
[b]Trend line: log y = 2.3008 + .0162t − .00005t$^2$, t = 0 = 1867.

**Table B-22** British Export Values, Original Data and Original Data as Deviation from Trend, 1820-1913 (in Millions of Pounds Sterling)

| Year | Exports[a] | Exports (trend removed)[b] | Year | Exports[a] | Exports (trend removed)[b] |
|---|---|---|---|---|---|
| 1820 | 36.4 |     | 1867 | 181.0 | 125 |
| 1821 | 36.7 | 137 | 1868 | 179.7 | 120 |
| 1822 | 37.0 | 132 | 1869 | 190.0 | 124 |
| 1823 | 35.4 | 121 | 1870 | 199.6 | 126 |
| 1824 | 38.4 | 125 | 1871 | 223.1 | 137 |
| 1825 | 38.9 | 122 | 1872 | 256.3 | 153 |
| 1826 | 31.5 | 94  | 1873 | 255.2 | 148 |
| 1827 | 37.2 | 107 | 1874 | 239.6 | 136 |
| 1828 | 36.8 | 101 | 1875 | 223.5 | 123 |
| 1829 | 35.8 | 94  | 1876 | 200.6 | 108 |
| 1830 | 38.3 | 97  | 1877 | 198.9 | 104 |
| 1831 | 37.2 | 91  | 1878 | 192.8 | 98  |
| 1832 | 36.5 | 85  | 1879 | 191.5 | 95  |
| 1833 | 39.7 | 89  | 1880 | 223.1 | 108 |
| 1834 | 41.6 | 90  | 1881 | 234.0 | 111 |
| 1835 | 47.4 | 98  | 1882 | 241.5 | 111 |
| 1836 | 53.3 | 106 | 1883 | 239.8 | 108 |
| 1837 | 42.1 | 81  | 1884 | 233.0 | 102 |
| 1838 | 50.1 | 92  | 1885 | 213.1 | 91  |
| 1839 | 52.2 | 93  | 1886 | 212.7 | 89  |
| 1840 | 51.4 | 88  | 1887 | 221.9 | 91  |
| 1841 | 51.6 | 85  | 1888 | 234.5 | 94  |
| 1842 | 47.4 | 75  | 1889 | 248.9 | 98  |
| 1843 | 52.3 | 80  | 1890 | 263.5 | 101 |
| 1844 | 58.6 | 86  | 1891 | 247.2 | 93  |
| 1845 | 60.1 | 85  | 1892 | 227.1 | 83  |
| 1846 | 57.8 | 79  | 1893 | 218.1 | 78  |
| 1847 | 58.8 | 78  | 1894 | 215.8 | 76  |
| 1848 | 52.9 | 67  | 1895 | 225.9 | 78  |
| 1849 | 63.6 | 78  | 1896 | 240.2 | 81  |
| 1850 | 71.4 | 85  | 1897 | 234.2 | 78  |
| 1851 | 74.4 | 85  | 1898 | 233.4 | 76  |
| 1852 | 78.1 | 87  | 1899 | 264.5 | 84  |
| 1853 | 98.9 | 106 | 1900 | 291.2 | 91  |
| 1854 | 97.2 | 101 | 1901 | 280.0 | 86  |
| 1855 | 95.7 | 96  | 1902 | 283.4 | 86  |
| 1856 | 115.8 | 112 | 1903 | 290.8 | 86  |
| 1857 | 122.1 | 115 | 1904 | 300.7 | 88  |
| 1858 | 116.6 | 106 | 1905 | 329.8 | 94  |
| 1859 | 130.4 | 115 | 1906 | 375.6 | 106 |
| 1860 | 135.9 | 116 | 1907 | 426.0 | 118 |
| 1861 | 125.1 | 103 | 1908 | 377.1 | 103 |
| 1862 | 124.0 | 99  | 1909 | 378.2 | 101 |
| 1863 | 146.6 | 114 | 1910 | 430.4 | 114 |
| 1864 | 160.4 | 121 | 1911 | 454.1 | 118 |
| 1865 | 165.8 | 121 | 1912 | 487.2 | 125 |
| 1866 | 188.9 | 134 | 1913 | 525.3 | 133 |

[a]Table B-19.
[b]Trend line: $\log y = 2.1616 + .0127t - .00007t^2$, $t = 0 = 1867$.

**Table B-23** British Deflated Exports, Original Data and Original Data as Deviation from Trend, 1820-1913 (in Millions of Pounds Sterling)

| Year | Deflated Exports at 1880 Prices[a] | Deflated Exports (trend removed)[b] | Year | Deflated Exports at 1880 Prices[a] | Deflated Exports (trend removed)[b] |
|------|------|------|------|------|------|
| 1820 | 15.5 |     | 1867 | 138.3 | 99 |
| 1821 | 16.4 | 113 | 1868 | 147.0 | 102 |
| 1822 | 18.0 | 116 | 1869 | 156.5 | 105 |
| 1823 | 17.8 | 108 | 1870 | 168.5 | 109 |
| 1824 | 19.8 | 113 | 1871 | 189.0 | 118 |
| 1825 | 18.5 | 103 | 1872 | 196.2 | 118 |
| 1826 | 17.0 | 84  | 1873 | 188.7 | 110 |
| 1827 | 21.3 | 101 | 1874 | 187.7 | 105 |
| 1828 | 21.6 | 97  | 1875 | 186.3 | 101 |
| 1829 | 23.2 | 97  | 1876 | 181.6 | 95 |
| 1830 | 24.2 | 101 | 1877 | 187.3 | 95 |
| 1831 | 24.5 | 94  | 1878 | 188.4 | 93 |
| 1832 | 26.2 | 89  | 1879 | 198.6 | 94 |
| 1833 | 28.0 | 97  | 1880 | 223.1 | 103 |
| 1834 | 28.5 | 97  | 1881 | 244.2 | 109 |
| 1835 | 31.0 | 97  | 1882 | 247.2 | 110 |
| 1836 | 33.3 | 100 | 1883 | 254.1 | 110 |
| 1837 | 28.6 | 70  | 1884 | 256.2 | 108 |
| 1838 | 36.0 | 96  | 1885 | 243.7 | 101 |
| 1839 | 37.9 | 96  | 1886 | 254.3 | 103 |
| 1840 | 40.0 | 98  | 1887 | 266.0 | 105 |
| 1841 | 41.5 | 93  | 1888 | 282.9 | 107 |
| 1842 | 41.5 | 86  | 1889 | 294.3 | 108 |
| 1843 | 46.7 | 96  | 1890 | 298.4 | 105 |
| 1844 | 51.0 | 102 | 1891 | 282.5 | 97 |
| 1845 | 50.8 | 94  | 1892 | 271.8 | 91 |
| 1846 | 49.7 | 93  | 1893 | 261.4 | 87 |
| 1847 | 49.8 | 85  | 1894 | 272.6 | 88 |
| 1848 | 50.0 | 85  | 1895 | 296.4 | 93 |
| 1849 | 63.1 | 100 | 1896 | 312.5 | 95 |
| 1850 | 70.8 | 104 | 1897 | 308.2 | 92 |
| 1851 | 75.1 | 106 | 1898 | 306.2 | 90 |
| 1852 | 79.6 | 104 | 1899 | 331.3 | 92 |
| 1853 | 91.5 | 109 | 1900 | 317.5 | 87 |
| 1854 | 89.4 | 102 | 1901 | 320.6 | 86 |
| 1855 | 90.2 | 105 | 1902 | 340.3 | 89 |
| 1856 | 106.8 | 115 | 1903 | 349.4 | 90 |
| 1857 | 109.3 | 109 | 1904 | 357.0 | 89 |
| 1858 | 106.9 | 111 | 1905 | 392.4 | 97 |
| 1859 | 116.9 | 116 | 1906 | 421.8 | 102 |
| 1860 | 122.9 | 119 | 1907 | 456.0 | 109 |
| 1861 | 112.6 | 104 | 1908 | 419.7 | 98 |
| 1862 | 106.1 | 87  | 1909 | 437.3 | 101 |
| 1863 | 113.8 | 86  | 1910 | 477.0 | 108 |
| 1864 | 113.5 | 85  | 1911 | 494.4 | 110 |
| 1865 | 123.2 | 96  | 1912 | 521.6 | 114 |
| 1866 | 135.8 | 102 | 1913 | 541.9 | 117 |

[a]Imlah, *Economic Elements in the Pax Britannica,* Table 8, Col. B, pp. 94-98.
[b]Trend line: $\log y = 2.1405 + .0165t - .00011t^2$, $t = 0 = 1867$.

**Table B-24** Index of British Domestic Investment, Original Data and Original Data as Deviation from Trend, 1871-1913[a]

| Year | British Domestic Investment | British Domestic Investment (trend removed) | Year | British Domestic Investment | British Domestic Investment (trend removed) |
|---|---|---|---|---|---|
| 1871 | 44 | 93.47 | 1893 | 68 | 84.88 |
| 1872 | 48 | 99.67 | 1894 | 76 | 92.59 |
| 1873 | 49 | 99.68 | 1895 | 82 | 97.67 |
| 1874 | 51 | 100.77 | 1896 | 94 | 109.51 |
| 1875 | 60 | 113.86 | 1897 | 89 | 102.34 |
| 1876 | 68 | 126.42 | 1898 | 106 | 119.95 |
| 1877 | 75 | 134.27 | 1899 | 120 | 133.85 |
| 1878 | 67 | 118.13 | 1900 | 115 | 125.25 |
| 1879 | 55 | 94.24 | 1901 | 108 | 116.12 |
| 1880 | 64 | 106.00 | 1902 | 104 | 110.08 |
| 1881 | 61 | 98.09 | 1903 | 108 | 112.85 |
| 1882 | 64 | 101.24 | 1904 | 114 | 116.27 |
| 1883 | 67 | 102.90 | 1905 | 125 | 124.25 |
| 1884 | 60 | 90.67 | 1906 | 115 | 114.10 |
| 1885 | 57 | 83.41 | 1907 | 100 | 98.31 |
| 1886 | 56 | 80.29 | 1908 | 98 | 94.54 |
| 1887 | 55 | 77.56 | 1909 | 99 | 95.06 |
| 1888 | 64 | 88.59 | 1910 | 100 | 94.30 |
| 1889 | 71 | 96.21 | 1911 | 96 | 90.35 |
| 1890 | 69 | 90.51 | 1912 | 92 | 85.32 |
| 1891 | 70 | 90.31 | 1913 | 107 | 98.00 |
| 1892 | 68 | 86.45 | | | |

[a]The original estimates are taken from A. K. Cairncross, "Home and Foreign Investment in Great Britain, 1870-1913" (unpublished thesis, Cambridge University), Table 12, as cited in Thomas, *Migration*, Appendix 4, Table 100, p. 290, with the trendless index.

**Table B-25** Index of British Share Prices, Original Data and
Original Data as Deviation from Trend, 1841-1913[a]

| Year | British Share Prices | British Share Prices (trend removed) | Year | British Share Prices | British Share Prices (trend removed) |
|------|------|------|------|------|------|
| 1841 | 56 | 102.56 | 1878 | 85 | 94.97 |
| 1842 | 56 | 101.08 | 1879 | 78 | 86.19 |
| 1843 | 57 | 101.24 | 1880 | 92 | 100.55 |
| 1844 | 63 | 110.33 | 1881 | 91 | 98.27 |
| 1845 | 65 | 112.26 | 1882 | 88 | 94.02 |
| 1846 | 62 | 105.44 | 1883 | 83 | 87.65 |
| 1847 | 56 | 93.80 | 1884 | 79 | 82.55 |
| 1848 | 52 | 85.95 | 1885 | 78 | 80.58 |
| 1849 | 51 | 83.06 | 1886 | 79 | 80.69 |
| 1850 | 53 | 84.94 | 1887 | 76 | 76.85 |
| 1851 | 55 | 87.03 | 1888 | 79 | 79.00 |
| 1852 | 56 | 87.36 | 1889 | 89 | 88.12 |
| 1853 | 60 | 92.31 | 1890 | 89 | 87.08 |
| 1854 | 60 | 91.05 | 1891 | 88 | 85.27 |
| 1855 | 62 | 92.81 | 1892 | 87 | 83.41 |
| 1856 | 66 | 97.49 | 1893 | 88 | 83.57 |
| 1857 | 65 | 94.61 | 1894 | 90 | 84.51 |
| 1858 | 65 | 93.39 | 1895 | 100 | 93.02 |
| 1859 | 72 | 102.13 | 1896 | 121 | 111.31 |
| 1860 | 73 | 102.10 | 1897 | 133 | 121.24 |
| 1861 | 73 | 100.83 | 1898 | 133 | 120.04 |
| 1862 | 85 | 115.80 | 1899 | 136 | 121.54 |
| 1863 | 90 | 121.13 | 1900 | 134 | 118.58 |
| 1864 | 102 | 135.45 | 1901 | 127 | 111.31 |
| 1865 | 94 | 123.20 | 1902 | 125 | 108.60 |
| 1866 | 87 | 112.55 | 1903 | 122 | 104.99 |
| 1867 | 74 | 94.51 | 1904 | 115 | 98.04 |
| 1868 | 75 | 94.58 | 1905 | 122 | 103.04 |
| 1869 | 78 | 97.14 | 1906 | 124 | 103.77 |
| 1870 | 87 | 107.01 | 1907 | 122 | 101.16 |
| 1871 | 98 | 119.08 | 1908 | 114 | 93.75 |
| 1872 | 110 | 132.05 | 1909 | 114 | 92.91 |
| 1873 | 113 | 134.05 | 1910 | 124 | 100.16 |
| 1874 | 110 | 128.96 | 1911 | 130 | 104.17 |
| 1875 | 104 | 120.51 | 1912 | 129 | 102.46 |
| 1876 | 97 | 110.98 | 1913 | 128 | 100.79 |
| 1877 | 92 | 104.07 | | | |

[a]Original data in P. Rousseaux, *Les Mouvements de Fond de l'Economie Anglaise, 1800-1913* (Louvain, 1938), p. 272; and K. C. Smith and G. F. Horne, "An Index Number of Securities, 1867-1914," *London and Cambridge Economic Service Special Memorandum*, No. 37, June, 1934, as cited in Thomas, *Migration*, Appendix 4, Table 99, p. 289, with the trendless index.

# BIBLIOGRAPHY

## BOOKS

Berry, Thomas. *Western Prices Before 1861: A Study of the Cincinnati Market.* Cambridge, Mass.: Harvard University Press, 1943.

Bogart, E. L. *The Economic History of the United States.* 2nd ed. New York: Longmans, Green, and Company, 1913.

Burns, Arthur. *Production Trends in the United States Since 1870.* New York: National Bureau of Economic Research, 1934.

Cairncross, A. K. *Home and Foreign Investment, 1870-1913.* Cambridge: Cambridge University Press, 1953.

Cole, Arthur H. *Wholesale Commodity Prices in the United States, 1800-1860.* Cambridge, Mass.: Harvard University Press, 1938.

Evans, G. H. *Business Incorporations in the United States, 1800-1943.* New York: National Bureau of Economic Research, 1948.

Fels, Rendigs. *American Business Cycles, 1865-1897.* Chapel Hill: The University of North Carolina Press, 1959.

Ferns, H. S. *Britain and Argentina in the Nineteenth Century.* Oxford: Clarendon Press, 1960.

Ford, A. G. *The Gold Standard, 1880-1914: Britain and Argentina.* New York: Oxford University Press, 1962.

Frickey, Edwin. *Production in the United States, 1860-1914.* Cambridge, Mass.: Harvard University Press, 1947.

Goldsmith, Raymond W. *A Study of Saving in the United States.* 3 vols. Princeton, N. J.: Princeton University Press, 1955.

Gurley, John G., and Shaw, Edward S. *Money in a Theory of Finance.* Washington, D. C.: The Brookings Institution, 1960.

Hammond, M. B. *The Cotton Industry.* American Economic Association. New York: Macmillan Co., 1897, New Series No. 1.

Hobson, C. K. *The Export of Capital.* New York: Macmillan Co., 1914.

Imlah, Albert H. *Economic Elements in the Pax Britannica.* Cambridge, Mass.: Harvard University Press, 1958.

Jenks, Leland. *The Migration of British Capital to 1875*. New York: Alfred A. Knopf, 1927.

Kindleberger, C. P. *International Short-Term Capital Movements*. New York, 1937.

Kuznets, Simon. *Secular Movements in Production and Prices*. New York: Houghton Mifflin, 1930.

Lewis, Cleona. *America's Stake in International Investments*. Washington, D. C.: The Brookings Institution, 1938.

Lipsey, Robert E. *Price and Quantity Trends in the Foreign Trade of the United States*. National Bureau of Economic Research. Princeton, N. J.: Princeton University Press, 1963.

Mann, James A. *The Cotton Industry of Great Britain*. London: Simpkin Marshall and Company, 1860.

Matthews, R. C. O. *The Business Cycle*. Chicago: University of Chicago Press, 1959.

———. *A Study in Trade Cycle History: 1833-1842*. Cambridge: Cambridge University Press, 1954.

Mitchell, Wesley C. *Gold Prices and Wages under the Greenback Standard*. ("University of California Publications in Economics," Vol. I.) Berkeley: University of California Press, 1908.

North, Douglass C. *The Economic Growth of the United States, 1790-1860*. Englewood Cliffs, N. J.: Prentice-Hall, Inc., 1961.

Poor, H. V. and H. W. *Poor's Manual of the Railroads of the United States, 1912*. New York: H. V. Poor and H. W. Poor, 1912.

Saul, S. B. *Studies in British Overseas Trade, 1870-1914*. Liverpool: Liverpool University Press, 1960.

Smith, W. B., and Cole, A. H. *Fluctuations in American Business, 1790-1860*. Cambridge, Mass.: Harvard University Press, 1935.

Spence, Clark C. *British Investments and the American Mining Frontier, 1860-1901*. American Historical Association. Ithaca, N. Y.: Cornell University Press, 1958.

Stovel, John A. *Canada in the World Economy*. Cambridge, Mass.: Harvard University Press, 1959.

Thomas, Brinley. *Migration and Economic Growth*. Cambridge: Cambridge University Press, 1954.

Ulmer, Melville. *Capital in Transportation, Communications, and Public Utilities: Its Formation and Financing*. National Bureau of Economic Research. Princeton, N. J.: Princeton University Press, 1960.

Williams, John H. *Argentina International Trade Under Inconvertible Paper Money, 1880-1900*. Cambridge, Mass.: Harvard University Press, 1920.

Wilson, Roland. *Capital Imports and the Terms of Trade*. Melbourne: Melbourne University Press, 1931.

Youngson, A. J. *Possibilities of Economic Progress.* Cambridge: Cambridge University Press, 1959.

## ARTICLES AND PAPERS

Abramovitz, Moses. "The Nature and Significance of Kuznets Cycles," *Economic Development and Cultural Change,* IX (April, 1961), 225-248.

———. "Long Swings in United States Economic Growth," *38th Annual Report of the National Bureau of Economic Research* (New York: National Bureau of Economic Research, 1958), pp. 47-56.

———. "Resource and Output Trends in the United States since 1870," *American Economic Review* (Supplement), XLVI (May, 1956), 5-23.

Bacon, Nathaniel T. *Yale Review,* November, 1900, pp. 265-285.

Bullock, Charles L.; Williams, John H.; and Tucker, Rufus S. "The Balance of Trade of the United States," *Review of Economic Statistics,* I (July, 1919), 213-268.

Cairncross, A. K., and Weber, B. "Fluctuations in Building in Great Britain, 1785-1849," *Economic History Review,* Second Series IX (December, 1956), 283-297.

Callendar, G. S. "Early Transportation and Banking Enterprise of the States in Relation to the Growth of Corporations," *Quarterly Journal of Economics,* XVII (1903), 111-162.

Cole, Arthur H. "Cyclical and Sectional Variations in the Sale of Public Lands, 1816-1860," *Review of Economic Statistics,* IX (January, 1927), 41-53.

Cooney, E. W. "Capital Exports and Investment in Building in Britain and in the U. S. A., 1856-1914," *Economica,* N. S. XVI (November, 1949), 347-354.

———. "Long Waves in Building in the British Economy of the Nineteenth Century," *Economic History Review,* Second Series XIII (December, 1960), 257-269.

Cranmer, H. Jerome. "Canal Investment, 1815-1860," *Trends in the American Economy in the Nineteenth Century* ("Studies in Income and Wealth," Vol. XXIV [Princeton, N. J.: Princeton University Press, 1960]), pp. 547-570.

Deutsch, K. W., and Eckstein, A. "National Industrialization and the Declining Share of the International Economic Sector, 1890-1959," *World Politics,* XIII (January, 1961), 267-299.

Feinstein, C. H. "Income and Investment in the United Kingdom, 1856-1914," *Economic Journal,* LXXI (June, 1961), 367-385.

Ford, A. G. "Flexible Exchange Rates and Argentina, 1885-1900," *Oxford Economic Papers,* N. S. X (October, 1958), 316-338.

Furth, J. H. "U. S. Balance of Payments in the Recession," *Quarterly Journal of Economics,* LXXIII (May, 1959), 197-206.

Graham, Frank D. "International Trade Under Depreciated Paper—the United States, 1862-1879," *Quarterly Journal of Economics,* XXXVI (February, 1922), 222-273.

Habakkuk, H. J. "Fluctuations in House-Building in Britain and the United States in the Nineteenth Century," *Journal of Economic History,* XXII (June, 1962), 198-230.

Hartland, Penelope. "Canadian Balance of Payments since 1868," *Trends in the American Economy in the Nineteenth Century* ("Studies in Income and Wealth," Vol. XXIV [Princeton, N. J.: Princeton University Press, 1960]), pp. 717-755.

Heath, Milton S. "Public Railroad Construction and the Development of Private Enterprise in the South before 1861," *Journal of Economic History* (Supplement), IX (1949), 40-53.

Imlah, Albert H. "British Balance of Payments and Export of Capital, 1816-1913," *Economic History Review,* Second Series V (1952-53), 234-239.

Kindleberger, C. P. "Foreign Trade and Growth: Lessons from British Experience since 1913," *Lloyds Bank Review* (July, 1962).

Kondratieff, N. D. "Die Preisdynamik der industreillen und land-wirtschaftlichen Waren (Zum Problem der relativen Dynamik und Konjunkten)," *Archiv für Socialwissenschaft und Sozialpolitik,* LX (1928), 1-85.

Kreps, T. J. "Import and Export Prices in the United States and the Terms of International Trade, 1880-1914," *Quarterly Journal of Economics,* XXXX (August, 1926), 708-720.

Kuznets, Simon. "Long Term Changes in National Income of the United States since 1870," *Income and Wealth.* Series II. Cambridge: Bowes and Bowes, 1952.

———. "Quantitative Aspects of the Economic Growth of Nations: I, Levels and Variability of Rates of Growth," *Economic Development and Cultural Change,* Vol. V (October, 1956).

———. "Long Secular Swings in the Growth of Population and in Related Economic Variables, *Proceedings of the American Philosophical Society,* CII (February, 1958), 25-52.

Lewis, W. A., and O'Leary, P. J. "Secular Swings in Production and Trade, 1870-1913," *The Manchester School of Economic and Social Studies,* XIII (May, 1955), 113-152.

Macesich, George. "Sources of Monetary Disturbances in the United States, 1834-1845," *Journal of Economic History,* XX (September, 1960), 407-434.

Mintz, Ilse. *American Exports During Business Cycles, 1879-1958.* Occasional Paper No. 76. New York: National Bureau of Economic Research, 1961.

———. *Trade Balance During Business Cycles.* Occasional Paper No. 67. New York: National Bureau of Economic Research, 1959.

Morgenstern, Oskar. *The Validity of International Gold Movement Statistics,* Special Paper in International Economics No. 2. Princeton, N. J.: Princeton University Press, 1955.

Murphy, G., and Zellner, A. "Sequential Growth, the Labor-Safety-Valve Doctrine and Development of American Unionism," *Journal of Economic History,* XIX (September, 1959), 402-421.

North, Douglass C. "Agriculture and Regional Economic Growth," *Proceedings of the American Farm Economic Association,* XLI December, 1959), 943-951.

———. "International Capital Flows and the Development of the American West," *Journal of Economic History,* XVI (December, 1956), 493-505.

———. "Location Theory and Regional Economic Growth," *Journal of Political Economy,* LXIII (June, 1953), 243-258.

———. "The United States Balance of Payments, 1790-1860," *Trends in the American Economy in the Nineteenth Century.* ("Studies in Income and Wealth," Vol. XXIV [Princeton, N. J.: Princeton University Press, 1960]), pp. 573-627.

North, Douglass C., and Heston, Alan. "The Estimation of Shipping Earnings in Historical Studies of the Balance of Payments," *Canadian Journal of Economics and Political Science,* XXVI (May, 1960), 265-276.

Nurkse, Ragnar. "International Investment Today in the Light of 19th Century Experience," *Economic Journal,* XLIV (December, 1954), 744-758.

Ripley, W. Z. *New York Journal of Commerce,* December 6, 1911.

Segal, Harvey H., and Simon, Matthew. "British Foreign Capital Issues, 1865-1894," *Journal of Economic History,* XXI (December, 1961), 566-581.

Shannon, H. S. "Bricks—a Trade Index," *Economica,* N. S. I (1934), 300-318.

Simon, Matthew. "The United States Balance of Payments, 1861-1900," *Trends in the American Economy in the Nineteenth Century.* ("Studies in Income and Wealth," Vol. XXIV [Princeton, N. J.: Princeton University Press, 1960]), pp. 629-715.

———. "The Hot Money Movement and the Private Exchange Pool Proposal of 1896," *Journal of Economic History,* XIX (March, 1959), 31-50.

Williamson, Jeffrey G. "International Trade and United States Economic Development: 1827-1843," *Journal of Economic History,* XXI (September, 1961), 372-383.

———. "The Long Swing: Comparisons and Interactions Between British and American Balance of Payments, 1820-1913," *Journal of Economic History*, XXII (March, 1962), 21-46.

———. "Real Growth, Monetary Disturbances and the Transfer Process: The United States, 1879-1900," *Southern Economic Journal*, XXIX (January, 1963), 167-180.

———. "Dollar Scarcity and Surplus in Historical Perspective," *American Economic Review* (Papers and Proceedings), LIII (May, 1963), 519-529.


PUBLIC DOCUMENTS

Hilgerdt, Folke. *Annual Figures for the Balance of Payments of the United States, 1850-1914*. United Nations Department of Economic Affairs. Research Memorandum No. 9 (n.d.).

Paish, Sir George. "Trade Balance of the United States," *Miscellaneous Articles*. Vol. XX. Report of the National Monetary Commission. Washington, D. C.: U. S. Government Printing Office, 1910.

Secretary of the Treasury. *Annual Report of the Director of the Mint, 1921*. Washington, D. C.: U. S. Government Printing Office, 1921.

———. *Annual Report of the Comptroller of the Currency, 1928*. Washington, D. C.: U. S. Government Printing Office, 1929.

———. *Report of the Comptroller of the Currency, 1876*. Washington, D. C.: U. S. Government Printing Office, 1876.

———. *Report of the Comptroller of the Currency, 1896*. Washington, D. C.: U. S. Government Printing Office, 1896.

U. S. Bureau of the Census. *Historical Statistics of the United States, 1789-1945*. Washington, D. C.: U. S. Government Printing Office, 1949.

———. *Historical Statistics of the United States: Colonial Times to 1957*. Washington, D. C.: U. S. Government Printing Office, 1960.

———. *Tenth Census of the United States*, Vol. IV: *Transportation*. Washington, D. C.: U. S. Government Printing Office, 1883.

U. S. Congress. *Hearings before the Joint Committee of the Congress of the United States*. 86th Cong., 1st Sess., 1959.

———. *Hearings before the Joint Economic Committee of the Congress of the United States*. 87th Cong., 2nd Sess., 1962.

U. S. Department of Commerce. *Exports of Farm Products from the United States, 1851-1908*. Bureau of Statistics. Bulletin No. 75. Washington, D. C.: U. S. Government Printing Office, 1910.

———. *Balance of Payments, Statistical Supplement*. Washington, D. C.: U. S. Government Printing Office, 1958.

——. *Commerce and Navigation of the United States, 1886.* Washington, D. C.: U. S. Government Printing Office, 1887.

——. *Foreign Commerce and Navigation, 1914.* Washington, D. C.: U. S. Government Printing Office, 1915.

## UNPUBLISHED MANUSCRIPTS

Cairncross, A. K. "Home and Foreign Investment in Great Britain, 1870-1913." Unpublished thesis, Cambridge University (n.d.).

Cootner, Paul H. "Transportation, Innovation, and Economic Development: The Case of the United States Railroads." Unpublished Ph.D. dissertation, Massachusetts Institute of Technology, 1953.

Dickens, Paul D. "The Transition Period in American International Financing: 1897-1914." Unpublished Ph.D. dissertation, George Washington University, 1933.

Friedman, Milton, and Schwartz, Anna J. "The Stock of Money in the United States, 1875-1955." New York: National Bureau of Economic Research, 1958. (Mimeographed.)

Kuznets, Simon. "Technical Tables Underlying Series in *Supplement to Summary Volume on Capital Formation and Its Financing.*" New York: National Bureau of Economic Research, 1956. (Mimeographed.)

Madden, John J. "British Investment in the United States, 1860-1880." Conference on Research in Income and Wealth. New York: National Bureau of Economic Research, 1957. (Mimeographed.)

Riggleman, J. R. "Building Cycles in the United States, 1830-1935." Unpublished Ph.D. dissertation, The Johns Hopkins University (n.d.).

# INDEX

Abramovitz, M., 6, 73, 77, 112, 188, 218, 223, 224
Alaskan gold discoveries, 180
Anglo-American building cycles, 13, 14, 68, 70, 189-93 *passim*, 208-16 *passim*. *See also* Atlantic economy, Kuznets cycles, long swings
Argentine development, 193, 214, 215. *See also* Latin American foreign investment
Atlantic economy, 5, 13, 14, 68, 99, 135, 193, 208, 214-15, 232. *See also* Anglo-American building cycles, Kuznets cycles, long swings
Australian foreign investment, 124, 146, 193

Balance of payments, stability, 10; secular disequilibrium, 221
Bank of the United States, 104, 109
Bell, P., 230
Biddle, Nicholas, 106, 186
Bonds, local, 97, 100, 103-9 *passim*, 120-21; state, 97, 100-9 *passim*, 120-21; British, 122-23, 155, 157; federal coupon, 125; federal registered, 125; railroads, 12, 114-16, 124-43 *passim*, 156. *See also* foreign investment
British, investment in America, 11-14, 90-101, 105-19, 121-23, 126-34 *passim*, 135-58 *passim;* export industry, 13, 14, 68, 70; home investment, 13; export prices, 68; share prices, 122-23, 155,

157; direct investment, 127-28; foreign investment, 208-16
Bryan, William Jennings, 218
Building, railroad, 3, 4, 12, 97, 107, 117-18, 129, 135-36; Riggleman index, 6, 41, 72-83 *passim*, 174; Anglo-American cycles, 13, 14, 68, 70; Long index, 72, 76, 78. *See also* Anglo-American building cycles, Atlantic economy, Kuznets cycles, long swings
Burns, A., 73

Cairncross, A. K., 135, 146-49, 152, 190-91, 196-98 *passim*
Canadian foreign investment, 124, 146, 193, 204, 212-15 *passim*, 232
Canal building, 4, 97, 104, 107, 115
Capacity limitation, 55
Capital flight, 218, 230-32. *See also* short-term capital
Cole, A. H., 65
Cooke, Jay, 125
Cooney, E. W., 198
Cootner thesis, 35, 40n
Cotton, markets, 9, 10, 18, 35-45, 107, 117, 120, 197; exports, 21, 35-45, 52, 98, 103-8 *passim*, 118, 134; prices, 23, 24, 35-45, 105-6, 192, 208; revenue, 24, 35-45, 106, 120; overexpansion, 35-45. *See also* North thesis
Crimean War, 100, 111-17, 122, 170
Crude foodstuffs, exports, 31-34, 118; imports, 59, 60-65, 226